Second edition
Copyright © November 2005
Alastair Sawday Publishing Co. Ltd

Published in November 2005
Alastair Sawday Publishing,
Yanley Lane, Long Ashton
Bristol BS41 9LR
Tel: +44 (0)1275 464891
Fax: +44 (0)1275 464887
Email: info@specialplacestostay.com
Web: www.specialplacestostay.com

The Globe Pequot Press
P. O. Box 480, Guilford,
Connecticut 06437, USA
Tel: +1 203 458 4500
Fax: +1 203 458 4601
Email: info@globepequot.com
Web: www.globepequot.com

Design:
Caroline King

Maps & Mapping:
Maidenhead Cartographic Services Ltd

Printing:
Butler & Tanner, Frome, UK

UK Distribution:
Penguin UK, 80 Strand, London

US Distribution:
The Globe Pequot Press, Guilford, CT 06437

ISBN 1-901970-65-5
      978-1-901970-65-4

A catalogue record for this book is
available from the British Library.

Paper and Printing: We have sought the lowest
possible ecological 'footprint' from the
production of this book, using super-efficient
machinery, vegetable inks and high
environmental standards. Our printer is ISO
14001-registered.

The publishers have made every effort to
ensure the accuracy of the information
in this book at the time of going to
press. However, they cannot accept
any responsibility for any loss, injury
or inconvenience resulting from the
use of information contained therein.

ALASTAIR SAWDAY'S
SPECIAL PLACES TO STAY

MOROCCO

Contents

Guide entries

Back

Alastair Sawday Publishing

We are the faceless toilers at the pit-face of publishing but, for us, the question of who we are and how we inter-react is important. For who we are shapes the books, the books shape your holidays, and thus are shaped the lives of people who own these 'special places'. So we are trying to be a little more than 'just a publishing company'.

New eco offices

By the end of 2005 we will have moved into our new eco offices. By introducing super-insulation, underfloor heating, a wood-pellet boiler, solar panels and a rainwater tank, we will have a working environment benign to ourselves and to the environment. Lighting will be low-energy, dark corners will be lit by sun-pipes and one building is of green oak. Carpet tiles are leased: some of recycled material, most of wool and some of natural fibres. We will sail through our environmental audit.

Environmental & ethical policies

We combine many other small gestures: company cars run on gas or recycled cooking oil; kitchen waste is composted and other waste recycled; cycling and car-sharing are encouraged; the company only buys organic or local food; we don't accept web links with companies we consider unethical; we use the ethical Triodos Bank for our deposit account.

We have used recycled paper for some books but have settled on selecting paper and printer for their low energy use. Our printer is British and ISO14001-certified and together we will reduce our environmental impact.

Thanks partially to our Green Team, we recently won a Business Commitment to the Environment Award – which has boosted our resolve to stick to our own green policies. Our flagship gesture, however, is carbon offsetting; we calculate our carbon emissions and plant trees to compensate as calculated by Future Forests. In 2006 we will support projects overseas that plant trees or reduce carbon use; our money will work better by going direct to projects.

Ethics

But why, you may ask, take these things so seriously? You are just a little publishing company, for heavens sake! Well, is there any good argument for not taking them seriously? The world, by the admission of the vast majority of scientists, is in trouble. If we do not change our ways urgently we will doom the planet and all its creatures – whether innocent or not – to a variety of possible catastrophes. To maintain the status quo is unacceptable. Business does much of the damage and should undo it, and provide new models.

Who are we?

Pressure on companies to produce Corporate Social Responsibility policies is mounting. We are trying to keep ahead of it all, yet still to be as informal and human as possible – the antithesis of 'corporate'. (We even have unofficial 'de-stress operatives' in the shape of several resident dogs.)

The books – and a dilemma

So, we have created fine books that do good work. They promote authenticity, individuality and high quality, local and organic food – a far cry from the now-dominant corporate culture. Rural economies, pubs, small farms, villages and hamlets all benefit. However, people use fossil fuel to get there. Should we aim to get our readers to offset their own carbon emissions, and the B&B and hotel owners too? That might have been a hopeless task a year or so ago, but less so now that the media has taken on board the enormity of the work ahead of us all.

We are slowly introducing green ideas into the books: the Fine Breakfast scheme that highlights British and Irish B&B owners who use local and organic food; celebrating those who make an extra effort; gently encouraging the use of public transport, cycling and walking. Next year we are publishing a book focusing on responsible travel and eco-projects around the globe.

Our Fragile Earth series

The 'hard' side of our environmental publishing is the Fragile Earth series: *The Little Earth Book*, *The Little Food Book* and *The Little Money Book*. They have been a great success. They consist of bite-sized essays, polemical and hard-hitting but well researched and methodical. They are a 'must have' for people from all walks of life – anyone who is confused and needs clarity about some of the key issues of our time.

Lastly – what is special?

The notion of 'special' is at the heart of what we do, and highly subjective. We discuss this in the Introduction. We take huge pleasure from finding people and places that do their own thing – brilliantly; places that are unusual and follow no trends; places of peace and beauty; people who are kind and interesting – and genuine.

We seem to have touched a raw nerve with thousands of readers; they obviously want to stay in special places rather than the dull corporate monstrosities that have disfigured so many of our cities and towns. Life is too short to be wasted in the wrong places. A night in a special place can be a transforming experience.

Alastair Sawday

Acknowledgements

Jose Navarro, once a lecturer at the University of Zaragoza in northern Spain, is an enterprising man. When he decided to settle in the UK, he resolved to get to know the country and went to live in the Hebrides for long periods. He cycles where he can, getting under the skin of the places he travels through. He is intrepid, curious and committed to authenticity – people being themselves and doing their own thing. Culture with a small 'c' is important to him. So Morocco has fired him up again, being a country that has not thoroughly embraced western culture and has therefore not denied its own.

He has travelled vast distances in pursuit of 'specialness', and has found places to stay of rare loveliness. Putting this book together is hard work, however, and involves huge amounts of paperwork. His is a fine achievement and we are much indebted to him.

Ann Cooke-Yarborough co-created our first Moroccan guide and has given steadfast and resourceful support to this one. She has done all the writing, a good chunk of inspecting and the final pre-production work, her eagle eye searching for error and opportunities for improvement. We owe her much, too.

Alastair Sawday.

Editors
Jose Navarro
& Ann Cooke-Yarborough

Series Editor
Alastair Sawday

Editorial Director
Annie Shillito

Managing Editor
Jackie King

Production Manager
Julia Richardson

Web & IT
Russell Wilkinson, Chris Banks, Brian Kimberling

Production
Paul Groom, Allys Williams, Kathy Purdy

Copy Editor Jo Boissevain

Editorial
Maria Serrano, Rebecca Stevens, Danielle Williams

Sales & Marketing & PR
Siobhan Flynn, Andreea Petre Goncalves, Sarah Bolton

Accounts
Sheila Clifton, Bridget Bishop, Christine Buxton, Jenny Purdy, Sandra Hassell

Writer Ann Cooke-Yarborough

Inspections
Ann Cooke-Yarborough, Jose Navarro, Guy Hunter-Watts, Emma Wilson

And many thanks to those people who did just a few inspections.

A word from Alastair Sawday

I am beginning to feel left out, with
no Moroccan experience to my name.
I know so many who love the country,
who sigh with inexpressible longing
to be there, who are unfulfilled if
they have not been recently, that
I know I am to be pitied.

So I will, by the time you read
this book, have put this pity to
rest. I will have walked in the Atlas,
explored a souk or two, reclined
upon a beach and wondered at
the colour and vitality of it all.
I will certainly have read one or
two of those wonderful books from
Eland Press, one by the Englishman
who loved it so much that he
lived there and passed himself off,
perilously, as a Moroccan. I will
have learned a little Arabic and
a song or two, and will have
quavered before the vastness of
the subject of 'Morocco'.

Jose and Ann, who have together
brought this edition to life, have
a deep fascination for this amazing
country. The mind-enriching variety
of Special Places here is witness
to the ebb and flow of peoples
and ideas, rulers and history. The
wonder is that so few English men
and women have taken to Morocco,
though an easy explanation is
that our imperial pretensions were
elsewhere. But the wonder remains,
so close it is to Gibraltar, British
visitors are still relatively few in
number. Be one of the few – you will
love it. The places we have selected
for you are there because they will
bring Morocco to life in a way
unavailable to large hotels and less
sensitive places. These places are
imaginative, personal, committed
and enterprising – and a delight to
stay in. Let us know if you agree.

Alastair Sawday

Introduction

MOROCCO IS DIFFERENT...

Be prepared for contrasts of all sorts, look forward to the unexpected and learn to trust those hooded figures – not sinister, just well protected against the strong and unpredictable elements. Marshal Lyautey, first Resident General of the French Protectorate in 1912, defined Morocco as *un pays froid au soleil brulant* (a cold country with a burning sun).

Morocco cannot be rushed so give it enough slow time. The country and the people are open to those who adapt to their rhythms and don't dash headlong from sightseeing to bracelet-buying to eating 'fast Moroccan'. If this is your first visit, the culture shock will probably last a while. If you find yourself recoiling from the gaudy cacophany and thronging smells of the medinas (the old Arab towns), slow down instead of running away, take the time to stand aside and watch. Look for patterns, gestures and expressions that reveal how things work, how people interact; connect into a new set of behaviours. Once you begin to sense the order in this apparent chaos, you will relax, others will notice that you have opened up and your senses of humanity and humour will take you inside the picture. Then you may fall for ever under the enchantment, despite the distressing poverty.

History, culture and religion
Because Morocco is North African and Islamic, which many of our readers will know less well than they know Europe or North America, Christianity or Judaism, we include a brief history of the country and an introduction to Islam by Morocco expert Barnaby Rogerson. You will find them at the back of the book. Islamic law applies here as in all Islamic countries; one of its decrees interests us directly: unmarried Moroccan-European couples are not legally allowed to share a room in a Moroccan hotel.

Photo left Kasbah Ellouze, entry 149
Photo right Riyad El Mezouar, entry 8

Introduction

Meanwhile, here is what Barnaby Rogerson says about contemporary Moroccan attitudes to the other two religions of The Book.

Multi-faith Muslim Morocco and religious tolerance

Morocco is a determinedly Muslim nation. It is also an example to the rest of the Muslim world in the tolerance and hospitality offered to other religions and cultures. There are as many church spires as minarets on the Tangier skyline to baffle a traveller on that first approach into this famous port-city. Just above the main square, among tombs and trees, stands an elegant Anglican church built in the Moorish style with the Lord's Prayer carved in Arabic script on the chancel arch. On one visit, the linen-suited expatriate congregation was completely swamped by Nigerians who, working their way up the continent (planning to enter Europe illegally), had stopped off in this home from home.

Away from the grand boulevards of Rabat and Casablanca, it is still possible to attend mass in a Roman Catholic cathedral as the call of the muezzin echoes through the whitewashed naves. Many thousands of Moroccan Jews continue to worship in their venerable synagogues, maintaining the old Hebrew cemeteries found in every ancient city as well as the shrine-tombs of saintly rabbis scattered over the most inaccessible mountain valleys. Every year – especially during the 'Jewish festival' months of March and October – more thousands of Jews of Moroccan descent are welcomed back as pilgrim-tourists. They have an easy time at the immigration desk for even though they might now live in Tel Aviv or New York, the Kingdom of Morocco has never withdrawn their passports, believing that some time they will return 'home'.

This tolerance is a testament to the Muslim faith of Morocco and in strict conformity to the Prophet's injunction to honour the "peoples of the Book", the Jews and Christians who, like Muslims, believe in one God, in honouring the scriptures, obeying the laws of the prophets and leading an ethical life.

There was a wise old sheikh from northern Morocco who, much to the scandal of his followers, had married an Englishwoman and never attempted to persuade her to convert to Islam. To explain his actions he would leave a cone of sugar in the centre of the room and bid his followers to watch silently. Soon the ants would discover this nectar and orderly columns would start marching towards the white rock. The sheikh would explain that just so are the peoples of the Book, dutifully following their own paths, blissfully unaware of each other as they ascend the mountain of sweetness.

Holy month of Ramadan

All Moroccans are expected to fast during Ramadan unless too old, too young, pregnant or sick. The rule for a practising Muslim is no food, no drink, no smoking, no sex between sunrise and sunset for one month. Families gather for a 'break-fast' meal every evening and another before dawn. This means less sleep – a lot less if Ramadan, a movable feast, falls in summer – and considerable hardship as the day wears on. But they soldier on, keep smiling and looking forward to the traditional harira soup. Most cafés, bars and licensed grocers close for the month and sensitive non-Muslims refrain from smoking, eating or drinking in public.

How to use this book
Regional breakdown

We have divided the country into the four essential areas of Moroccan geography and culture, then into sub-sections based on a logic for touring.

Tangier, Essaouira and the Atlantic coast

Despite our Euro-centric conceptions, Morocco is an Atlantic rather than a Mediterranean country with a seaboard that runs for over 2,000km and land that produces most of the country's food.

Photo Dar Zarraba, entry 97

Marrakech and the High Atlas

A cultural rather than a geographical area that drains over half Morocco's tourist traffic and has the highest density of places to stay; the ultimate must, it occupies 40 per cent of this book.

Fez, Meknès and the Middle Atlas

The great central area of Morocco has played a major part in her history and Fez claims proudly to have seen the birth of the university as medieval Europe came to understand it. It is without doubt the country's grandest, most cultural metropolis.

The South

Lastly, the southern Atlantic stretch, the desert and the oases, the harsh and the gentle that have forged the character and wealth of the region's inhabitants, as well as the history of the whole country.

Introduction

What to expect

Staying in this country of extremes can take you from the luxuriously sublime to the ridiculously simple, from near-celebrity status in an ancient palace to the most human warmth and the least facilities of a roadside inn. 'Special' does not mean perfect, it means that something makes a place stand out – it may be its architecture, position, people, interior design or history. In our wide selection of places, most of them classified as guest houses of varying sizes and degrees of luxury, we hope to have made the differences clear in the descriptions so that you only choose places that suit you.

Proper names

Transcriptions from Arabic to Roman letters vary a lot. Some of our place names do the same, to prepare you for life on the ground.

Contact and bookings

Most bookings can be made by email, telephone or fax direct to Morocco but read the entry carefully: some owners only accept fax or on-line bookings, others give a French, Spanish or British telephone number (codes +33, +34, +44 respectively) alongside the local number.

• Telephones are not always reliable so some owners have more than one line and a mobile number.
• The national code is 212; all Moroccan numbers start with 0 (for inland calls only, not to be used when calling from abroad) followed by eight digits.
• Mobile (or GSM)* numbers start with (0)6 or (0)7. Numbers given here follow on without repeating identical elements.

e.g.: +212 (0)44 44 55 55/77 77
+ : the international access code from the telephone you are using from outside Morocco
212 : code for Morocco from outside the country
(0) : dial only if calling from within Morocco
44 44 55 55 : the owner's first land-line which reads in full (0)44 44 55 55
/77 77 : the owner's second land-line which reads in full (0)44 44 77 77

*GSM (pron. "jay ess em") is the term used in Morocco for mobiles. This edition includes a specific GSM slot as more and more owners are relying on this system.

Photo left Auberge de Tameslohte, entry 96
Photo right Dar Beida, entry 13

Introduction

Rooms and bathrooms

We tell you the types of rooms available (doubles, twins, suites, etc). Unless otherwise stated, they have their own bath or shower with wc, and suites are for two people. Given the country's limited water supply, showers are the rule, baths the exception. It may be possible to add beds for children; ask when booking.

A Berber salon or dormitory is a dual-purpose room with a few low tables and two to twelve typical padded benches round the walls that are converted into beds for the night. Bedding may be provided or brought by the sleepers, depending on the category of the inn.

Suite has a special Moroccan meaning: in a traditional riad house, there are three big to very big rooms leading directly off the patio through those four-metre high carved doors. These rooms are often used as salons or dining rooms but when they are used as bedrooms they are, by unspoken agreement, called suites. i.e. their generous rectangular space easily contains a large double bed, often a four-poster, at one end, and a sitting area at the other.

Prices

The basic price listed is for a room for two for one night with breakfast, unless otherwise stated. If we give a range, it means either that some rooms are more expensive than others or that some seasons are more expensive than others, or both. If breakfast is not included, its price will appear under Meals.

Prices are often negotiable, especially outside the spring and Christmas/New Year peaks (when they may be higher than published). Many places offer terms for children, half or full board, long stays, etc., or package deals with desert treks, spa treatments, golf. Ask when booking.

Some prices are quoted with local *taxe de séjour* included, others not. You may find this small amount levied per guest per night by the town council added to your bill. The same goes for VAT.

Photo Riad Norma, entry 118

Published at the end of 2005, the prices printed here are liable to be altered at any time and most will be changed for autumn 2006.

Breakfast

Generally included in the price, it varies from basic continental to a feast that will have delicious little Moroccan pancakes, eggs and cheese – enough to set you up for the whole day.

Other meals in guest houses

Most guest houses employ a permanent cook and do dinner if you book in advance. The commonest menu is delicious mixed Moroccan salads followed by tagine or couscous then a pastry or fruit, but some houses pride themselves on real gourmet food. They will often do light lunches too, or pack a picnic. Small hotels in towns generally leave the provision of meals to their restaurant neighbours.

Meals in hotels

Tourism in Morocco is still very group-based and, in the south, mostly open-air. As a result, apparently small hotels may have intimate interiors for their residents but feeding space for coachloads in their gardens, so the bower where you had settled down for a quiet lunch beneath the acacia tree can suddenly be invaded by bevvies of excited tourists just in from the

carpet bazaar who will have a quick lunch and be shepherded off to the next delight.

Alcoholic drinks

Some places sell wine, others allow you to bring you own (BYO); some do not specifiy but this does not always mean no wine. In this constitutionally Islamic country, the situation is delicate. Some places will neither sell alcohol nor accept that guests bring it in. However, many guest houses and small hotels sell wine with meals but do not have a licence so cannot announce the fact. On the other hand, they want you to drink their wine – which can be good and interesting Moroccan – rather than bring in something from the local supermarket. So please understand this before arriving with bags of clanking bottles and asking for a corkscrew.

Photo Riad Al Zahia, entry 24

Introduction

Directions

We have been as clear as possible but always check the itinerary when booking. Guest houses in the medinas can be hard to find the first time; they will generally arrange for someone to meet you at an agreed spot and escort you in. Thereafter, you will quickly learn the route – it's a great way of taming one corner of an inscrutable medina.

Out in the country, when we say, for example, 'from Marrakech for Amizmiz 24km...' this generally means that at or very near the 24km 'milestone' there will be a sign or a turning, so no need to worry about the exact distance from some undefined spot in Marrakech.

Disabled and limited mobility

Morocco is behind Europe and America in providing for the disabled but if rooms and especially bathrooms lack the specific equipment, the traditional architecture is in your favour: many places have a ground-floor bedroom and communal life is lived around the patio so once you have negotiated the two or three steps from the front door, it should be plain sailing.

Animals

There are cats absolutely everywhere in towns so even places without the 'pets live here' symbol is likely to have them wandering around.

Photo Riad Maizie, entry 79

Types of places to stay
Guest house: *Maisons d'hôtes* or B&B Moroccan style

The Moroccan breed of *maison d'hôtes* is comparable to no other I know and the English is an inadequate translation. They all employ permanent staff, the minimum being a handyman, a chambermaid and a cook. Remember, this is the country where the guest palace – *palais d'hôtes* – was invented.

Over 90% of guest houses in Morocco are owned by non-Moroccans. The owners may live elsewhere in the town, or even in another country, in which case they employ a good manager. This is still a new phenomenon, new houses are opening and old houses are changing hands fast, so some of our addresses are bound to have different owners and managers before the next edition is out (2007); others will have been sold to people who are not continuing the B&B activity. We have tried to include guest houses where the owners are present at least for the essential moments: arrival (when tea or a cool drink will probably be offered), aperitif time and possibly dinner if you are dining in, then breakfast the next day. Where the owners are more often absent than present, the atmosphere will be less immediately 'family' but

Introduction

managers and housekeepers, be they Moroccan or European, are generally friendly, knowledgeable and helpful – "smiling to break your heart".

The traditional architecture of a house with blank outside walls and welcoming courtyard inside usually means that bedrooms give onto the patio only. This makes the smaller riads and dars feel pretty intimate. It's always cooler on the ground floor than up under the roof. In big houses, rooms may be different sizes as the women's quarters were narrower and more secret than the men's quarters, where people from outside were received and a grander display was required.

Auberge: travellers' resting place with a few rooms and a good family restaurant open to non-residents; or a relatively remote hostel/base camp for excursions and organised adventures into the desert or the mountains, possibly with an overnight bivouac; or the two combined.

Small hotel: place with presence and character; can have up to about 25 rooms and widely differing levels of comfort and price.

Hotel: can have 25 to as many as 60 rooms but, even if less intimate, has been chosen for some specific quality of history, atmosphere or setting.

Catered house: either a B&B guest house that can be rented exclusively by one group or family by the day or the week, or a flat or house that is only offered for sole occupancy. As the terms generally include breakfast and staff remain to do the cleaning and provide meals if you want, this doesn't really count as 'self-catering'. We give rental prices where available.

The advantage of having someone who asks you what you want to eat and then does the shopping needs no emphasising; you can even ask to go with her and see how it's done. If you reckon your catering for the week would come to €150, you will probably find that you can spend a little less here and have the work done for you. This could be a novel way of doing your annual family gathering.

Even houses and flats let as 'self-catering' will come with cleaning and laundry included, though the staff will be less present.

Staff
The men and women who staff the Moroccan places to stay are, almost without exception, charming, smiling, friendly and helpful without being obsequious. They hope guests will treat them with the same degree of respect and friendliness. Certain guest-house owners like

them to wear the traditional jellabah, others are happy for them to work in civvies, though many women wear headscarves with their T-shirts and trousers.

Extra services

Places to stay often have an arrangement with a taxi driver or a local rental agent and can offer very good deals compared to the big car-hire companies.

Inside Morocco
Medinas

Medinas are not western cities. Both their architecture and way of life are specific and ancient. You should visit the three main medinas – Fez, Marrakech and Essaouira – for an idea of how different they can be. Know that in Fez street signs are in Arabic only and that house signs are more or less forbidden in all the old cities. Arm yourself with a good map (see Reading List at back of book) and plenty of time.

● **Fez** the ancient, the grand, the proud, is the centre of Morocco's intellectual and religious heritage. Built on several hills, encircled by others, it has a marvellous, organic shape and masses of personality. Grand palaces, crumbling or restored, hide at every turn, their ceilings higher, their decoration more finely elaborate than anywhere else.

● **Marrakech** the red rambles dustily across a vast, totally flat area – a foretaste of the desert. High red-earth walls lead you past anonymous doors, sometimes along endless twisting *derbs* – to perdition? No, you always find your way in the end. The legendary Jemaâ El Fna square may now be paved – that dreamy sunset dust cloud no longer covers the scene as you look down from a high terrace in the early evening – and its stall-holders provided with identical twee little chariots, it is still the authentic centre of the old Arab city and home to story-tellers and snake-charmers, performing monkeys and henna-painters.

● **Essaouira** the white is smaller, cooler, has sea air, more open streets, alleys hung with carpets and an inimitable shipyard and fish market out by the harbour. It has had more contact with the rest of the world because of its desirability as an Atlantic coast haven but its houses are more modest, more inward-looking and darker than in Fez or Marrakech, their central patios smaller and often covered with a glass top or tarpaulin in cold wet weather. Terraces can be bracingly windswept and gull-perched.

Medinas were designed by and for a thrifty, resource-conscious people

People and practices of Morocco
Bargaining, hassle and carp\et sellers
Bargaining is part of the Moroccan way of life: you are expected to take time doing important things like spending your money. It is a sign of respect, not a tourist-fleecing plan, a civilised way of relating human to human, not a battle to the death. So relax, smile, enjoy it – and aim to reduce most prices by about one third. And if you don't want an object, don't begin the process, however pressing your merchant may be. Use all your acting skills and be properly appreciative of his.

In towns other than Marrakech and Fez, where local police enforce the law against pestering people with offers of goods and services, you may be bothered by sellers of minerals, fossils, brasses, etc and by unofficial guides demanding to show you the sights. If it's your first visit, you may want an official guide – if you don't mind an occasionally disdainful attitude to less fortunate compatriots. You can find one at the Tourist Office and he will 'protect' you against the others (while pointing you out by virtue of his conspicuously neat jellabah or shiny medallion). Or you can choose the most honest-looking chap on the square – at your own risk. Most guides have commission agreements with merchants in the bazaars – but he do know their way around when you don't.

and are ill-adapted to the greed of our western habits. Water supply, for example, is a serious problem and pressure can be erratic, even non-existent. The situation is bound to get more crucial as each new guest house, swimming pool and golf course forces the demand up, ever up, depriving first the poorer Moroccan inhabitants then even us, the wealthy water-guzzling tourists. Be prepared for occasional drops in pressure while you shower and remember that if you are aware of the impending crisis and make it quick, your shower will be less of a drain on limited resources

Photo Riyad Al Moussika, entry 44

Carpet selling is not confined to shops or bazaars. We were asked by a 'hotel worker' in the Todra Gorge to "drive him back to town for his three-weekly visit to his mother". On arrival, he offered us money which we naturally refused. This created a debt: he was obliged to return our generosity with tea at home, "just to meet my family and say goodbye". At 'home', we met his 'brother and sister'. They took us up to a big empty room with six looms round the walls – each with a work in progress – and the tea tray. Our hitch-hiker had vanished. Two hours, six cups of tea and dozens of carpets later, we left with two of the latter and minus a substantial cheque in euros.

Getting things done

An old Morocco hand once told us "Asking for the man in charge can be a lengthy procedure; if possible, in any office, try and find a woman." She will not be 'in charge', she will be overworked, a bit taciturn and stiff, but she will probably be the only one who knows how to use the computer, make a booking, print a ticket, etc.

Always check telephone numbers on a card or flyer with the person handing it to you. Telephone numbers change frequently and may well have changed since the print job was done.

Photo Riad Aïda, entry 75

Women – Moroccan and visiting

It is perhaps understandable that, as western women coming from decades of "if you've got it, flaunt it", we should initially feel uncomfortable, even rejected by being looked at askance in our normal clothes and hailed with "gazelle! bonjour gazelle!" From the other side, some of us rise in feminist fury at veiled women, though I have never heard anyone remark that the man in the hooded jellabah is downtrodden and needs a defence society to save him from oppression.

Vive la différence! Our cultures, traditions and unwritten rules are different, neither better nor worse, just different, and if we want to reach into the very real cultural, aesthetic and human pleasures that Morocco offers us, including its simpler way of

Introduction

life and lack of consumer frenzy, then we must be tolerant of the ground rules of that simplicity. When I hear that rooftop swimming pools are, in fact, only allowed if bathers in bikinis cannot be seen from neighbouring roofs, I feel it is perfectly reasonable: the Moroccan sense of decency is similar to ours some 50 years ago. When I am told that bare midriffs, miniskirts and shorts shock the inhabitants of the old Arab towns, I feel that is reason enough for not wearing them in public.

In Moroccan towns, one sees women wearing a whole range of dress, from smart hairdo and lipstick over trendy denim trousers and jacket to tidy white scarf over designer suit to full flowing robe, veil and black lace face mask (often competing with a pair of glasses for space on the nose). Then I remember that my grandmother would never have worn trousers but found it perfectly all right that her daughter did and that her grand-daughters wore skimpy bikinis in front of her friends. In Morocco today, women are less hassled when soberly dressed without too much skin showing.

Here is some advice from Holly Larsen Boissevain, who visited Morocco with two girlfriends.

Photo Chez Momo, entry 104

"Morocco is a stunning country to visit but young women travellers should be aware of the implications of journeying through a semi-medieval land unescorted by a man.

"The key to avoiding harassment lies in donning long skirts, scarves and shawls. Etiquette becomes even more crucial off the beaten track and should be taken very seriously in the remote towns. If you still get pestered to an unreasonable degree, don't confront those who follow you! Instead, learn a few Arabic phrases (French won't get you far at all). A simple "min fadhlik" (please) and "shukran" (thank you) will help you gain the respect of Moroccans and demonstrates a respect for their culture.

"The best way of avoiding these social perils is to employ an official guide. Offers from men on trains who happen to bump in to you and 'know the city' should not be accepted. The tourist offices have excellent guides who have a set price and will not overcharge. They take you to areas of the medinas you would otherwise be nervous to approach and are wonderfully helpful, not least at providing mid-tour Arabic pronunciation lessons! Some of the medinas are so vast that it might be best to have a guide for two half days rather than one, so you can take things at your own pace."

Introduction

Poverty

First-time visitors are often surprised, even shocked, to see evidence of poverty in the streets, the markets and the tourist sights of Morocco, alongside some demonstrations of almost overbearing luxury. Like others, you may feel uncomfortably privileged all of a sudden. It is, however, still true that traditional family solidarity holds the worst effects of deprivation in check, especially in rural areas. Once people leave the drought-stricken countryside to look for work in the towns, their family ties get overstretched and their situations become more precarious. This is the hardest part of our learning curve of this extraordinary country.

Begging

Moroccans are generous with their beggar population – the Koran encourages believers to give money or at least a smile. We found it proper to follow their example. One dirham is more than fair but smaller change is hard to come by. When you are guiltily and silently cursing the little children grabbing at your garments, their mothers sitting in corners with babes in their arms, their grandfathers chanting religious homilies to the rattle of a begging tin, it's worth remembering that in 2005 the official minimum monthly wage was 2010Dh, (roughly 200 euros or dollars), that very many workers are not even paid this much and that unemployment is high. But don't give money to children (now read on).

An example among others: under the guidance of the Moroccan-European team at the Kasbah du Toubkal, the villagers of Imlil are teaching their children not to ask tourists for coins or pens or sweets and a neat little message is handed to guests reminding them that children who beg money or biros from foreigners are not in school. If you withhold the easy gift and contribute to the local school books fund instead, you will be helping those children learn their way to prosperity rather than beg their way to a lifetime of poverty.

The section on Conservation and Development at the end of this book gives ideas for useful contributions that should reach their proper destinations.

Litter

A national disaster, especially plastic. No-one can fail to be horrified at the reams and streams of coloured plastic that are thrown by the winds in garlands across the shanty towns, waste lands and scrub of city borders. One of our owners got parliament to pass a bill outlawing the sale and distribution of small supermarket plastic bags. A brilliant move, it has yet to be enforced – because industrial interests would suffer.

Language: Arabic or Berber, French or Spanish

Arabic is the official language but this is a multi-lingual country, its history illustrated by the languages its people speak. The presence of the original Berber inhabitants from early pre-history is proven. In the eighth century, the Arabs invaded, brought Islam in their wake, and continued into Spain. For seven centuries, Morocco and Andalucia were interwoven by dynastic currents and cross-cultural influences until the Andalucian Moors were expelled from rechristianised Spain in the 15th century. In the 19th century, various European countries tried to gain a foothold until, eventually, Spain and France were allowed to share the task of 'protecting' Morocco.

Half the population are of Berber (properly Amazigh) descent and speak one of three Amazigh languages and Arabic. In towns, almost everyone also speaks French but in the north many people are more comfortable with Spanish. Moroccans are excellent linguists and you will find great willingness to try and speak English but remember that this is, from a traveller's point of view, a francophone country. Children in the street want to practise the French they are learning at school. It is a joyous hubbub of sense-making, not a tower of Babel.

Photo Riad Merstane, entry 49

Modernities

When you stay in a medina and stand on one of those wonderful roofs, you will be astounded by the forest of satellite dishes growing there. The effects are not always visible on the ground but world television is entering practically every Moroccan home.

Photography, rural exodus and urban poverty

The culture of modesty, in women and girls especially, is part of traditional Amazigh upbringing, where women are to be respected and not looked at – a woman is always tied to someone else, first her family then her husband. Coachloads of loud tourists brandishing cameras make them retreat even further into their haïks (veils) and they are reluctant to be photographed. In other families things are more relaxed and it's not a problem. Always ask before taking a picture of a Moroccan; asking for an address to send them the printed picture (only if you really intend to do this, of course) is much appreciated.

Introduction

Do not give money for photographs, particularly to children. Ten dirhams, a minute sum for us, represents one third of a farm worker's daily wage. Children, quickly learning to skip school for the sake of these coins, just as quickly come to despise their parents' way of earning a living and take off as early as possible for the 'city paved with gold'. There, the hideous truth of slums and shanty towns forces them into begging, drug-dealing and prostitution. Once again, don't give money to children.

Speaking the social and body language of Morocco

Moroccans appear to spend half their lives out in public and are naturally friendly and helpful – if you share a language. From another point of view, they are very secret people, draping their bodies in coveralls, living in houses that face inwards, denying any but the faithful a look into their places of worship. They live quite differently inside their own homes among their own clan. However, out in public you will see the men embrace with great vigour, walk hand-in-hand and behave in other surprisingly demonstrative ways. Moroccans also have a very different concept of personal space from ours: their way of huddling close is not threatening and should not make you feel uncomfortable.

Food and drink

Water People living here drink the water from their wells or from their taps when they know it is safe but it is advisable to stick to bottled water until you are acclimatised. Flat spring water is *eau pure*, fizzy water is *eau gazeuse*. Waiters will automatically bring you a big bottle unless you specify small.

Alcohol Consumption of alcohol, specifically wine, is forbidden by the Koran. Morocco is an Islamic monarchy, the King is a direct descendant of the Prophet Mohammed with the title of Commander of the Faithful, and Moroccan Muslims are theoretically forbidden to buy alcoholic drinks. In fact, only hotels and guest houses may serve alcohol in the medinas but bars, cafés and restaurants in other parts of town are often licensed, though drinking alcohol out of doors is still prohibited. A bottle of drinkable Moroccan table wine should cost about 100Dh in a restaurant.

Non-alcoholic specialities Mint tea, the national drink, is offered as "Moroccan whisky" by gently-smiling half-apologetic waiters; it comes with excessive amounts of sugar – you can ask for *sucre à part* (sugar separate) and dose your own – and it can turn out to be an unexpected pep-up. They may offer many other

drinks with healing properties.
Try their herbal infusions, especially
romarin or *thym* (rosemary or thyme)
for an upset stomach. Alternatively,
if you choose *thé noir* it will most
probably be that familiar yellow-
labelled echo of tea.

The freshly-squeezed juice of several
oranges is a recurring delight – you
should get it for breakfast and find it
at market stalls or in any café when
you collapse from sights-overload.

Food Moroccan food can be
remarkable – memorable mixes
of ultra-fresh vegetables, meat
and fish in subtle sauces. Most
meat is mutton or chicken as the
climate is not good for bovines.
Unfortunately, the tourist menus
found all over the country tend to
be repetitive and bland. One tip is
to eat cheaply – vegetable
couscous, salads – for two or three
days and save up for a good
restaurant at the end. It's really
worth it, the contrast is so striking.

Vegetarians Moroccan cooking
uses a lot of vegetables but,
paradoxically, it isn't an easy
place for pure vegetarians. Lovely
vegetables are generally cooked
with meat, or at least steamed
above it. So flexibility is needed.
You can always get vegetables
only, you can't often avoid all
traces of meat.

Photo Kasbah Mohayut, entry 134

Organic produce It is quite difficult
to give a true organic label to food
grown in Morocco because a lot of
the water used to irrigate crops is
polluted and the land tends to be
used and used until it is exhausted
and another piece brought into
exploitation. However, crops are
subjected to far fewer pesticides
and chemical fertilizers than in the
west and in this sense are 'cleaner'.
The budding Moroccan organic
industry is mostly for export at this
early stage.

Practical tips
Packing reminder
Bring a rubber bung plug, a torch,
ear plugs, a corkscrew, your
favourite pillow and a remedy
for diarrhoea.

Introduction

Pillows

Big thick pillows are considered The Best – if they don't suit you, bring your own skinny one.

Baths and basins

Take a flat rubber bung plug as even in the best houses plugs disappear and it's especially upsetting to waste water here (see Conservation and Development at the back of this book).

Driving

Avoid driving after dark. Roads may be pot-holed, lorries drive determinedly down the middle, cars and bicycles cannot be relied on to carry decent lights, pedestrians and donkey carts disappear into the night.

Electricity

The current is 220 volts and Moroccan sockets are two-pin style, like French ones, so you will need an adaptor for your plugs and a transformer for 110-volt appliances.

Lighting seems to be planned for its capacity to create atmosphere rather than to make things visible and dinner is very often served by candlelight. Take a good torch for reading in bed! Also, power cuts are not infrequent, particularly outside the cities, and some country places only have electricity from 6pm to 10.30pm. The rest of the time it's candles and lanterns.

Health

Though not inevitable, it is likely that you will suffer a bout of *la turista*. Take a reliable diarrhoea remedy. However, classic remedies in traveller's first-aid kits such as Imodium work by simply disabling your gut, i.e. they prevent the desperate dashing to the loo but don't help you get over the bug. In normal circumstances it's much better just to go as frequently as you need to, making absolutely sure you replenish both loss of fluid and salts after each trip. Your chemist will sell you rehydration packs for exactly that.

Maps

Our general maps are not for use as road maps and if you are planning to drive, get a good map such as the Michelin: clear and accurate, it even shows the types of trees that grow in different areas. For detailed walking maps, consult a specialist bookshop such as Stanfords (www.stanfords.co.uk).

Photo Riad Lune et Soleil, entry 110

Money

The national currency, the dirham, is divided into 100 centimes. It is illegal to take dirhams out of Morocco or bring them in so you need to change money at your point of arrival (or at a French airport). You may be asked when leaving to change any dirhams you have left into hard currency – at a relatively unfavourable rate, so aim to have as few as possible in your pocket when you get to the airport.

Cash dispensers are found in the most out-of-the-way places and your hosts are usually happy to be paid in cash – some only take cash. Unless they have the  symbol, owners accept payment by credit card, (often excepting American Express or Diner's Club). However, the card machines in guest houses, hotels and petrol stations do not always work, in which case you have to go to the nearest cash dispenser.

Should you ever find you need to write a cheque, be prepared to be asked to do it in blue ink, not black. There is a belief that black ink does not make legal tender.

Small change is rare – you may begin to wonder what 50 centimes look like. There appears to be a dirham economy and a centime economy: foreigners join the former and are seldom given centimes in change so if you want change for tips or alms or you are simply curious, buying individual stamps should bring in the little ones. And you quickly learn to hoard small coins like a miser gathering gold.

Noise

Not all hotels are protected from street noise so take your ear plugs.

Passport & Time zone

A passport valid for six months from the date of entry is required. Morocco is on GMT all year round.

Taxis

They come in two sizes, big and little. *Petits taxis* are restricted to inner city areas. They are numerous, battered, quick and cheap – this is the best way to get around, even over short distances inside the medinas. *Grands taxis* are, indeed, bigger and more comfortable for the longer distances. Always either make sure the driver turns the meter on (it

Introduction

seem a rather superior, wealthy westerner's attitude but, interestingly, locals welcome it because you save them having to wait for the grand taxi to achieve its six-person quota.

Your silent reaction when you get your first taxi may be "I'll choose better next time, it looks and sounds so worn and patched-up."
But you soon realise that they are all like that, as hard-working and enduring as the donkeys. Moroccan taxi drivers are highly skilled and you will learn to trust them as they weave and hustle through alleyways already filled to the brim with pedestrians, animals and pavement stalls.

is illegal not to) or, in a *grand taxi*, agree on the total charge – and the cost of carrying your bags – before driving off. It is normal for visitors to tip about 10% over the meter charge.

A grand taxi will not normally leave unless there are six paying passengers (two at the front, four at the back). In my own experience, travelling by *grand taxi* is the least comfortable way to travel in Morocco – if you exclude the Berber truck in the High Atlas. One way to get round this is to be willing to pay for one or two imaginary passengers as well as your own fare. By doing so you can be the only passenger at the front, or travel far more comfortably at the back. This might

Telephoning
Telephone connections are pretty good and everyone has a mobile but using your own mobile can be very expensive. Some old hands buy the cheapest Moroccan mobile on offer when they arrive plus a card – after the initial outlay, it costs very little. Or you can have your own mobile 'deblocked' and buy a Moroccan SIM card. Otherwise, the *téléboutiques*, found in the remotest spots, are brilliant. Quieter and easier than outdoor call boxes, they are like old post office boxes where you can stand and talk for hours, sheltered from sun and rain, feeding coins into the slot. It's 2Dh for any

Photo above Riyad Charaï, entry 47
Photo left La Villa des Orangers, entry 76

local call, more for long distance; the boutique manager has a bottomless stock of coins.

Tipping

It is normal to tip waiters, taxi drivers, porters, petrol pump attendants etc. something like ten per cent. When you park your car, look for the *gardien* to make sure he has taken you underhis wing: a picturesque ancient or a young boy, he will ward off all marauders. The normal rate is about 2Dh an hour.

Trekking and adventure – at your own risk

Many hotels and guest houses offer to organise excursions and treks, often with their own guides. There are also dozens of little shopfronts, especially in the desert-edge south, proclaiming their guiding skills on desert and mountain treks and bivouacs on foot, mule or dromedary or in 4x4 vehicles. You should know that few of these 'organisations' are registered or insured and you join their expeditions at your own risk. To be totally insured, choose a travel agent who displays his *Numéro de Patente*.

We have found the Moroccans to be among the gentlest and most tolerant of people. They are easy with foreigners and, as long as you don't appear to be aiming to offend their sensibilities, they are helpful and hospitable and sharing. However, it's useful to know that permits of all sorts, including driving licences and mountain guide certificates, appear to be obtained as often by connections as by practical testing of skills. Thus, one young Parisian Moroccan visiting her family in Casablanca was offered a driving licence as a birthday present; one competent, knowledgeable and committed young

Introduction

Berber was unable to pass his mountain guide exams because he could not afford the 'personal fee' charged by the examiner.

And beware of 'false guides' in the desert who are said to lay false trails, then leap to your succour when you get stuck in order to earn a goodly sum for your salvation.

Subscriptions

Owners pay to appear in this guide. Their fee goes towards the cost of inspections (every entry has been inspected by a member of our team before being selected), of producing an all-colour book and of maintaining a sophisticated web site. We only include places and owners that we find positively special. It is not possible for anyone to buy their way into our guides.

Internet

www.specialplacestostay.com has online pages for all of the places featured here and from all our other books – around 4,500 Special Places in Britain, Ireland, France, Italy, Spain, Portugal, India, Morocco, Turkey and Greece. There's a searchable database, a taster of the write-ups and colour photos.

Disclaimer

We make no claims to pure objectivity in choosing our Special Places to Stay. They are here because we like them. Our opinions and tastes are ours alone and this book is a statement of them; we hope that you will share them.

We have done our utmost to get our facts right but apologise unreservedly for any mistakes that may have crept in. Feedback from you is invaluable and we always act upon comments. With your help and our own inspections we can maintain our reputation for dependability.

You should know that we do not check such things as fire alarms, swimming pool security or any other regulation with which owners of properties receiving paying guests should comply. This is the responsibility of the owners.

And finally

A huge 'thank you' to all of you who have taken the time and trouble to write to us about your experiences and to recommend new places.

Ann Cooke-Yarborough & Jose Navarro

Photo Riad 72, entry 7

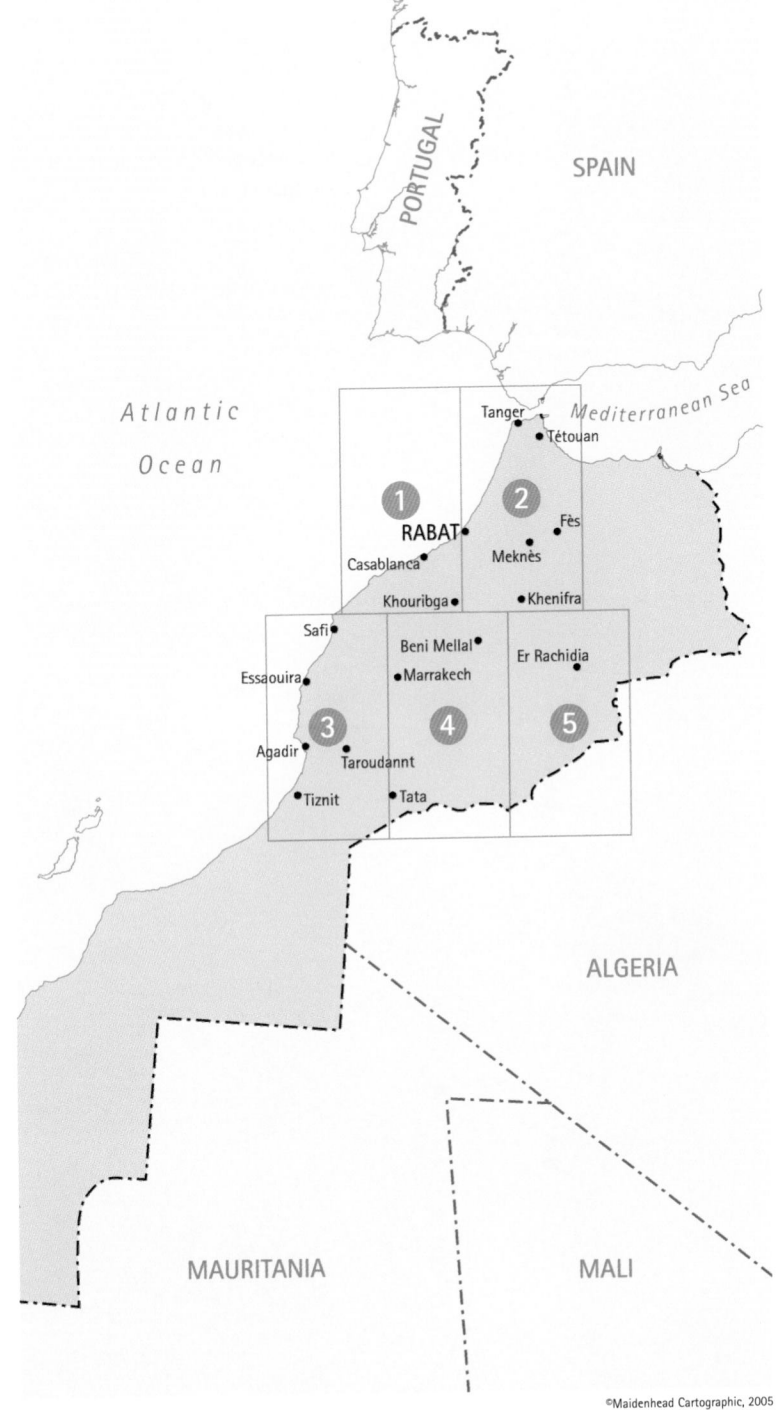

©Maidenhead Cartographic, 2005

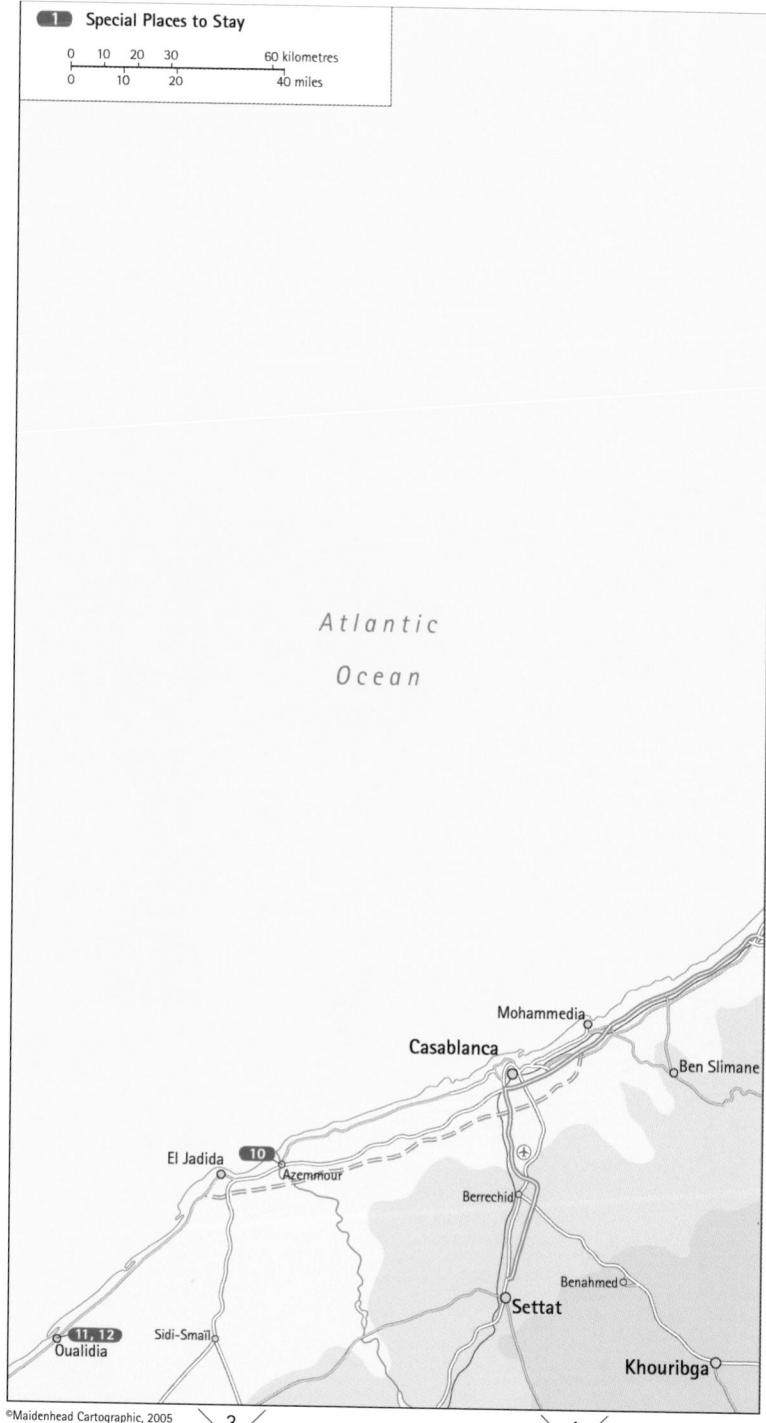

1 Special Places to Stay

0   10   20   30   60 kilometres
0   10   20   40 miles

Atlantic

Ocean

Mohammedia

Casablanca

Ben Slimane

El Jadida **10**

Azemmour

Berrechid

11, 12
Oualidia   Sidi-Smaïl

Benahmed

Settat

Khouribga

3   4

Map 2

37

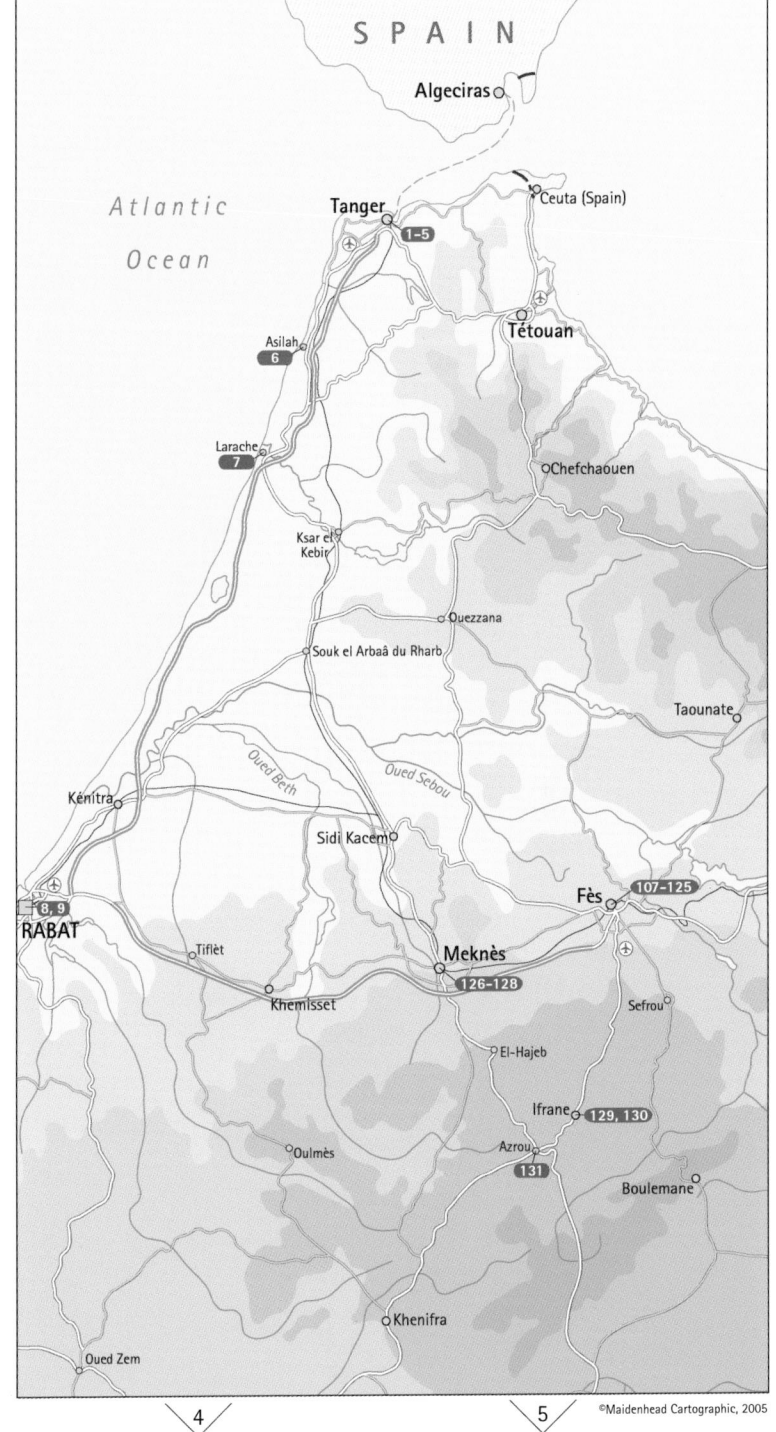

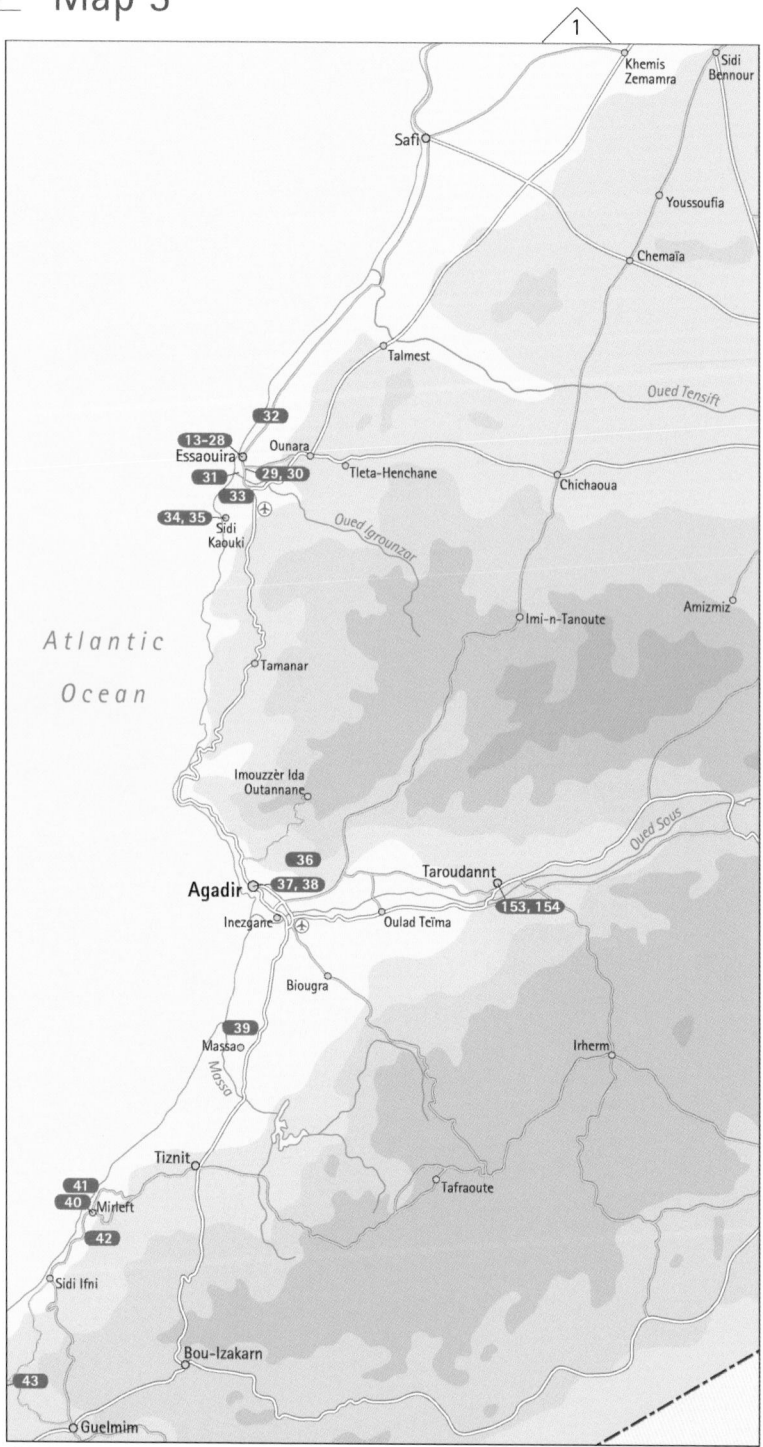

Map 4

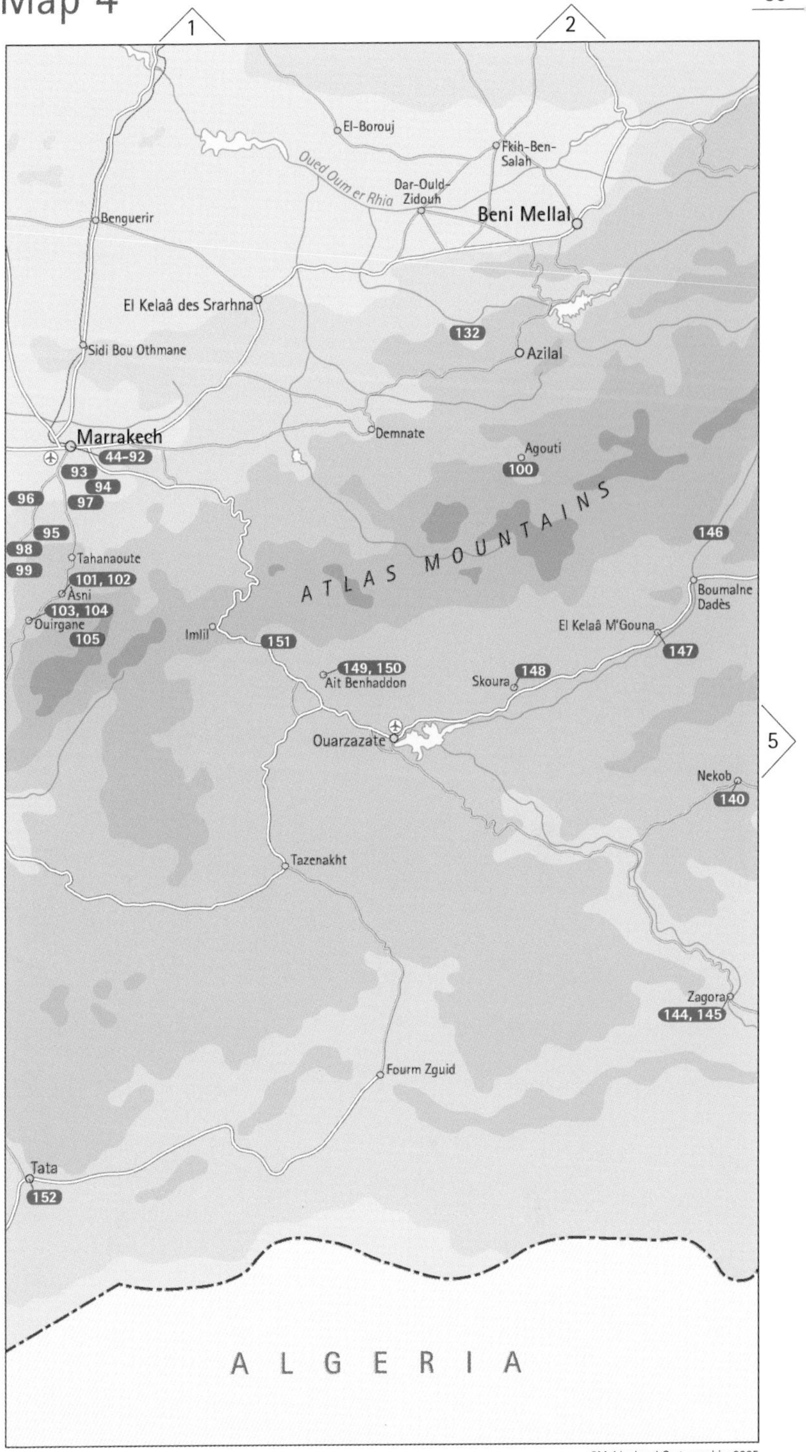

El-Borouj

Fkih-Ben-Salah

Oued Oum er Rhia

Dar-Ould-Zidouh

Beni Mellal

Benguerir

El Kelaâ des Srarhna

Sidi Bou Othmane

132

Azilal

Marrakech

Demnate

Agouti
100

44–92
93
94
96
97
95
98
99
146

Tahanaoute

ATLAS MOUNTAINS

Boumalne
Dadès

101, 102
Asni
103, 104
Ouirgane
105

Imlil
151

El Kelaâ M'Gouna

149, 150
Aït Benhaddon

Skoura
148
147

Ouarzazate

Nekob
140

Tazenakht

Zagora
144, 145

Fourm Zguid

Tata
152

A L G E R I A

©Maidenhead Cartographic, 2005

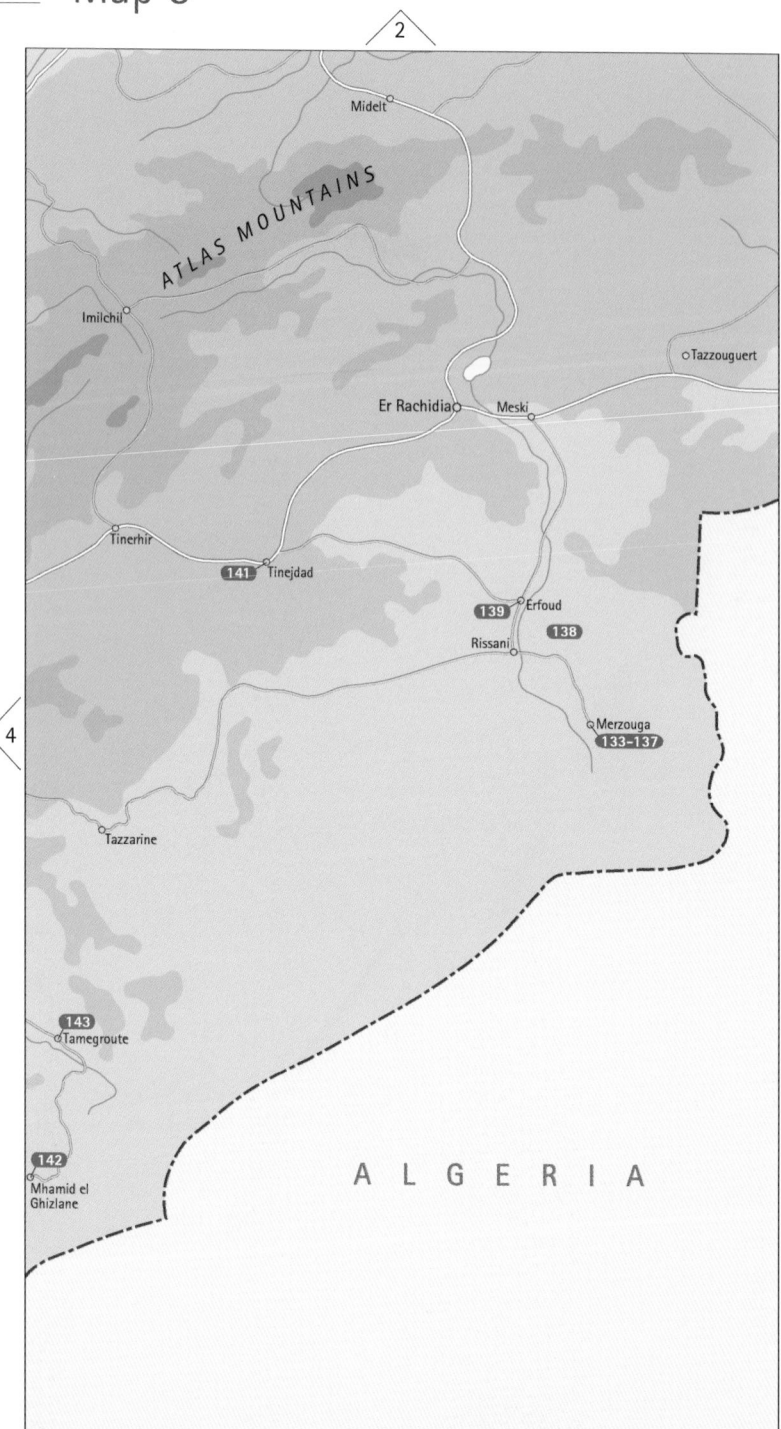

How to use this book

❶ region, district

❷ write up
Written by us.

❸ rooms
Assume rooms are en suite,
unless we state otherwise.

❹ price
The price shown is for two
people sharing a room. Half-
board prices are per person.
A price range incorporates
room/seasonal differences.

❺ meals
Prices are per person. If
breakfast isn't included we
give the price.

❻ closed
When given in months, this
means for the whole of the
named months and the time
in between.

❶ Desert oases

❷ Dar Azawad
Douar Ouled Driss, BP 16, M'Hamid

The desert sand flows seamlessly up the solid walls of this very civilised base for
exploring the barren lands and fabulous dunes that lie beyond M'Hamid, the
southernmost village of Morocco. Vincent, a charming, energetic Arab-speaking
art collector, has fulfilled his dream of creating a high-class trekking centre in a
tiny palm grove. He has done it with true French refinement: sober, local style
outside, some zinging colours on tiles, sabra-silk bedcovers, bright Berber rugs
and remarkably original bathrooms inside. You sleep either in an individual
miniature kasbah or in a bright-doored cabin with a camel-hair roof (they can get
very hot). Each room is different, full of personality, yet calm and comfortable
with a fascinating tadelakt bathroom. The tent corral washroom is unbelievably
smart – tadelakt basins topped with copper taps and brass-framed mirrors; the
dining room is a mass of fabulous pieces from Vincent's collection; the lovely pool
is in the centre of the 'hamlet'. Come to discover the desert – on foot, dromedary
or 4x4. It may seem expensive but there's none other like it.

❸ rooms	6 + 7: 5 doubles, 1 suite. 7 tents for up to 4.
❹ price	Half-board 1,000Dh-1,200Dh for two. 700Dh per tent for two half-board.
❺ meals	Half-board only. Lunch 110Dh.
❻ closed	Never.
❼ directions	From Zagora south to M'Hamid 86km. House on right 900m after Ouled Driss sign.

Small hotel

	Vincent Jacquet
tel	+212 (0)44 84 87 30
mobile	+212 (0)61 24 70 18
fax	+212 (0)44 84 87 30
email	vincent@darazawad.com
web	www.darazawad.com

❽

❾ Map 5 Entry 142

❼ directions
Use as a guide and travel with a good map.

❽ symbols
see the last page of the book for a
fuller explanation:

&#9831;	wheelchair facilities	🅥	good vegetarian dinner options
🏃	easily accessible bedrooms		
👶	children of all ages are welcome	🐱	owners' pets live here
		🔑	at least one bedroom has air-conditioning.
✗	no smoking anywhere		
💰	payment by cash or cheque only	🏊	pool on the premises
		🚲	bikes on the premises to borrow or hire
(Hello)	your hosts speak some English	🎾	tennis on the premises
		👟	information on local walks

❾ map & entry numbers

tangier, essaouira & the atlantic coast

Busily trading since the Phoenicians, this seaboard has been a meeting point for merchants and marauders, pirates and power-seekers from far and wide who have left historic cities, architecture and rich craftsmanship. Its rare pearls, jealously protected by heavy ramparts, are the medinas of Asilah, El Jadida, Essaouira. The cities of Tangier, Rabat, Casablanca and Agadir are variously interesting and the delightful hinterland, with some simple, authentic places to stay, must not be neglected.

We don't tend to see seaside resorts when we summon visions of Morocco but there are hundreds of miles of gorgeous, mostly empty, beaches along the beautiful and varied Atlantic coast. The ocean beats the shore relentlessly, be it rock or sand, the fish and seafood are superb, the swimming is exhilarating (but can be dangerous: there is a strong constant undertow).

Economically, most of the phosphates, the country's primary resource, mined here are exported from Safi. Almost all fishing - another major resource - takes place off the Atlantic coast, from the ports of Tan-Tan, Agadir, Essaouira, El Jadida and Casablanca, and much of Morocco's agricultural wealth is fed by Atlantic-driven clouds that are stopped by the Atlas mountains.

The southernmost part of the Moroccan Atlantic coast is where the Sahara Desert meets the Atlantic Ocean - a fearsome, hostile land of outstanding wild beauty.

Photo: Bénédicte & Damien Lecire, entries 40-41

Dar Sultan

49 rue Touila, La Kasbah, Tangier

Built in the 18th century on the ruins of the old kasbah (burnt down by the English) and a still-springing spring, this old *dar* is a bright, amusing gem. Maïté, passionate about her new life and ladling as much love on her guests as on her house, couldn't be more welcoming. There are flowers everywhere and oceans of candles on your dinner table; it always feels like a feast day here. The small bejmat patio flutters with ferns and potted palms, zellige highlights the natural background (22,000 tiles were cut), the house climbs up, up to the fourth floor. One room is slathered in stucco, stencilling and musical instruments (a G'naoua brotherhood once lodged here), another is a jackdaw's nest of colourful things and an amazing Turkish lamp, the terrace room has a staggering view across to Gibraltar; rent this high delight and the terrace is yours to enjoy. Bathrooms are small and pretty and may have Balinese camels or Tahitian shells on show; the tiny reading corner includes all the coffee-table classics on Morocco: come here to prepare your whole trip. The Durands are involved in Kasbah conservation.

Guest house

rooms	6: 2 doubles, 2 twins, 2 suites.
price	€80–€100, including airport transfers & parking.
meals	Lunch, 3 courses, €20. By arrangement.
closed	Never.
directions	From Place du Grand Socco take Rue d'Italie to 'La Porte de la Kasbah'. Ring for escort from here; guests can also be met off boat.

	Jean-Pierre & Maïté Durand
tel	+212 (0)39 33 60 61
mobile	+212 (0)71 18 15 80
fax	+212 (0)39 33 60 61
email	darsultan@menara.ma
web	www.darsultan.ma

Map 2 Entry 1

La Tangerina
19 Riad Sultan, Kasbah, Tangier

Jürgen and Farida took three years to accomplish this meticulously crafted conversion, done with materials salvaged from other period buildings, and create Tangier's newest kasbah guest house. The roof terrace, its absolute crowning glory, has indescribable views across the straits to Spain: what a place to chill out and watch the sun set after a pampering in the hammam. Jürgen, who is German, has very high standards and finishes are impeccable (the tadelakt in the bathrooms is luscious), yet he is the easiest, most affable company. After 20 years in Spain, he met the lovely, Farida – she is Moroccan, warm and friendly, too, as are their two young children – and they decided to move just across the narrow water. That original oriental hammam is what prompted them to buy this particular house. Three of the bedrooms have that straits view, all are done in soft colours and a style that is more colonial than Moroccan, reminders of Tangier's rich history, with an Arab, English or French… theme. They share a special love of breakfast so look forward to something special each morning.

rooms	10: 5 doubles, 2 twins, 3 suites.
price	€70-€200.
meals	By arrangement only.
closed	Never.
directions	From port up hill to main entrance of Kasbah then call La Tangerina for escort. Car access directions on request.

Jürgen Leinen & Farida Kanario
tel   +212 (0)39 94 77 31
mobile   +212 (0)72 20 90 83
fax   +212 (0)39 94 77 33
email   info@latangerina.com
web   www.latangerina.com

Guest house

Map 2 Entry 2

Dar Nour

20 rue Gourna, Kasbah, Tangier-Medina

After taking a guided mystery tour ever deeper and higher into the medina, you will be glad to find this civilised, hospitable house at the end of it. Not only is it beautiful, it is unusual, perfectly positioned and serves memorable breakfasts. Pure Tangier white outside, the 'house of light' is utterly personal inside. Philippe adopted Morocco decades ago, owned the famous Colonnes bookshop here and rubbed shoulders with the literary lights. His house exudes the energy of rich culture: books galore, a desk in every room, eye-catching pictures and sculpture, antiques and hangings against white walls, yet nothing overdone. With his willing aides Khadija and Abdellatif you will be well and intelligently cared for. Rooms are as vertical as the house with level changes, the odd duplex, a bed squeezed into a corner, those rather unforgiving pillows, two staircases, two restful windowless womb-like salons and two kitchens. Then you climb to the flowering terraces to contemplate the evening light over the panorama and dine on superb food. Everything here is seeking the light – you may join in.

rooms	7: 2 doubles, 1 single, 4 suites.
price	300Dh-1,100Dh.
meals	Dinner 150Dh. By arrangement.
closed	Never.
directions	From Kasbah car park 1st right to fountain on little square, immediately right 30m, lime green door.

Guest house

	Philippe Guiguet Bologne
tel	+212 (0)62 11 27 24
email	pgb.tanger@caramail.com
web	www.darnour.com

Map 2 Entry 3

Hôtel Continental

36 Dar Baroud, Tangier

Staying at the Continental means living, however briefly, inside a legend, breathing an air of friendly nostalgia and fun. Tangier's first hotel, built in 1865 for the cosmopolitan élite, used by spies on both sides in wartime, the Continental has seen many incarnations and never lost its charm or its heavenly marble staircase. Imaginatively renovated by the present owner and a young Fassi designer, the hand-painted bedrooms, stylish and bold, have thoughtful colour schemes, hangings and paintings old and new and decent bathrooms. The writer/poet/painter atmosphere, the whiffs of Graham Greene, are part of the fabric, in there among the keyhole arches and geometric tiles of the grand hall, on the vastly beautiful terrace whence Spain can be seen on fine days, in the dining room with its dripping chandeliers. The people here are relaxed and friendly, happy to swim in such rich streams and share their luck with fortunate guests. Right on the port, this is the place to be in summer when the city's windows are open east and west every hot afternoon and the draught cools it so blissfully.

rooms	60: 28 doubles, 21 twins, 6 triples, 3 quadruples, 2 suites.
price	396Dh–456Dh.
meals	Lunch/dinner 50Dh–100Dh.
closed	Never.
directions	Visible from port entrance but ask taxi to guide you in.

Landmark hotel

	Mohamed Soussi
tel	+212 (0)39 93 10 24/37 58 51
fax	+212 (0)39 93 11 43
email	hcontinental@iam.net.ma

Map 2 Entry 4

Le Mirage
Grottes d'Hercule, BP 2198, Tangier

Hunkered down on an Atlantic-battered headland, the Mirage's brilliantly flowered, manicured garden, and above it the superb plum-coloured restaurant, look south to golden sands – incomparable, no beach hotel could be better sited. They call it a club, in fact, and the words 'exclusive' and 'out-of-this-world' do come to mind. Sheltered from the unfettered elements in salons of classic European comfort, you have a sense of intimacy and secret magic, fed by original paintings and prints, some of remarkable quality, an excellent piano bar, world-renowned cuisine. White steps hurry down the cliff to the vast empty beach where the Caves of Hercules and the ancient Roman site of Cotta lie waiting. Sumptuous suites, each hidden in its own ground-hugging villa, come in several sizes of big, done in rich fabrics, smelling of traditional carved cedar, with luxurious cushions, marble bathrooms and private terraces onto palms and pool. Opulent, chic and nurturing, the Mirage is a place to be cocooned in exclusive peace (celebrities love it) and staff are appropriately top-class.

rooms	25 bungalow suites (double room & salon).
price	1,380Dh–8,000Dh.
meals	Lunch/dinner 100Dh–500Dh.
closed	Never.
directions	From Tangier for Rabat & airport 9km; right for Grottes d'Hercule. Hotel on left at 1st r'bout.

Small hotel

	Ahmed & Abdeslam Chakkour
tel	+212 (0)39 33 33 32
fax	+212 (0)39 33 34 92
email	mirage@iam.net.ma
web	www.lemirage-tanger.com

Map 2 Entry 5

Berbari

Dchar Ghanem, Cercle de Tnine Sidi El Yamani, Asilah

Out in the country, in the middle of the village, three hefty pillars bend under the weight of the years and the iron roofs so typical of this region, and you find storks on their scruffy great nests, the widest starriest skies in the north (Berbari uses candles or dim bulbs so as not to compete), a grand piano with a few good old armchairs under the sweeping tataoui salon roof and a splendidly light-hearted approach to décor, all items resuscitated from other lives and full of soul (quirky plumbing, too). Beamed, lime-washed rooms are all different in their simplicity of bright local fabrics against rough white walls, the Moroccan salon with its comfortably cushioned benches and uncluttered style is much favoured and your private space, be it sitting area or piece of garden, is a delight. Relax, stop dashing, take time to talk to the owners and staff – they love their land and customs – and discover genuine rural Morocco, the neolithic village, the braying, praying dawn chorus. In summer, you can rent one of their beach huts and sleep in splendid isolation. Real undiluted Morocco is here.

rooms	7: 4 doubles, 3 suites, each with salon or garden.
price	250Dh-700Dh for two. Summer beach huts 200Dh per night. Book ahead.
meals	Snacks 60Dh. Lunch/dinner 120Dh-200Dh. By arrangement.
closed	Never.
directions	If you have no 4x4 vehicle, it is essential to ring from Asilah for escort last 4km.

Guest house

	Louis Soubrier & Rachida Youdra
tel	+212 (0)62 58 80 13
email	louis.soubrier@caramail.com
web	www.berbari.com

Map 2 Entry 6

La Maison Haute
6 Derb Ben Thami, Larache

As you pass under the great old arch from colonial Hispania into eternal Arabia, this jewel of a medina house promises exoticism, with its ground floor of centuries-old souk shops, and gentle rest. Rising tall above that friendly bustle of an unsmartened medina, so far from the sophisticated frenzy of our cities, it is no deluxe tourist trap but a place to make contact with other people's reality and possibly your own. The owners have kept their renovation of the old house discreet and simple, respecting its original shapes and atmosphere. Sea light caresses the vibrant colour-washed walls until the sun dips and tinges the world with fire – you'll want to climb the four floors to the incredible terrace every day for this. Rooms are furnished with taste, rich Moroccan rugs and colonial furniture, the fruit of many *brocante* hunts, in an attractive mix of red velvet armchairs, dark old Spanish trunks, iron candlesticks. On the two bedroom floors, the central patio/landing is the place for cool-weather breakfasts and the terrace, of course, a must for dinner, all served with smiles and intelligence.

rooms	7: 5 doubles, 1 triple, 1 suite.
price	352Dh-572Dh.
meals	Lunch/dinner. By arrangement. BYO.
closed	Never but advance booking essential October to May.
directions	From Place de la Libération enter medina by Bab El Khemis: house is opposite.

Guest house

	Bertrand Capet & Marc Louis
tel	+212 (0)39 91 65 37
mobile	+212 (0)65 34 48 88
email	info@lamaisonhaute.com
web	www.lamaisonhaute.com

Map 2 Entry 7

Dar Baraka
26 rue Jamaâ, Kasbah des Oudaïas, Rabat

The austere kasbah, a huge circle of buff walls pushing right up to the estuary's edge, was built by Sultan Al Mansour as a centre for launching soldier monks against the heretics. From Dar Baraka's fabulous terrace, a simple wonderland of citrus, billowing bougainvillea and birdsong, you gaze down on the quiet cemetery, out to Salé and the sea (baraka means divine blessing). Immense care has been taken over the restoration of this magical house, light pours in from all sides onto the gentle colourless colours of the walls and hangings – ivory, beige, ecru, white – and the contrasting richnesses of carpets and cushions, antique mirrors and 1920s inlaid furniture, books and music in the cosy living room. The two fine big bedrooms, fresh, uncluttered and welcoming, carry a sense of colonial times, bathrooms are full of old-style chrome fittings. Jean, a refined, cultured and fascinating old Moroccan resident, suits the house perfectly and Hamza, his righthand man, as friendly and helpful as you could wish, will take you shopping or show you the astounding double vaulted cellar dug into the cliffside.

rooms	2: 1 double, 1 twin.
price	900Dh–1,300Dh. Sole occupancy 2,100Dh (max 5).
meals	French dinner 330Dh, Moroccan dinner 260Dh. By arrangement.
closed	Never.
directions	Enter Kasbah des Oudaïas at main gate Bab Al Qasha into Rue Jamaâ; last house in street.

	Jean Vassort
tel	+212 (0)37 73 03 62
fax	+212 (0)37 26 34 71
email	jvassort@iam.net.ma
web	www.darbaraka.ma

Guest house & catered house

Map 2 Entry 8

Villa Mandarine
19 rue Ouled Bousbaa, Souissi, Rabat

Art historian and lover of all Islamic arts, Claudy Imbert, dreaming her own architectural dreams, decided to transform her family's holiday mansion, with a Moroccan architect's valuable advice, into a very special hotel. You do indeed feel you are a personal guest of a delightful, lively, cultured family, not a client of a 36-room hotel. Son-in-law Antoine and three daughters make a great team. Set in delirious gardens, it has enough private corners for everyone: *Eden au Maroc*. In the original house are the glorious ochre-washed, Marrakech-red communal spaces – blue-tiled bougainvillea patio, 'African' bar, serene library, wide-open restaurant where the garden rushes in through glass. Round the generous patio are the sophisticatedly simple rooms, each with its own balcony-terrace, its own warm colours, its own pretty rugs and lamps, its own share of Claudy Imbert's personal and rewarding gallery of Morocco-linked pictures, from Michelangelo to local landscape to modern abstract. Sheer delight. And moreover – a famous restaurant, a real spa, a hammam, a jacuzzi and a resident massage lady.

Small hotel

rooms	36: 31 doubles, 5 suites.
price	1,800Dh–2,800Dh.
meals	Lunch/dinner 260Dh.
closed	Never.
directions	From west-bound ring-road, right Ave Mehdi Ben-Barka; pass two sets traffic lights; right Rue Ouled Saïd; 2nd right Rue Ouled Bousbaa; hotel on left (sign).

	Claudy Imbert
tel	+212 (0)37 75 20 77
fax	+212 (0)37 63 23 09
email	reservation@villamandarine.com
web	www.villamandarine.com

Map 2 Entry 9

L'Oum Errebia
25 Derb Chtouka, Azemmour-Medina

The most authentic little medina in the country at your back, a light-giving estuary sweeping out to sea before your eyes, an art gallery all around you: this is a groovy, boutiquey inn with a young heart and a sense of fun. It reflects the progressive spirit at work in Azemmour, once a thriving centre of Jewish culture. Because this is a residential medina – the souk is outside the old Portuguese ramparts – l'Oum Errebia is a haven of peace, an ideal environment for contemplating the myriad paintings, sculptures and art books – Moroccan and foreign – that greet you behind every arch, in every room of this pale water-lit house. Its traditional bones (it was once the caïd's kitchens and servants' quarters) have been renovated with a modern touch and the lovely river views just outside are centre stage. An unusual and beguiling place with bright-tiled sunken baths, pale rooms whose paintings leap out at you, intriguing modern furniture and lamps, the odd antique: some have inside windows, the best two are the diaphanous *Verte* and *Rouge*. Charming people, too.

rooms	6 twins, 2 sharing bathroom.
price	350Dh-700Dh. Breakfast 50Dh.
meals	Lunch/dinner 150Dh. By arrangement.
closed	Never.
directions	Arriving in Azemmour follow signs for Medina; park by Bab Maghzen (old door into medina) and ring for escort.

	Saïd Tlemçani	Guest house
tel	+212 (0)23 34 70 71	
mobile	+212 (0)66 82 42 33	
fax	+212 (0)23 34 77 05	
email	contact@azemmour-hotel.com	
web	www.azemmour-hotel.com	

Map 1 Entry 10

Maison de l'Ostréa II

Parc à Huitres et Coquillages No 7, Oualidia

Not only is the food divine at this restaurant with rooms, it is in one of the most beautiful spots on Morocco's Atlantic coast, the exquisite lagoon where the Phoenicians once fished and Jacques Pinscloux's beds grow most of the country's oysters. The lunchtime crowd scrambles for the freshest possible shellfish prepared by a brilliant chef. Manager Adbelhadi knows all there is to know about oysters, their lives and times and always has a helpful suggestion. Book a lagoon tour on the Ostréa's own barge. Later, sleep over the restaurant and the oyster beds. Each small, simple room has one wide double and one single bed, soft colouring, a walk-in cupboard and a plain white bathroom with all the necessary bits and good towels. You can fling wide the big square windows and breathe in the invigorating sea air or close their double-glazing against wind and wave. This is a peaceful place to sleep, then wake to the morning activity of fishermen and gulls in that limpid view across calm water and gleaming sands – an ornithologist's dream. Highly unusual and a very special spot.

rooms	5 family rooms for 3-4.
price	600Dh.
meals	Breakfast 50Dh (children free). In-house restaurant 80Dh-250Dh. 10% discount for bearers of this guide.
closed	Never.
directions	From Casablanca, on right as you enter Oualidia; signs.

Guest house

	Jacques Pinscloux & Adbelhadi Mounadi
tel	+212 (0)23 36 64 51
fax	+212 (0)23 36 64 53
email	ostreacasablanca@menara.ma
web	www.ilove-casablanca.com/ostrea

Map 1 Entry 11

Villa La Diouana
Douar Moulay Abdesalam, Oualidia

Dreaming of a refuge from the pandemonium of city life? La Diouana is it. There can be few places to stay anywhere in Morocco with so seductive a view: this exquisite house looks straight out across the enchanting lagoon. Inside, a harmoniously crafted understatement creates a relaxing, uncluttered mood of well-being with everything to soothe the senses. Nothing in these perfectly fitting blues and whites - with the occasional escapade into pinkness - distracts you from simply being with the mesmerising beauty that lies outside. Done by Belgian designers and tadelakt experts, the rooms are of the very best: natural-coloured tadelakt floors, deeply comfortable sofas, armchairs and beds, piles of cushions, a raised bath where you gaze on the horizon and wallow. All the comforts are here, the music system is excellent, lots of CDs and DVDs, a beautiful metal writing table. Kind, smiling Abdillah, the perfect manager, can also take you to the Pirates' Caves in his boat. Fishing rods are provided and Fatima will cook your catch, or prepare your oysters, or anything else you care for.

rooms	1 house for 6. 1 cottage for 2.
price	House £950-£1095 p.w. House + cottage £1,150-£1,350 p.w.
meals	Self-catering, or cook available. Lunch/dinner £6 p.p. by arrangement.
closed	Never.
directions	Entering Oualidia from Marrakech stop at Café La Jeunesse on left to ring Abdillah for escort (house 2 min walk, near old kasbah).

Self-catering

	James von Leyden
tel	+44 (0)7810 543951
mobile	+212 (0)66 55 16 46
email	james@33degreeslatitude.com
web	www.33degreeslatitude.com

Map 1 Entry 12

Dar Beida

141 rue Ibn Khaldoun, Essaouira-Medina

When Emma met Morocco, it was love at first sight – she bought a house rather than a bunch of souvenirs. She and Graham, both designers, uncovered a treasure trove of stone arches and rebuilt the shapes with loving artistry, creating an enchanting white womb of a house with not an ugly thing or a right angle in sight. Everywhere you sense their lightness of touch, love of beauty and quirky humour; if they are in town, their company is a huge bonus. From the front door you get your first vision of raw wood, books, African masks, 1960s collector bits, arts and crafts – just enough of everything, skilfully put together. Indoors are two sitting rooms, five pot-bellied fireplaces, bright cushions, benches, a wonderful modern-old kitchen, one double room by the shower and two fine cats. On the first terrace, a post or two support the Berber canopy over comfy benches and two rooms flank the big bathroom; up again, the most private room has its own terrace. Rachid organises, Amina cleans (and can cook), Mustafa can drive – the perfect setup. *Also Dar Emma, self-catering 'hippy' house for 2-4, £500-£600 per week.*

Catered house

rooms	House for 8 (4 doubles, 1 bathroom, 1 shower). Only let to members of same party.
price	£300 p.p. per week. (£100 supplement if under 4 people.)
meals	Self-catering, or cook available.
closed	Never.
directions	10 minutes walk from Place Moulay Hassan. Directions given on booking.

Emma Wilson & Graham Carter
tel   +44 (0)776 835 219
mobile   +212 (0)67 96 53 86
email   emma@castlesinthesand.com
web   www.castlesinthesand.com

Map 3 Entry 13

Dar Nafoura-Mogador

30 rue Ibn Khaldoun, Essaouira-Medina

This solid Breton couple's bounding enthusiasm for life in their new seaside town, and for all of magic Morocco, will inspire you to explore the treasures. Anyway, Jacky simply loves taking people to see the fish market, the village souk, the medina craftsmen. Sylvie stays happily tweaking the careful details of their warm open house that she so easily shares with her guests, closing the roof sail at night, opening it to the heavens in the morning so the sparrows can fly right down to gather your crumbs on the patio. Everyone said they were mad to up sticks for the unknown – it has been a huge success from day one. Through its narrow keyhole door, your big room, be it an ochre-red mezzanine suite or a cool blue double, will have *haïk* curtains, bejmat floors and a strong proud colour scheme: purple, red and ginger for example. The wicker or iron furniture, firm new beds and personal ornaments – local carved and inlaid tables, rugs, hangings, African carvings, paintings, typical lamps – give great character. But it's Jacky and Sylvie's infectious joy that make Nafoura so special.

rooms	8: 4 doubles, 1 twin, 3 suites for 2-5.
price	460Dh-730Dh.
meals	Dinner 110Dh.
closed	Never.
directions	From Bab Marrakech Avenue Mohamed El Qorry; 3rd right Rue Ibn Khaldoun; right at Dar Nafoura sign to house.

	Sylvie & Jacky Renan-Uguen
tel	+212 (0)44 47 28 55
mobile	+212 (0)61 69 70 76
email	s.renan@menara.ma
web	www.essaouiranet.com/dar-nafoura

Guest house

Map 3 Entry 14

Dar Liouba

26-28 impasse Moulay Ismaïl, Essaouira-Medina

Light rushes in from all sides, exceptional for a medina house. Maria, a cosmopolitan designer brimming with spirit and talent, is reputed for her furniture and her renovation of this former imam's house (the mosque sings out nearby) which celebrates her love of light, subtle colour, form and texture. From the fine stone arch you enter a broad living room where a little indoor garden thrives beneath the octagonal light and open moucharabieh galleries. Sit over tea in the clean-cut elegance of white, sand and warm-flame cushions, then move up to the serenity of soft pale bedrooms decked in lustrous cottons, interesting objects, carved alcoves. Her shower rooms are little gems, her linen so silky, her terrace charming and her top-floor apartment a restful pink and grey nest. She has respected the ethos of her old medina house without betraying her European eye. If possible, dine with this fascinating, eccentric, voluble artist who receives so brilliantly. When it's his turn, Peter is the perfect cultured host. "There is nothing ugly anywhere in this house," said one reader – nor any contrived Moroccanisms.

Guest house

rooms	6 + 1: 4 doubles, 2 twins. 1 apartment.
price	€60-€80. Sole occupancy €450 per day.
meals	Dinner, 3 courses, 180Dh. By arrangement.
closed	10-31 January.
directions	Enter medina at Bab Marrakech: Rue Mohamed El Qorry; 3rd right Rue Ibn Khaldoun; 1st right Rue Moulay Ismaïl; 2nd impasse on right, 2 lanterns at door.

	Maria Pergay & Peter Cheung
tel	+212 (0)44 47 62 97
mobile	+212 (0)63 18 29 60
fax	+212 (0)44 47 64 13
email	lallaliouba@menara.ma
web	www.darliouba.com

Map 3 Entry 15

Chez Rebecca

42-44 rue Boutouil, Essaouira-Medina

Rebecca's flats are a comfortable choice if you want to be independent with your family and don't mind sharing the panoramic terrace with other tenants. From the quiet little medina street where children play in the daytime, push the blue door and climb the clean wide tiled stairs. Each opens with a pale, airy, uncramped living area where stripped wood, white cushions on built-in benches and a hand-made wooden table set the scene. This easy minimalistic design is ideal with children as there's nothing to worry about. Rebecca provides a music centre and some CDs; bring your own, too. Bedrooms are similarly simple, lit by big windows onto the street, enlivened by red Moroccan rugs, alcoves and the occasional traditional hand-painted wall motif. Bathrooms are in the same vein: a good size, very clean, warm and dry with plenty of space to put your stuff and romantic lighting as well as daylight from the window. Each kitchen is small and simple with all the basics. Finally, Rebecca or Abdellatif will be welcoming, friendly and helpful. *Minimum stay 1 week.*

rooms	2 apartments for 6.
price	£295-£395 per week.
meals	Self-catering. Breakfast 25Dh. Lunch/dinner 150Dh-300Dh. By arrangement.
closed	Never.
directions	From Bab Doukkala take Avenue Zerktouni; left Rue Boutouil; road wiggles round to left; house on left at No 44.

Self-catering

	Rebecca du Plessis
tel	+212 (0)70 72 92 90
mobile	+212 (0)70 72 92 90
email	rebecca_du_plessis@hotmail.com
web	www.chezrebecca.co.uk/info

Map 3 Entry 16

Riad Marosko
66 rue d'Agadir, Essaouira-Medina

Ancient North African Essaouira is now twinned with historic French La Rochelle – two fortified ports – and this colourful house has become the heart of a gentle connection between them. Your hosts came from La Rochelle, witnessed the fascinating G'naoua music festival, fell under the windswept Souiri spell, and stayed. A most welcoming couple, they love modern art and their quiet personality informs a soft-textured, interesting house: a pale yellow *bhou* and patio where quiet water trickles, *haïk* veils as curtains, weavings, rugs and local artists' paintings on the walls. The colour scheme changes from floor to floor in rooms that are a good size, some with steep mezzanines under high, timbered, *tassioute* ceilings, (wood and bamboo) all with space, good storage, a sitting corner, a Berber rug or pot to decorate and a pretty tadelakt bathroom. In the superb G'naoua salon, musical instruments and paintings tell the story of the festival: the atmosphere is palpable. Stay a while: these thoughtful people are worth getting to know.

rooms	7: 2 suites, 5 family rooms for 3 to 5.
price	500Dh-600Dh.
meals	Restaurants nearby.
closed	Never.
directions	Enter medina at Bab Marrakech; 1st left 100m; follow signs (5 mins).

Guest house

	Mari & Rosko Becquet
tel	+212 (0)44 47 54 09
email	marosko2000@yahoo.fr
web	www.riad-marosko.com

Map 3 Entry 17

Casa Lila

94 rue Mohamed El Qorry, Bab Marrakech, Essaouira-Medina

The grand old house on the busy avenue is a funky-chic lilac hymn to Nat's taste (*lila*: night in Arabic, lilac in French) who else would dare lay a mauve floor, encrust it with coloured glass stars then leave it to age? In 2000, she and Philippe fell in love with Essaouira and created this open, welcoming house. Her cheerful personality radiates from every cushion, hammock and piece of music, she comes daily to do the flowers and make sure guests are happy. Great potted plants dangle down the pillars and ironwork, mauve cushions beckon from benches in the long Moroccan salon with its bulbous purple and white fireplace. Bedrooms, draped, fireplaced and ornamented, varying in size and mauveness, have country antique armoires, clever storage niches in the walls and small sweet bathrooms, some behind curtains (separate loos); the lovely duplex suite has a steep spiral staircase. It is a house that inspires serenity and imagination where you are well cared for by trilingual staff under the delightful Jamila. The hall also serves as a clothes, jewellery and oils shop – great fun.

rooms	9 + 1: 5 doubles, 4 suites. 1 apartment for 4.
price	680Dh-1,130Dh. Apartment 1,480Dh.
meals	Dinner 180Dh. By arrangement.
closed	Never.
directions	Casa Lila is a 2min walk from Bab Marrakech on left - signposted.

	Nathalie & Philippe Vignal
tel	+212 (0)44 47 55 45
mobile	+212 (0)61 10 88 49
fax	+212 (0)44 47 55 45
email	riadcasalila@hotmail.com
web	www.riad-casalila.com

Guest house

Map 3 Entry 18

Hôtel-Restaurant-Hammam Lalla Mira

14 rue d'Algérie, Essaouira-Medina

Morocco's first organic hotel! An unusual, passionate person, in love with Morocco, its people and food, Felicitas left organic farming in Germany to build her dream here. She restored Essaouira's oldest bathhouse as a traditional green and yellow hammam for 30 so that the locals could still use it for just 10Dh. Above it she built a house in natural, untreated materials and opened a little yellow and green organic restaurant (choose a balcony table) where local ingredients and spices are cooked with northern know-how; Berber breakfast is a tremendous experience. House and hammam are solar heated (another first), in sober rooms, mattresses, blankets and linen are non-allergic kapok or organic cotton. It is virtuous yet anchored in Moroccan style: carved keyhole-arch doors, lots of wrought iron in the soft yellow patio, four-posters in the double rooms, good use of one colour on white – blue, purple, red, green or terracotta. An elegantly light-hearted atmosphere, charming helpful staff under excellent Khalid, greenery growing apace – and a new organic farm venture in the offing.

Small hotel

rooms	13: 6 doubles, 1 suite for 2-4, 6 family rooms.
price	412Dh-752Dh. Includes use of hammam.
meals	Breakfast 20Dh-60Dh. Lunch/dinner 90Dh-120Dh, or à la carte.
closed	Never.
directions	From Bab Marrakech into Rue Mohamed El Qorry; 2nd left Rue d'Algérie.

	Felicitas Christ
tel	+212 (0)44 47 50 46
mobile	+212 (0)61 14 50 87
fax	+212 (0)44 47 58 50
email	lallamira@lallamira.ma
web	www.lallamira.ma

Map 3 Entry 19

Ryad Watier

16 rue de Ceuta, Essaouira-Medina

Kids playing ball in the square, women collecting water from the fountain – and a huge carved-stone doorway behind: Riyad Watier. Built in 1913 as Essaouira's first school for Muslim children, closed as derelict in 1982, it was rediscovered by Jean four years ago and named after the man who saved Essaouira by fixing the dunes with woodland. A fascinating character, Jean used to run a gallery in Alice Springs and lots of aboriginal art hangs here alongside French landscapes painted by his forebears over a 100 years ago. Despite the size of the place, you feel you're in someone's house: books galore, including a great collection on art, plants all over the little courtyard, opera music coming from the living room, Moroccan lanterns hanging from ornate ceilings, more art and photography against white bedroom walls, colourful saffron rugs and lots of lovely thuya wood furniture. These rooms are big, light and comfortable, some even have working fireplaces. Dining is communal and Jean hopes guests may visit him in his patch of woodland or join him on his boat. He wants you to have a different sort of holiday.

rooms	10: 7 doubles, 3 family.
price	935Dh-1,650Dh.
meals	Dinner 150Dh. By arrangement.
closed	Never.
directions	From Place Moulay Hassan take Avenue Ben Abdellah; Rue de Ceuta along on left (5min walk). Ryad on right, large stone entrance.

	Jean-Gabriel Nucci
tel	+212 (0)44 47 62 04
mobile	+212 (0)61 34 68 18
fax	+212 (0)44 47 62 04
email	contact@ryad-watier-maroc.com
web	www.ryad-watier-maroc.com

Guest house

Map 3 Entry 20

Dar Adul

63 rue Touahen, Essaouira-Medina

After the bright windy light of the street, with shops and restaurants on your doorstep, this house is quiet and restful, nothing to shock your eyes or ears. Pale and interesting with pleasing details – soft brick floor patterns, pretty tiling, carved wooden chairs, mosaic tables – it is done in ochres, gingers, yellows against the stone and no wild decorative flourishes. The warm-toned square sitting room has a good fireplace to magic away any dampness; you will eat either in the patio (glass-canopied in bad weather) or in the long soft dining room; hidden lamps highlight a fine old jar or a contemporary carving. Bedrooms have windows to the patio and personality – a couple of mezzanines, a straw pouffe, a draped bed alcove, sunny colour schemes – and attractive bathrooms. Marie is the strong presence here: with her long experience of further-flung exotic continents and lifestyles, she is fiery good company, has high standards and a marvellous team to staff the house under the firm humorous guidance of Fatima who knows the place backwards. Excellent value and good fun.

rooms	5: 4 doubles, 1 triple.
price	605Dh-825Dh.
meals	Dinner 150Dh.
closed	Never.
directions	From La Sqala remparts take Rue Laâlouj, 2nd right, house on left.

Guest house

	Marie B.
tel	+212 (0)44 47 39 10
mobile	+212 (0)71 52 02 21
fax	+212 (0)44 47 39 10
email	dar_adul@hotmail.com
web	www.dar-adul.com

Map 3 Entry 21

La Maison des Artistes

19 rue Laâlouj, Essaouira-Medina

Is it an art gallery? a museum? a jumble sale? You decide. It's zany, funky, totally endearing. A wide airy street, a darkly arched alley, two steep flights – out into the dazzle of a rooflit, sealit organised chaos of uneven rugged floors, gaudy kitchen chairs, carvings, musical instruments, copperware, some strong paintings. Each piece of furniture oozes personality, be it an iron-framed glass table or a blue leather armchair, a carved bed or an old tea set. In one room, fake neon-daylit windows make up for only one rooflight, in others the sea crashes onto the rocks beyond the ramparts where people stroll. The 'marine lookout' room (above) on the terrace is astounding: the wind and waves are always with you beyond the wraparound windows, you hang your clothes behind a free-standing Berber door and bath sybaritcally with a sea view. All bathrooms are fun and each has a bath. Cyril, young and energetic, rules his crazy kingdom with relaxed bonhomie and managerial talent: new bedding throughout and good friendly service. An endlessly fascinating place, if not for the purist or the minimalist.

rooms	6: 5 doubles, 1 suite.
price	550Dh-1,300Dh, including soft drinks.
meals	Dinner 150Dh (non-residents 190Dh). By arrangement.
closed	Never.
directions	From back of Place Moulay Hassan, through left arch; 1st right, 1st left, 1st arch on left; 1st door on right, 2nd floor.

Cyril Ladeuil

tel	+212 (0)44 47 57 99
mobile	+212 (0)62 60 54 38
fax	+212 (0)44 47 57 00
email	lamaisondesartistes@hotmail.com
web	www.lamaisondesartistes.com

Guest house

Map 3 Entry 22

Dar Loulema

2 rue Souss, Essaouira-Medina

You reach this pretty little 18th-century house through a tunnel hung with myriad carpets. Dar Loulema was on the damp side of the medina, so the last owners simply dismantled it, dug a damp-proof pit and put every stone back in place, creating a cocoon of warm dry comfort. Nathalie's refreshing and happy presence has brought it all to life: she has travelled a lot and is open, straightforward, energetic – and fun. The little white patio carries the house up to the sky, past galleries and light-filtered sitting spaces to the fabulous furnished terrace with its wraparound view. A rare, soberly perfect staircase of unglazed tiles, wood and zellige will take you up to a festival of bedroom décors: *Marrakech* is rich red, of course, with a superb orientalist picture over the vaulted bed; calm, sandy *Todra* has the shapes, colours and textiles of the southern kasbahs; *Majorelle* celebrates the cobalt-blue artist; then there's *Mogador, Zagora,*… all with soft sensuous bathrooms. Every rug, lamp, chair and fabric is thought through and put in just the right place.

rooms	7: 3 doubles, 1 twin, 3 mini-suites.
price	780Dh-1,300Dh.
meals	Lunch 80Dh. Dinner 180Dh. By arrangement.
closed	Never.
directions	From Place Moulay Hassan, Rue Sqala, 1st right Rue Souss, 1st impasse on right.

Guest house

	Nathalie Burnet
tel	+212 (0)44 47 53 46
mobile	+212 (0)61 24 76 61
fax	+212 (0)44 47 53 48
email	info@riadloulema.com
web	www.riadloulema.com

Map 3 Entry 23

Riad Al Zahia

4 rue Mohamed Diouri, Essaouira-Medina

The relaxed and charming owners of darkly mysterious Riad Al Zahia greet their guests with tea and pastries, smiles and interest, as generous as their miraculously sheltered, light-flooded terrace. Art lovers both, they show the best local painters in their salon while media folk fill the house every year for the G'naoua music festival. It's an experience to meet Pascale – astonishingly, elegantly French – in these narrow alleyways, with her deep interest in many subjects; Alain the former rally driver with his sunny humour and easy contact; and, of course, Attila the Pasha tomcat, purring as you watch the fountain flicker in the lantern light, sit by the fire in the womb of the byre-like earth-brown salon and feel the quality of old furniture and modern art. Bedrooms, with sublime kaftans as wall hangings, wear their Moroccan rugs and fabrics, their colours and patterns, to perfection; muslin shimmers over beds, colourful tadelakt bathrooms have the latest equipment. Finally, the nicest possible staff will look after you with intelligent smiles and delicious breakfasts.

rooms	8: 4 doubles, 2 twins, 2 suites for 4.
price	700Dh. Suites 1,000Dh–1,100Dh.
meals	Plenty of choice nearby.
closed	10 November–20 December.
directions	From Place Moulay Hassan, pass 'ONE'; arched street on left, 2nd right, house on right.

Guest house

	Pascale Robinot & Alain Crozet
tel	+212 (0)44 47 35 81
mobile	+212 (0)61 34 71 31
fax	+212 (0)44 47 61 07
email	zahia@essaouiranet.com
web	www.riadalzahia.com

Map 3 Entry 24

Les Matins Bleus

22 rue de Draâ, Essaouira-Medina

Having owned this house for generations, the delightful Mahboul family have joined heartfelt forces with a French couple of adopted Souiris to prepare it for others to enjoy. It seems fitting: their grandfather was guide to the first Frenchman to cross the Sahara to Smara and they have not allowed the house to be over-prettified for foreigners. You will find its wide welcoming porch at the end of a damp and rather scruffy impasse. Reading and sitting rooms have black and white floors, cool wall tiling and simple furniture; the pink, white and blue patio is as traditional as ever, lifting to the blue wind-blown sky or to the transparent windsurfer sail that keeps cold wet weather out; the brothers' willing, eager, smiling hospitality spreads friendly warmth. They are also multilingual. Bedrooms are straightforward with unadorned or painted Souiri wooden furniture and some wickerwork, no knick-knackery or overstated authentics. There are three good mezzanine suites for families, a couple of four-posters, four smaller, more private rooms on the terrace and good little shower rooms. Simple good value.

Guest house

rooms	8: 3 doubles, 2 twins, 2 suites, 1 family.
price	420Dh. Suites 540Dh-840Dh.
meals	Dinner 80Dh; children under 12, 50Dh. By arrangement.
closed	2 weeks in November.
directions	From back of Place Moulay Hassan right Rue Sidi Mohamed Ben Abdellah, right Rue Lattarine, left at sign to end of impasse.

	A. Belliot, C. Marandon, F. El Mahboul
tel	+212 (0)44 78 53 63
mobile	+212 (0)66 30 88 99
fax	+212 (0)44 78 53 63
email	lesmatinsbleus@free.fr
web	www.les-matins-bleus.com

Map 3 Entry 25

Jack's Apartments
1 Place Moulay Hassan, Essaouira–Medina

Jack's Kiosk is a focus and he is a central actor in the microcosm that is Essaouira. His apartments are higgledy-piggledy in three old houses out on the ramparts facing the pounding sea, the rocks and the Mogador Isles: one of the best views in town. He has respected the old architecture, painted everything white with Essaouira blue woodwork, ingenious use of unusual corners and really charming results. Each flat has a sitting area, a cooking/eating space and an excellent, if occasionally snug, shower room: Jack's Swiss origins show in the quality of fittings, finishes and maintenance. Superb bedding, too. The decoration is simple, modern, delightful with some bold colour schemes: Berber blankets, Moroccan lamps of iron character, super rugs on tiled floors, pretty furniture – string-back chairs, glorified deckchairs, bamboo cupboards. The light bounces off the sea into the windows, some flats are a steep climb but worth it for the wider view and sense of freedom. (The two doubles have patio windows only, and no sea views.) Self-catering couldn't be sweeter. *Daily cleaner included.*

rooms	2 + 10: 2 doubles sharing kitchen. 1 studio for 2; 3 studios for 3; 4 apartments for 4; 1 for 6; 1 for 8.
price	300Dh (double room)-1,300Dh (apartment for 8), per day.
meals	Breakfast 45Dh. Lunch/dinner from 60Dh. Delivered by arrangement. BYO.
closed	Never.
directions	In Place Moulay Hassan on SW edge of medina, go to Jack's Kiosk for keys (open until 11pm).

Catered house

	Jack Oswald
tel	+212 (0)44 47 55 38
mobile	+212 (0)62 20 19 19
fax	+212 (0)44 47 69 01
email	apartment@essaouira.com
web	www.essaouira.com/apartments

Map 3 Entry 26

Dar Ness

1 rue Khalib Ben Walid, Essaouira-Medina

Your hosts, both strong, interesting individuals, clearly know how to make guests happy and their house is as full of warm careful intelligence as their lovely terrace is flooded with ocean light and a great view of Place Moulay Hassan, Essaouira's heart. The fine 18th-century architecture has pride of place: the patio soars on its stone columns, some bedrooms have trefoiled Moorish arches, doorways are crowned with stone 'spy' holes. There are two attractive salons, one Moroccan, one European, furnished with fireplaces and a mix of typical thuya-wood and French country pieces. The bedrooms, on two floors round the patio, are big with good storage space, wide beds and simple yet unconventional bathrooms in colourful Safi zellige; some have their own sitting area. The décor is Berber carpets on warm brick floors, blankets in cactus-silk sabra stripes or thick soft Berber wool, rich curtains. With her committed and endearing personality, Élisabeth is the heart and soul of Dar Ness, ever ready to advise or chat to you over a cup of coffee, and very involved with a project to help local street kids.

rooms	9: 6 doubles, 2 twins, 1 single.
price	640Dh-740Dh.
meals	Dinner 165Dh. Picnic possible. By arrangement.
closed	Never.
directions	Rue Khalib Ben Walid gives directly into the main square Moulay Hassan.

Guest house

James Desforges & Élisabeth de la Bourdon
tel	+212 (0)44 47 68 04
fax	+212 (0)44 47 68 04
email	contact@dar-ness.com
web	www.darness-essaouira.com

Map 3 Entry 27

Madada Mogador

5 rue Youssef El Fassi, Essaouira-Medina

The entrance is so worn you can't imagine the rich modernity of the renovation Christine has wrought on the upper floors of this old Souiri house. The breathtaking terraces, virtually on top of the ramparts, provide deep wicker chairs and eyefuls of plunging sea. The deceptively simple interior was done by well-reputed furniture designer Jonathan Amar, the light is the ineffable Atlantic – possibly more fascinating in the evening than by day – though the enclosed central reception area and two of the bedrooms have no view. Pale colours, clean modern lines, fabulous finishes and Moroccan cactus silks in matt and gloss, just enough of the right furniture and a few Grecian urns. Bedrooms, two with terraces, are sober, soft and quiet with books and music and a gentle pastel touch to lift the natural background. A refined hostess, Chris produces fabulous breakfasts and even more interesting conversation. Add a brilliant sense of presentation (lights, scents, music), a great sense of humour, inventive vegetarian cooking in her partner's restaurant downstairs and you have a cocoon of enormous class.

rooms	6: 5 doubles, 1 suite for 4.
price	1,100Dh-1,320Dh. Suite 1,650Dh.
meals	Lunch/dinner 150Dh. By arrangement.
closed	Never.
directions	Just inside ramparts opposite Orson Welles Garden.

	Christine Dadda	Guest house
tel	+212 (0)44 47 55 12	
mobile	+212 (0)61 77 53 13	
fax	+212 (0)44 47 55 12	
email	info@madada.com	
web	www.madada.com	

Map 3 Entry 28

Villa Flora
7 quartier des Dunes, Essaouira

For sunset enchantment, the roof terrace looks straight out to the beach, the dunes and old Essaouira, so if you feel that staying in the medina may be slightly claustrophobic, try this discreet, modern little family hotel where seven of the rooms, each with its own bit of terrace, give onto the pretty rose garden and quiet comfort is assured. Bedrooms are splendid for the price with good beds, local thuya furniture and plenty of storage, while the odd Moorish arch gives that authentic touch. Bathrooms are excellently fitted and fixtured. The new 'Moroccan' salon, slathered in thick red rugs, cushions and astounding objects, gives onto the back garden and you can have breakfast at the little mosaic tables outside if you wish. Khalid, a modest, attentive host, wants breakfast to be a relaxed and memorable event and is eager that his guests lack nothing. He was born here, knows Essaouira and the area inside out, can tell endless tales and advise on all sorts of visits. Villa Flora, a great base for exploring the region, invites you to settle in among her flowers and stay a while.

rooms	9: 7 doubles, 2 twins.
price	600Dh-700Dh.
meals	Dinner from 100Dh.
closed	Never.
directions	Entering Essaouira, pass sea-front roundabout, 1st right, 1st left.

Small hotel

	Khalid Rahham
tel	+212 (0)44 47 39 46
mobile	+212 (0)61 20 71 79
fax	+212 (0)44 78 47 91
email	villaflora@menara.ma
web	www.essaouira-villa-flora.com

Map 3 Entry 29

Riad Zahra

90 quartier des Dunes, Essaouira

The atmosphere here will gather you up in easy welcome. Mohamed – 'Simo' –
came home after 20 years in America, bringing his relaxed and dynamic
Quebecoise partner Céline. They mustered his family and built the simplest,
friendliest hotel in Essaouira with mother and sisters making delicious Moroccan
crêpes for breakfast and brothers serving super Moroccan or international dishes
later in the day. Traditional Beldi design and décor inspired the generous open hall
with its sandstone pillars and baronial staircase, the big luminous rosy-red
Moroccan salon/dining room, the giant pots that stand guard everywhere, their
leafy green sentries waving at you, the total absence of frilliness. Bedrooms wear
the red and green of the Moroccan flag, the larger ones have Moroccan cushioned
bench-beds for two extra sleepers, all have good shower rooms and top-floor
rooms give great views over the pool to the dunes. Laughing and attentive, Simo
and Céline can't do enough to make your stay memorable – they love their new
life and, just 150 metres from beach and dunes, their riad is excellent value.

rooms	20: 8 doubles, 12 family rooms for 3-4.
price	450Dh-600Dh. Extra person 100Dh.
meals	Lunch/dinner 90Dh. By arrangement.
closed	Never.
directions	From Marrakech into Essaouira, at sea-front roundabout, right then 1st left.

	Céline Bélanger & Mohamed Najid
tel	+212 (0)44 47 48 22
fax	+212 (0)44 47 43 12
email	riadzahra@menara.ma
web	www.riadzahra.com

Small hotel

Map 3 Entry 30

Baoussala
Douar El Ghazoua, Essaouira

In a green eucalyptus oasis far from the wild windy coast, this wonderful womb of a house with its kasbah water tower and earthy ochre curves, centres on a brilliantly rug-strewn circular patio. Original, organic shapes and spaces are the norm, then shimmering fabrics, unusual traditional weaves, warm colours and wood – wicker, oleander, eucalyptus. The generous round salon with leaping white arches and a mini-amphitheatre before the sunken hearth is irresistibly attractive. The same sense of drama rings in the marvellous bedrooms: platforms and draperies, superb Berber blankets, modern art, fireplaces and mosquito nets – you could stay all year and never tire of it or its warm friendly atmosphere. Big bathrooms are naturally lovely in oodles of taste and colourful tadelakt. Dominique is the strong, dynamic owner whose flair and personality have created this exceptional place and keep it alive with convivial candlelit dinners, musical evenings, delicious food, books and music everywhere, even a tiny pool. Relax deeply and make yourself at home this utterly special place which so effortlessly welcomes you.

Guest house & catered house

rooms	6: 1 twin, 4 doubles, 1 suite for 4.
price	€85. Extra bed €10. Children under 6 free. Sole occupancy possible.
meals	Lunch €5-€7. Dinner €15. Picnic possible. By arrangement.
closed	Never.
directions	From Essaouira, coast road for Agadir 8km to Douar El Ghazoua; right on track, 3km to last telegraph pole; house on left.

	Dominique Maté
tel	+212 (0)44 47 43 45
mobile	+212 (0)66 30 87 46
fax	+212 (0)44 47 43 45
email	dchoupin@yahoo.fr
web	www.baoussala.com

Map 3 Entry 31

La Maison

Essaouira

Out on the flat coastal plain – you can see the sea, over in the distance – surrounded by trees and flowers, Thérèse's new, traditionally-built house is a refuge from Essaouira's medina and harbour bustle. The building stone, gathered here on the site, stands unrendered and at peace on home ground; the house rests in neutral colours with just the odd dash of spice in a burnt orange or rich red cushion. Once the plants have grown and the salt air has weathered it all, the arched patio and superb antique front door will look as if they have stood here for ever. Through that door you find a fountain and a small shop selling local delights (jams, kaftans, argan oil) then a relaxed country-rustic interior: Berber-striped benches on their knees before locally-crafted tables, bamboo ceilings overhead, bits of fine Berber pottery and weaving to intrigue you. Simply decorated bedrooms, with colourful, functional tadelakt bathrooms, look onto the patio, and the pool is a decent distance. Thérèse loves having guests, loves cooking her own Franco-Moroccan fusions for you, loves sharing her passion for Morocco.

rooms	5: 3 doubles, 1 triple, 1 quadruple.
price	490Dh. Quadruple 730Dh.
meals	Lunch/dinner 100Dh.
closed	Never.
directions	From Essaouira for Marrakech approx. 9km; left R301 coast road for Safi 3km; house on left.

	Thérèse Roche
mobile	+212 (0)61 19 73 74
email	roche_therese@yahoo.fr
web	www.la-maison-essaouira.com

Guest house

Map 3 Entry 32

Villa Juba

Ida Ougourd, BP 8, Essaouira

Magnificent in its 15-hectare walled hilltop estate, this surprising Moroccan take on the Palladian mansion is named after Rome's vassal Juba, renowned for his knowledge of the arts and sciences around 25BC: Giulio's new venture for culture and relaxation is anchored in history. There will be theatre, poetry and painting, an artist in residence, a garden (sow one year, reap – with your eyes – the next), a hammam and fitness space, all informed by Giulio's search for meaning and talent for communication. Renovated from top to toe, the pasha's 19th-century villa is a feast of unaffected comfort and mellow intelligence. Big bedrooms, all differently decorated, have arches, alcoves and pure white linen; salons and terraces, library, gallery and stables. Explore the countryside on a camel, hear a rehearsal, eat delicious food, lounge by the spectacular pool. But Villa Juba's rarest offerings are of the soul: close encounters with artists and their works, with like-minded guests, and Giulio's passion for culture. *Horse & camel rides included. Also, his country inn Tangaro and Essaouira hotel Desdemona.*

Small hotel

rooms	11: 7 doubles, 4 suites.
price	Half-board (dinner) 900Dh-1,500Dh for two.
meals	Half-board only. Lunch 100Dh-150Dh, by arrangement.
closed	Never.
directions	From Essaouira for Agadir; in El Ghazoua fork left for Marrakech & Casablanca 6km; right small road for Ida Ougourd 4km; yellow house on hill.

	Giulio Siry
tel	+212 (0)44 78 47 84
mobile	+212 (0)61 60 10 81/61 16 09 69
fax	+212 (0)44 78 57 35
email	g.siri@menara.ma
web	www.villa-juba.com

Map 3 Entry 33

Auberge de la Plage
Sidi Kaouki

Enter the courtyard, discover the charming garden and its giant mimosa – you'll see why we like this place. A square modern building above Sidi Kaouki, the 'beach inn' sees riches from its newly-fitted terrace: beyond the surrounding uglies, the bay view with its wind-driven surfers is so wildly alive you could sit and watch for hours. A team of four – from Germany, France, Ivory Coast and New Caledonia! – own the hotel and, most originally, run it for a season each. Their various personalities and interests make it a welcoming, ever-lively house of inspiration and smiling seriousness. Spaces are wide and luminous, colourful recently-renovated rooms stand in their simplicity round the covered patio or the terrace, and almost all windows look out to sea. The warmly atmospheric restaurant has instant appeal, books for guests to borrow and lanterns in the evening: no electricity yet, just solar heating, hot water at set times, hot-water bottles at bedtime. Marvellous. Renewal continues – restaurant, pool, garden – and the whole place is awash with friendly, spirited expectancy.

rooms	10: 2 doubles, 1 twin, 1 triple, 1 suite for 4; 2 doubles, 1 twin, 2 triples sharing 2 bathrooms.
price	410Dh–540Dh with bathroom; 260DH sharing bathroom.
meals	Dinner 90Dh; brunch, lunch, tea à la carte. By arrangement.
closed	Never.
directions	Entering Sidi Kaouki, take track immediately on left and follow signs.

Small hotel

	C. Fisher, D. Alabert, Corine, Natalie
tel	+212 (0)44 47 66 00
email	info@kaouki.com
web	www.kaouki.com

Map 3 Entry 34

Le Kaouki

Route d'Agadir - km 20, Sidi Kaouki

Down near the sea, at the bottom of a rather dusty, scruffy village, you enter Le Kaouki through an arch into a sheltered patio where a pergola flooded in bougainvillea shades the lounging benches, tables stand waiting for outdoor drinkers and an open door invites you into the red-checked embrace of a sweet little country inn: beams are made of eucalyptus, furniture is Moroccan rustic, colours are Souiri blue and white and a log fire roars in winter. Philippe, himself a surfer, spreads fraternal conviviality and the happy serenity of south-west France. Roro also loves this place like her own child. They manage the inn alternately and are both proud to introduce you to Myriam and Khadiya, a couple of really good Berber cooks. A recipe for success. The bedrooms are monastic in their simplicity: a pretty-blanketed bed and a bedside table for the candlestick (no electricity); the communal washing facilities are basic and spotless; the place charms instantly by its position, its atmosphere, the interesting people one always meets here – and its excellent value, of course. Super big terrace on top, too.

Auberge

rooms	10: 2 doubles, 5 twins, 2 triples, 1 family, all sharing 3 showers, 2 wcs.
price	260Dh. Sole occupancy possible.
meals	Lunch 50Dh-100Dh. Dinner 100Dh. Picnic available. By arrangement.
closed	Never.
directions	From Essaouira for Agadir 12km; right to Sidi Kaouki; at entrance to village left 300m, sign on left.

Philippe Lions & Roro Viallon

tel	+212 (0)44 78 32 06
mobile	+212 (0)68 05 16 27
fax	+212 (0)44 47 54 47
email	info@sidikaouki.com
web	www.sidikaouki.com

Map 3 Entry 35

Hôtel des Cascades

Imouzzèr Ida Outanane

Wind a thousand spectacular metres up through palm groves and plunging gorges to this relaxing retreat and its well-tended gardens: the drive alone is worth it. Birdsong and the water music flood in; long views of the Atlas foothills – and to the distant sea on clear days – unwind you further. Monsieur Atbir couldn't be more charming. He has been gradually expanding his hotel with its growing bedroom wing where rooms are a generous size and open to the view. Upstairs rooms have balconies, from the ground floor rooms you can go straight into the garden to wander down to the pools (there's one for children) without running the corridor gauntlet. Eat, excellently, at wooden tables on the terrace or in the dining room – rather formal with cool marble mosaic floors and central fireplace. Helpful staff can arrange donkey-rides, trekking, mountain biking, you name it. The famous waterfall is generally a winter phenomenon but the welcome and the views make it worth a visit all year round, be you rambler, bird-lover, painter or honeymooner.

rooms	27: 14 doubles, 13 twins.
price	570Dh.
	Half-board from 820Dh for two.
meals	Lunch/dinner 100Dh-200Dh.
closed	Never.
directions	From Agadir N1/N8 for Marrakech approx 100km; after Abdelmoumen dam left 43km to Imouzzèr; signs. Airport transfer possible.

	Jamal Eddine Atbir
tel	+212 (0)48 82 60 16/23
mobile	+212 (0)60 16 05 05
fax	+212 (0)48 82 60 24
web	www.cascades-hotel.com

Small hotel

Map 3 Entry 36

Hôtel Riad des Golfs

Route des Golfs, Aghrod Ben Sergao, Agadir

You will eat and sleep extremely well here, in a stylish mixture of modern and classical Moroccan moods. Designed remarkably by your host, this luxurious oasis celebrates local tradition: strong geometric forms, arches and colonnades, sunken mosaic fountain, cool interiors with high high ceilings, angles and perspectives. Round the lofty light-filtered atrium, the big sitting and dining areas, decorated in a hot-house version of French styles, mix Louis XV and modern, softness and clarity, in a symphony of ivory, indigo and magenta: clean lines, a velvety finish, all the details. Once you're inside, all living happens within the walls, the patio and the split-level pool area are your garden (shared with many happy birds) – it feels intimate and safe. Bedrooms are just as cool, calm and sophisticated with tempting big beds, lots of space, a terrace or balcony each and outstanding porticoed bathrooms. Bernard and Paule indulge in extravaganzas of fresh flowers, love their new life here, consider their guests as friends they have not yet made and really enjoy sharing their passion for food.

rooms	8 suites for 2-3.
price	1,650Dh–2,640Dh.
meals	Dinner 330Dh. Lunch 165Dh. By arrangement.
closed	Never.
directions	From Agadir airport for Agadir Centre 5km then 'Centre Touristique'; at Marjane shopping centre follow signs for Golf des Dunes & Golf du Soleil.

Guest house

	Bernard & Paule Brilhault
tel	+212 (0)48 33 70 33
mobile	+212 (0)61 23 71 61
fax	+212 (0)48 33 54 55
email	riadgolf@menara.ma
web	www.riaddesgolfs.com

Map 3 Entry 37

Hôtel Atlantic
Boulevard Hassan II, BP 53, Agadir

Exceptionally convenient, bang in the middle of Agadir and just 15 minutes from the beach, the Atlantic has an uninspiring façade that belies the old-style/modern charm you find inside. The recent and well-inspired renovation brought some genuine old Moroccan elements into the public areas – splendid carved doors, intricate brass lamps, bits of brass and copper – and unusually interesting modern Moroccan paintings. Also a fountain in the lobby, lots of zellige and carved plaster, so it all feels thoroughly Moroccan but not at all tacky or repro. The beautifully done garden and pool area, however, is the star turn here. Palm trees and birdsong in the middle of the city, deck chairs on rough grass round a superb crystal-clear pool and, presiding over the whole scene, an extraordinary water wall made of local stone in colours ranging from pale sand to rich earthy ochre, like a great Berber carpet. Rooms are functional and less characterful, each floor having its own colour theme, water for the European-class bathrooms being solar heated. Add really friendly staff and you have excellent value.

rooms	50.
price	465Dh.
meals	Lunch/dinner 110Dh.
closed	Never.
directions	From Agadir airport for 'Centre Ville'. In Boulevard Hassan II. pass stadium floodlights on left; hotel 800m on right (set back from main avenue, easy to miss).

	Najia Ounassar	Hotel
tel	+212 (0)48 84 36 61/62	
fax	+212 (0)48 84 36 60	
email	atlantichotel@wanadoo.ma	

Map 3 Entry 38

Ksar Massa

Complexe balnéaire de Sidi R'bat, Commune Rurale de Sidi Wassay, Chtouka Aït Baha

Fabulously remote, deep in the Souss-Massa national park, a place for rare and wonderful birds: flamingoes, cranes and bald ibis hang out on this stretch of coast. Join them in the dune-anchored ksar, a huddle of low 'rustic' houses offering… refined cooking, high-pressure hot water and superb towels. With its rich, strong atmosphere, it is a very special place for lovers of space, peace and real comfort. All earthy red and yellow ochre tones with flashes of blue, excellent rugs and objects to pick up the colours, it is deep Morocco. The impressive bedrooms – wrought-iron screens, carved furniture, original mirrors, more lovely rugs, superb bedding – look out to sea or onto the garden where newly-planted mature palms wave. Bathrooms are brilliant: moulded, deep-coloured, intended to look old but with immaculate modern fittings. Unostentatious and outstanding, it has a friendly, efficient, philanthropic owner who works with the local community, organises sports days and loves his sandcastle house. This is active conservation of natural, architectural and rural resources.

rooms	12: 2 doubles, 9 suites, 1 villa for 4. Also 15 tents for workshop/seminar groups.
price	1,420Dh. Half-board 2,040Dh (dinner) or 1,720Dh (lunch) p.p. Full-board 2,340Dh p.p.
meals	Half- or full-board options.
closed	Never.
directions	From Agadir for Tiznit about 50km; 4km after Had Belfa (aka Aït Bella), right for Ksar Massa & follow signs for Sidi R'bat: 7km of track.

Small hotel

	Nasser Laraki
tel	+212 (0)61 28 03 19
mobile	+212 (0)62 80 24 85
fax	+212 (0)48 25 57 72/22 47 13 72
email	ksarmassa@ksarmassa.com
web	www.ksarmassa.com

Map 3 Entry 39

Hôtel Restaurant Atlas

Mirleft

Sitting on the pavement terrace of the Atlas you will come to know the dogs, the eccentrics and the tradespeople of relaxed, sandy Mirleft; also the fat contented hotel cat. It's a great atmosphere. The Atlas and its brother the Abertih are the Lecire family's new life: in 2004, parents and adult children abandoned the rain and bureaucracy of France for a business adventure and are doing it easily and well. Their colourful renovation of the open, airy house has one red and one green corridor, space, lightness and youth, easy laid-back comfort, Moroccan weavings and dishes of pebbles in the big restaurant and the upstairs salon/breakfast room. Also a roof terrace that's ideal for balmy barbecues. Bénédicte, wedded to a local man, is a ray of sunshine: dynamic and attentive, she cares immensely that her food is fresh and her rooms, as simple as her prices, are spotless. These have unpretentious charm in vibrant colours, new bedding, basic storage (hooks on doors and bamboo shelf units); half have washbasins. Come for the trekking, parapenting, watersports, fishing – and the superb-value Atlas hotel.

rooms	17: 16 sharing 3 showers, 3 wcs; 1 double with bathroom.
price	80Dh-150Dh.
meals	Breakfast 15Dh-25Dh. Lunch/dinner 80Dh; one course 40Dh.
closed	Never.
directions	From Tiznit enter Mirleft; right into main street, hotel on left.

	Bénédicte Lecire
tel	+212 (0)48 71 93 09
mobile	+212 (0)72 22 58 74
email	benedicte@atlas-mirleft.com
web	www.atlas-mirleft.com

Small hotel

Map 3 Entry 40

Hôtel-Restaurant Abertih
Mirleft

Even if friendly, dusty Mirleft looks like a western film set, your young host Damien, whom we met at his sister's Hôtel Atlas nearby, is unmistakably, charmingly French. He has run his little hotel for two years now, with imagination, verve and enthusiasm. Continents away from boutiques or designers, it flashes such youthful colour from walls, ceilings and fabrics that you step in and smile. A gentle house whose smallness and unaffected simplicity make it a quiet, intimate place where slow time favours long conversations and thoughtful reading. Rooms are basic and… colourful; bedding is new; bathrooms are small, plain and practical. The roof terrace looks left to the mountains, right to the sea about 900 metres away; Damien occasionally organises eat-all-you-can sardine-kebab dinners here, or traditional Berber music sessions. Strong on outdoor activites – fishing, surfing, bathing on dramatic Atlantic beaches, trekking or donkey hikes, the area also has ruins and *marabouts* to visit. One guest booked for a night and stayed for five weeks. Genuine hospitality and really good, fresh food.

Small hotel

rooms	11: 5 twins/doubles; 2 doubles, 3 twins, 1 single sharing 2 showers, 3 washbasins, 4 wcs.
price	120Dh-200Dh. Half-board only in July & August: 330Dh-440Dh for two.
meals	Lunch/dinner 60Dh-120Dh.
closed	Never.
directions	From Tiznit enter Mirleft; right into main street, hotel on left.

	Damien Lecire
tel	+212 (0)48 71 93 04
mobile	+212 (0)77 22 58 72
fax	+212 (0)48 71 93 05
email	damien@abertih.com
web	www.abertih.com

Map 3 Entry 41

Kasbah Tabelkout
Tabelkout, Mirleft

In an attitude of defiant power, the brand new kasbah-mansion perches on the edge of its cliff, daring the wild-alive ocean to reach up the rockface and grab it. Nicole has put all her love of Moroccan buildings and finishes into her southern kasbah: floors are sensual-soft bejmat or old-style tiles, walls are beautifully smooth-hued tadelakt, the patio is wafer bricks, the double-height hall it topped by a great dome, the library is the quiet spot you may need from time to time. Arches and high, carved antique Marrakchi doors are everywhere, a magnificent four-pillared fireplace brings extra punch to the dining room, the salon, with two more fireplaces, leads out to the great brick terrace and the patio gives the house a perfect heart. Bedrooms, each in a different style (African, Fassi, Art Deco,...), have space and comfort to spare, carefully-chosen furnishings and really super bathrooms. Most have their own fireplace and terrace, too. And at every turn, from every window, a view to die for. An ideal base for exploring the coast, north and south, and the unsung delights of the Anti-Atlas. *Opening early 2006.*

rooms	7 twins/doubles.
price	550Dh.
meals	Lunch/dinner 150Dh. Picnic 50Dh. By arrangement. BYO.
closed	Rarely.
directions	From Mirleft for Sidi Ifni 4km; on top of rise overlooking bay.

	Nicole Arbousset
tel	+212 (0)44 38 75 67
mobile	+212 (0)61 58 27 49
email	nicolearbousset@yahoo.fr

Guest house

Map 3 Entry 42

Hôtel Fort Bou-Jerif
Fort Bou-Jerif, Guelmin

The beaten track? It's miles behind you once you've bumped through the rolling stony wilderness to this remote and confidential meeting place. Adventurous spirits, aged 18 to 80, have been coming for years. Bou-Jerif is a hybrid of hotel, motel and camping site where you bask in the fraternal bonhomie of desert addicts. But it's also a fabulous place for walking, star-gazing (the generators stop at 11pm and the shimmering sky is all yours), sand-yachting and buggy expeditions (Bruno will come to initiate and guide you), nature-loving (the desert flowers heartbreakingly when it rains, we saw a lone wolf cross the track ahead of us). Pierre, the quiet new owner of this extraordinary creation, will be sprucing up the five big plain and comfortable hotel rooms in the solid *petit château* (it has a daft medieval look) and the simpler motel cabin rooms. He also plans to develop more open-air motorised activities and the big garden. Come for space, more space, excellent food and the sweetest team of willing, unpushy people to serve and advise you. *Self-catering riad house for 6-10, tents for 60 & camper spaces.*

Small hotel

rooms	10: 5 twins/doubles; 5 motel rooms sharing 2 showers, 2 wcs. Also tents for 60 & camper spaces.
price	Half-board dinner 584Dh-770Dh for two. Tents 242Dh half-board p.p.
meals	Half-board only. Lunch 44Dh-165Dh. Picnic 55Dh.
closed	Never.
directions	Leaving Guelmin for Sidi Ifni, left for La Plage Blanche approx. 35km; right at sign to Fort Bou-Jerif: 9km rough track. GPS N. 29°04'93" W. 010°19'87".

	Pierre Gerbens
tel	+212 (0)72 13 00 17
mobile	+212 (0)72 13 00 17
fax	+212 (0)48 87 30 39
email	contact@fortboujerif.com
web	wwwfortboujerif.com

Map 3 Entry 43

marrakech
& the high atlas

Without the Atlas, Morocco would be a desert and it is easy to forget that more than half the country is mountains. The majestically high narrow valleys of the High Atlas and untouched Amazigh villages are much sought after by climbers, hikers and even skiers. To make the most of these regions, to explore still-virgin areas of unspeakable beauty, it is best to travel in a 4x4 vehicle.

A short drive from Marrakech are the lovely green and temperate lands at the foothills of the High Atlas and some ideal refuges from the city's blazing summer heat or simply its year-round hubbub: inns and guest houses that serve good local or organic food in natural surroundings where a walk is always a voyage of discovery.

What makes Marrakech the mythical, magical magnet it is? Its melting-pot position between desert nomads and 'civilised' northern tribes has always encouraged the meeting of uneuropeanised African cultures with sophistications from Spain and beyond. "Black Africa starts at Marrakech" is what the locals say. They could also say that Andalucia stops here.

Within the dauntingly blank walls of the medina are marvels of Moorish art, gardens imitating Eden, over 350 mosques, gastronomic delights and some exceptional people. Non-Muslims may not enter the mosques but their very being vibrates into the streets with calls to prayer and white robes.

Places to stay, in the medina or in the legendary *Palmeraie* (it is said that the palms grew from pips spat out in 1071 by Youssef Ben Tachfine's army as it marched in conquest), vary from simple and authentic to extravagantly designed and decorated. Each is the expression of an owner's dream.

Photo: Jose Navarro

Riyad Al Moussika

62 Derb Boutouil, Kennaria, Marrakech-Medina

Riyads don't come more manicured than this careful orchestration of form and colour "where mansion meets Alhambra" and roses float in gurgling fountains: Giovanni is a powerful perfectionist. He studied Moroccan arts in depth, then turned his eye to every last detail, from zouaké paintwork, carved furniture and geometric zellige to Andalucian pool, tadelakt hammam and candy-striped sofas, then supervised the best craftsmen during hours of painstaking labour. He is rightly proud of his handiwork, it is a most cultured house: a music room with a Pleyel grand piano, interesting modern art and lots of recordings: as befits an Italian, Giovanni knows a lot about opera; a library, for perfect peace, a remarkable degree of comfort in the fine big bedrooms, excellent bathrooms and nothing synthetic anywhere. Every corner has been thought through into quiet luxury and done to a tee without stinting. He then trained his smiling staff. People who want first-class everything will enjoy this experience, and some say Giovanni's son makes the best Italian food in Marrakech. *Minimum stay 3-7 nights.*

Guest house & catered house

rooms	6: 3 suites, 2 doubles, 1 single.
price	Half-board lunch €250-€340; singles €155. Sole occupancy €1,370 per day. Includes airport transfers.
meals	Half-board only. Dinner €45-€55. By arrangement.
closed	Never.
directions	Enter at Bab Ghemat, left at Lycée Mohamed V: Douar Graoua to Place Palais Moulay Idris; door at No 17 Derb Cherkaoui on corner of square.

	Giovanni Robazza & Khalid Essafa
tel	+212 (0)44 38 90 67
mobile	+212 (0)61 26 76 71
fax	+212 (0)44 37 76 53
email	riyad.al.moussika@menara.ma
web	www.riyad-al-moussika.com

Map 4 Entry 44

Villa El Arsa

18 Derb El Arsa, Kennaria , Marrakech-Medina

A peaceful, unshowy house, where furniture is of the rustic string-back type plus masses of cushions in the salons. Ranks of potted plants adorn the citrus/banana courtyard beneath deeply attractive wrought-iron balustrading, and a tiny tadelakt pool is tucked off to one corner: really lovely, though the fountain doesn't always play. The restoration was done by a Frenchman and the Scotts, who have owned El Arsa for five years, but only come occasionally so it is managed by easygoing Simo and Brahim who make sure the house instructions in English are clearly visible. All the very handsome bedrooms have remarkable antique doors, light white cotton curtains that waft gently in the breeze, pale tadelakt walls that provide the perfect backdrop for bright cushions and a wonderful feel for textures as well as colours. And bathrooms are just as attractive in their pastel or plum colours. If you are feeling Marrakech-worn, there are books for distraction, a chess set for concentration and some glorious painted ceilings for contemplation. Brilliantly close to Jemaâ El Fna, it is a house of well-worn, welcoming sobriety.

rooms	4 doubles.
price	800Dh-1,000Dh.
	Sole occupancy by arrangement.
meals	Lunch/dinner 150Dh.
	By arrangement.
closed	Never.
directions	Ring for escort from Jemaâ El Fna or from Préfecture by Palais Bahia. Transfers to/from airport by arrangement.

	David & Susie Scott
tel	+212 (0)44 42 63 26 (& fax)
mobile	+212 (0)68 41 72 38
fax	+44 (0)1584 861 325 (& tel)
email	susiescott451@hotmail.com
web	d.scott.free.fr

Guest house

Map 4 Entry 45

Riad Oasis

86 Derb Makina, Arset El Baraka, Bab Aylen, Marrakech-Medina

An oasis indeed, with citrus trees, banana plants and three vast cypresses seething with bird life in its outstanding courtyard, this fine, rather unusual riad once belonged to a grand Marrakchi family. Ornate sculpted white plaster contrasts with smooth polished tadelakt, oriental touches add another vibration: Riyad Shama's imaginative design team have been at work here. Bathrooms are almost regal with their double beaten-copper basins and bathrobes, beds are imperially comfortable, television sets imperiously present. The bedrooms all have something theatrical about them – a surprising dark colour combination, a china cockatoo, a set of curly French Empire furniture – and each fireplace is a flight of fancy. The most appealing room is *Bougainvillea* right up on the terrace with its natural-coloured tadelakt. Up here, a mass of potted plants guards the hammam and your breakfast. The staff, with Asma to manage them and Tariq to shoot trouble, are quite delightful, the food is excellent, the décor somewhat baroque. And the birds try every morning to harmonise with the muezzin's call.

rooms	6: 4 doubles, 2 suites.
price	€90–€150.
meals	Lunch/dinner 150Dh–300Dh. By arrangement.
closed	Never
directions	From Bab Aylen ring for escort. 15 minutes from Jemaâ El Fna.

Guest house

Map 4 Entry 46

	Nazik Selmouni
tel	+212 (0)44 38 64 64
mobile	+212 (0)61 24 24 74
fax	+212 (0)44 38 06 66
email	riadoasis@menara.ma
web	www.riadoasis.com

Riyad Charaï

56 Diour Jdad, Zaouia Abassia, Marrakech-Medina

Once past the dark entrance you forget all about the medina because you've been gobbled up by the leafy world of the big, beguiling patio garden (one of the largest riad gardens), its lovely bejmat floor and the twittering citrus trees. This mansion is where Pacha Glaoui's secretary lived, in grandeur, and it certainly has an old, authentic feel to it, with oodles of charm, floods of light, plenty of space. The uncontrived décor takes a soft minimalist approach, leaving room for the house to breathe – natural wood, plain ecru upholstery – with an occasional whimsical flourish such as an extraordinarily ornate mirror, a loo in a cupboard, a fanciful fireplace. Colours are studied and subtle, dark tadelakt here and there, few patterns, just a restful quiet mood and more of those living breathing bejmat tiles leading up to the pool. Bedrooms are all different with excellent beds and very fine bathrooms but the loveliest feature is the beautiful first-floor gallery closed in by high wooden windows and intricate ironwork. A great place to call home for a while – and, exceptionally, you can park right outside.

rooms	3 + 2: 3 suites. 2 apartments for 4.
price	€168-€195.
	Apartments €189-€220.
	Sole occupancy €5,125-€6,030 p.w.
meals	Dinner 250Dh-400Dh.
closed	Never.
directions	From Bab N'Qob, walk up Kaat Al Machraa to house or ring for escort.

	Nazik Selmouni
mobile	+212 (0)61 24 32 01
fax	+212 (0)44 44 81 55
email	info@riyadcharai.com
web	www.riyadcharai.com

Guest house

Map 4 Entry 47

Riyad Shama

22 Derb Taht Sour, Lakbir, Zaouia Abbassia, Marrakech-Medina

A cool elegant exercise in interior loveliness, Riyad Shama breathes an air of repose and contentment. And the staff are such a likeable, attentive lot: it's a really good place to be. The gorgeous use of pale tadelakt on columns, floors and fireplaces as well as in bathrooms, sings harmonious life into the high walls, white curtains catching the breeze flutter over dark wooden bench sofas, masses of oriental silk cushions on embroidered bedcovers, heart-stoppingly subtle colour mixes (grey-brown, pink-mauve, lemon-ivory) and excellent lighting turn each space into a small symphony. There's some super bejmat tiling, too, always so naturally sensual. Every room has a fireplace, the bathrooms have the same air of sumptuous elegance that is never ostentatious or brash, despite all the pots and potions, and the public areas will tempt you to hang around: by the lovely green-tiled patio pool or up on the terrace under its tented chill-out area. Breakfast should meet all your expectations, the suites are worth every last dirham, it's all brand new — and remarkable value.

rooms	7: 5 doubles, 2 suites.
price	€144–€160.
	Sole occupancy €5,500 per week.
meals	Lunch/dinner 130Dh–300Dh.
closed	Never.
directions	Riyad is 100m from Bab Taghroute car park.

Guest house & catered house

	Nazik Selmouni
tel	+212 (0)44 43 72 11
mobile	+212 (0)61 24 32 01
fax	+212 (0)44 44 81 55
email	contact@riadshama.com
web	www.riadshama.com

Map 4 Entry 48

Riad Merstane

13 Derb El Merstane, Zaouia El Abassia, Marrakech-Medina

An old, historic house this, originally an annexe of the Sidi Bel Abbès mosque where troubled minds were soothed with music, now a guest house with an exceptionally welcoming attitude that greets you with an open front door. Then comes manager David, the quiet Scot who has lived in Marrakech for four years, knows all the lore and makes sure there are fresh flowers in your room. You may use the kitchen, too, though Myriam's *briouats* (little savoury pastry triangles) should make you want to taste her cooking every night. The Elliotts have renovated and furnished their second home in mostly muted colours with simple, local furniture and nothing contrived or pretentious: a lovely wrought-iron bed from Essasouira here, a Tataoui ceiling or a claw-footed bath there, pastel tadelakt finishes, some admirable old encaustic tiling, pretty sabra cushions and an open hearth surrounded by soft sofas and rugs in the big first-floor salon. There's also a small Berber-matted lounging room off the patio. A simple, no-frills riad, it is comfortable, friendly and remarkable value.

rooms	4: 3 doubles, 1 twin.
price	400Dh-640Dh. Sole occupancy 1,760Dh.
meals	Lunch 50Dh. Dinner 150Dh. By arrangement.
closed	Never.
directions	In the Zaouia district; ring for escort from Bab Taghzout.

Guest house

	Alan & Kate Elliott
tel	+212 (0)44 42 63 90
mobile	+212 (0)67 75 57 21
fax	+212 (0)44 42 63 90
email	avelliott@hotmail.com
web	www.riadmerstane.com

Map 4 Entry 49

Riad El Ouarda

5 Derb Taht Sour Lakbir, Zaouia El Abbassia, Marrakech-Medina

The old mansion's nobility stands proud in the powerful white verticals that protect the central space and its exceptional brand of civilisation. Rooms are big and high, the restored antique stucco is perfect, bathrooms are well done in tadelakt and copper, suites have a suggestion of opulence as well as luxuries of space. Thierry and Laurent have decorated their little palace with loving sensitivity, colours rich and soft, nothing busy or overdone; their Mauritanian 'wall mats', for example, are original but don't shout. The main house brings gentle reminders of traditional design – velvet wall hangings as seen in aristocratic salons, glorious stylised Berber patterns over a plain white fireplace; the Douiria is unexpectedly modern, its patio, warmed with log fires in winter and greened with banana plants in summer, leading to a brilliant great grey and white bed-and-bath suite. Split-level terraces offer plenty of private spaces – and 360° medina-to-mountain views. But most important of all is the impeccable, attentive and genuinely friendly service from the owners and their delightful staff.

rooms	9: 5 doubles, 4 suites.
price	1,100Dh-2,100Dh.
meals	Lunch 100Dh-200Dh. Dinner 350Dh. By arrangement.
closed	Rarely.
directions	In medina, go to Bab Taghzout and telephone for guide to riad.

Guest house

Thierry Saint Marc & Laurent Bocca
tel	+212 (0)44 38 57 14
fax	+212 (0)44 38 57 10
email	elouarda@yahoo.fr
web	www.riadelouarda.com

Map 4 Entry 50

Dar Warda

266 Sidi Bouamare, Riad Laârouss, Marrakech-Medina

Wafer bricks zigzag round the patio, water trickles, birds chirrup: all is peace. Restored with a Tuscan touch by former owner and talented designer Christiane Mèche, the house melds her original lamps and furniture with traditional Moroccan architecture and contemporary objects into a soberly warm, harmonious city retreat. Paintings over mauve-grey divans in the long dining room are by French *orientalistes*; bedcovers are thick natural cotton with hand-sewn velvet or wide sabra stripes, always in keeping with the gentle colour scheme; there's a proudly arched winter salon and some fascinating leather chairs, vibrating with African influence. No wonder the discerning new owners, who live in Paris, kept most of her ideas. Bathrooms are a delicious mix of brick, zellige and tadelakt. Up two floors and you find yet more space on the split-level terraces among white canvas chairs and divans, superb local pots and a splendid view. Finally, Fatiha and Abdellatif, as well as being gentle and efficient, give guests such a relaxed and charming welcome that you'll be tempted to stay a while.

rooms	4: 2 double, 1 twin, 1 suite.
price	€120-€160. Sole occupancy €450 (max 10) or €2,900 per week.
meals	Dinner 200Dh-250Dh. By arrangement.
closed	Never.
directions	From Place Riyad Laârouss take Rue Sidi Bouhamaar; 2nd left; house at end on left.

	Isabelle & Charles-Henri de Sainte Croix
tel	+212 (0)44 37 83 56
mobile	+212 (0)61 92 96 53
fax	+212 (0)44 38 74 57
email	darwarda@menara.ma
web	www.darwarda.com

Guest house & catered house

Map 4 Entry 51

Riad Zina

38 Derb Assabane, Riad Laârouss, Marrakech-Medina

The architecture of the gently renovated Riad Zina takes centre-stage here against the serenely uncluttered backdrop of white walls and blue shutters. A delightful, strong, intelligent woman whose company you will appreciate, Beate has faithfully adapted the original intentions of her mansion: four symmetrical beds grow spiky cacti among great smooth pebbles; a daily libation of rose petals blesses the octagonal pool; in the simple pale rooms, alcoves and corners play with the light, pools of colour ripple in rich curtains, covers, rugs and wall hangings, contemporary pictures call for real attention, smooth bathrooms relax. The Great Moroccan star here is the suite, a fine high room with a breathtaking ceiling, said to be 350 years old, inside it there's a delicately excised and gaudily painted frieze of Koranic verses – you sleep in heavenly peace; there are heaps of cushions and a fireplace; through one set of towering double doors is the sitting space. And moreover... Beate was once a professional cook so expect mouth-watering French dishes one day, Malika's Moroccan delicacies the next.

rooms	4: 2 doubles, 1 triple, 1 suite.
price	1,000Dh–2,000Dh including afternoon tea.
meals	Lunch 50Dh–150Dh. Dinner 200Dh. By arrangement.
closed	Never.
directions	Directions given on booking.

Guest house

	Beate Prinz
tel	+212 (0)44 38 52 42
mobile	+212 (0)61 24 31 37
fax	+212 (0)44 38 52 42
email	beate.prinz@laposte.net
web	www.riadzina-marrakech.ma

Map 4 Entry 52

Dar Soukaina

19 Derb El Ferrane, Riad Laârouss, Marrakech-Medina

In its plain white robe, Dar Soukaina is a perfect example of a modest medina house where Alain has preserved the traditional, almost monastic atmosphere: simple furniture, light-handed decoration, spots of colour to remind one of the brilliant sun outside. The little patio sums it up: a small, light square with one humble tree and arches and doorways in the palest of pale mauves. Swathed in contrasting red, orange and crimson, the bed in the ground-floor *Marjoram* room lies proudly in an elaborate alcove, at the windows are curtains of rough natural cotton, built-in storage spaces look as original as the steep little staircases, the shower is through a narrow arch. Each room is coloured to fit its spice name with fabrics of real quality, simple yet stylish. Floors in ecru tadelakt, white walls, the odd gossamer mosquito net, excellent bathrooms, together give a sense of peace and rest. Alain will generally be here for breakfast or evening drinks on the warm ochre terrace and the intelligent attentive staff are ever at your service with gentle smiles and not a scrap of obsequiousness.

rooms	5: 3 doubles, 1 twin, 1 triple.
price	650Dh–800Dh. Sole occupancy 3,000Dh per day.
meals	Dinner 220Dh. By arrangement.
closed	Mid-July to end August.
directions	Directions given on booking.

Alain Bonnassieux

tel	+212 (0)44 37 60 55
fax	+212 (0)44 37 60 54
email	darsoukaina@hotmail.com
web	www.darsoukaina.com

Guest house

Map 4 Entry 53

Hôtel Sherazade

3 Derb Jemaâ, Riad Zitoun El Kdim, Marrakech-Medina

The studded door looks tough but beyond the smiles of the little reception hall you discover the cool sweet light of a tiled and tinkling courtyard. This delightful hotel spreads over two old mansions: two courtyards, two histories, one frondy pot-planted terrace that stretches amply across the lot. The atmosphere up there is delectable: intimate corners with little garden tables, a breakfast tent with its generous buffet and the four simpler, white, light-filled rooms that share washing facilities. The Sherazade, restored by friendly, attentive Sabina who hails from Pakistan and Germany, and her warmly intelligent Moroccan husband, is a simple, attractive place to stay, done in those reds, blues and greens that are so well suited to the Moroccan light, striped fabrics, multi-coloured zellige and brass trays, all with space round the network of galleries and staircases. Every room feels different in shape and décor, most give onto the galleries, beds are good, bathrooms are spotless, some bigger than others, and the staff are exceptionally welcoming – in all simplicity. *Day trips to mountains and desert.*

rooms	19: 8 doubles, 4 twins, 3 triples; 2 doubles, 2 twins, all sharing 2 showers, 2 wcs.
price	200Dh-600Dh.
meals	Buffet breakfast 50Dh. Lunch/dinner 60Dh-140Dh. BYO.
closed	Never.
directions	From Place Jemaâ El Fna, through archway into Riad Zitoun El Kdim, 3rd turning on left.

Small hotel

	Ahmed & Sabina Benchaira
tel	+212 (0)44 42 93 05
fax	+212 (0)44 42 93 05
email	sharazade@iam.net.ma
web	www.hotelsherazade.com

Map 4 Entry 54

Dar Limoun
25 Derb Ben Amrane, Riad Zitoun El Kdim, Marrakech-Medina

In one of the medina's liveliest neighbourhoods, the sudden quiet as you turn into Derb Ben Amrane is striking. The Hotel Sherazade's annexe is the neatest little Moroccan house you could imagine: deeply, peacefully welcoming, unpretentiously authentic and warmly lived-in (spots of peeling paint will prove it). Its low front door opens onto a Berber rug pointing the way to the arcaded patio where greenery climbs out of earthenware pots towards the sky while others hang from the roof to shelter the house from the summer sun. In a Moroccan salon off the patio you will find books and music, a fireplace for chilly days, a cool space in summer. Lanterns flicker on the stairs every evening and paintings of life in early 20th-century Morocco call your eye as you climb to the good simple bedrooms (the best are 2 and 3) with their tribal rugs, sitting corners, new beds and little shower rooms, then on up to the two terraces with all those plants, a lemonwood table and space above for sunbathing. The staff are as quiet as the house and most attentive; it is intimate, appealing, excellent value.

rooms	4: 3 doubles, 1 triple.
price	400Dh–450Dh.
meals	Breakfast 40Dh. Lunch/dinner 120Dh, or à la carte. By arrangement.
closed	Never.
directions	From Place Jemaâ El Fna take Riad Zitoun El Qdim, left into Derb Djemâa to Hôtel Sherazade. Call Dar Limoun from here.

Guest house

	Michel & Nadia Orcel
tel	+212 (0)44 42 66 43
mobile	+212 (0)66 59 17 59
fax	+212 (0)44 42 66 43
email	darlimoun@hotmail.com
web	www.darlimoune.com

Map 4 Entry 55

Riad Kaïss

65 Derb Jdid, Riad Zitoun El Kdim, Marrakech-Medina

Christian Ferré's talent has married two riads with the best of France and
Morocco. His sense of volume is impeccable, his eye for detail unerring, his
hidden pool one of the most beautiful ever: pure form, like an abstract painting.
Kaïss is Marrakech red, the patio garden bathes you in cool green light and
running water, competition for those birds, the paintwork is quintessential
Majorelle blue. Each bedroom is touched with personality: a few choice hangings
and objects that let you into a meeting of tradition and modernity, subtle colour,
sensual texture… and bathrooms as little jewels. Christian is the discreetest host,
there with knowledge and intelligent conversation when you want them, glad that
you appreciate his achievement. The salons, one small and French, the other
magnificently oriental, are soberly opulent with enough original pieces to keep
you gazing for days. The courtyard turns to lantern magic at night, the terrace has
a colonnade for refined dinners, the gym is green marble. And Volka the German
shepherd gives hours of amusement.

rooms	8: 5 doubles, 2 twins, 1 mini-suite with own terrace; connecting rooms possible.
price	1,245Dh-2,355Dh.
meals	Lunch 150Dh. Dinner 300Dh. By arrangement.
closed	Never.
directions	From Place Jemaâ El Fna, Riad Zitoun Kedim to Dar el Salaam restaurant; left into little street; house along on right: red building.

Guest house

	Christian Ferré
tel	+212 (0)44 44 01 41
fax	+212 (0)44 44 01 41
email	riad@riadkaiss.com
web	www.riadkaiss.com

Map 4 Entry 56

Dar El Souk

56 Derb Jdid, Riad Zitoun El Kdim, Marrakech-Medina

Be you jet-setter or budget-hopper, Jean-Michel hopes you will arrive as a guest and leave as a friend. And a friend of Morocco, too, of the gentler Morocco that he has known and loved for years. Knowledgeable, enthusiastic and thoroughly integrated, speaking fluent English, he is the ideal person to point you towards the things you won't find in the guide books. And his riad house, unusual in having four floors, is exceptionally restful: could it be the vibes from those lowly tortoises in the patio? 'Less is more' has been his theme here, no visual overwhelm, no cluttersome collections, just a few fine bright rugs, the occasional cushion or flashing door and an unusual pair of high sofas in the salon. His quietly pale rooms are fresh and light with calico curtains, dark wooden furniture and carefully chosen lamps, their pastel tadelakt bathrooms (five showers, one bath) utterly in keeping. There are plenty of corners to sit in but the best spot is surely the lovely terrace; higher than most, it gives remarkable views. Jean-Michel lives here and, the final flourish, loves cooking.

rooms	6: 4 doubles, 1 twin, 1 quadruple.
price	660Dh-825Dh. Quadruple 1,320Dh. Sole occupancy 5,000Dh.
meals	Lunch/dinner 130Dh-200Dh. By arrangement.
closed	Never.
directions	Between Jemaâ El Fna & Palais El Badi. Detailed directions given on booking.

Guest house

	Jean-Michel Buf
tel	+212 (0)44 39 15 68
mobile	+212 (0)61 17 04 70
email	contact@darelsouk.com
web	www.darelsouk.com

Map 4 Entry 57

Riad Habiba
Riad Zitoun Jdid, 82 Derb Jemaâ, Marrakech-Medina

Marrakech meets simplicity meets humanity: the house, the team, the food combine to make this a really special place. Gorgeously sober black, white and natural-coloured tadelakt create an elegant, soothing mood, the Moroccan furnishings dovetail perfectly with the minimalist feel and the occasional spectacular chandelier gives just the right baroque flourish. Dark furniture, bright silk cushions on low benches, interesting wall hangings and modern French Canadian art are enhanced by lack of clutter, careful clever lighting and magical evening candlelight. Brilliant black bathrooms, too. Frédéric's experience of running top-class hotels in Paris stands him in good stead but it is the human touch that he and Laurence have brought and the willing friendliness of their staff that give the place an exceptional family-run atmosphere. Jamila's cooking is a must: her own bread and yogurt for breakfast, her pastilla or couscous for dinner – unforgettable. Another must: Laurence's hammam in the new town: Les Secrets de Marrakech. One of the most attractive group of rooms and people one could wish for.

rooms	4: 3 doubles, 1 twin.
price	€90–€150.
meals	Lunch/dinner €25.
closed	Never.
directions	From Palais Bahia car park for Dar Si Saïd museum, first right, 2nd left.

Guest house

	Laurence & Frédéric Charmoy
tel	+212 (0)44 38 21 04
mobile	+212 (0)64 99 05 07
fax	+212 (0)44 38 26 36
email	fcharmoy@yahoo.fr
web	www.riadhabiba.com

Map 4 Entry 58

Riad Azzar

94 Derb Moulay Abdelkader, Derb Dabachi, Marrakech-Medina

Cees and Maryk are so interesting. Starting from Holland, they spent years in corporate spheres seeing more hotel rooms than their own bedroom. Then they discovered the medina and a new life called Riad Azzar. They are a warm, caring, integrated couple who live here, say this is pleasure not work and give you the chance to see more than skin-deep Morocco. Bring your heart – and any old toys you have: they sponsor the local orphanage. Their refreshingly all-white house is furnished in dark soothing colours and comforts for a sense of peace, quiet music brings your mind to rest as you walk in, the giant banana tree and green-mosaic plunge pool in the patio tell you that they want it Moroccan with their own twist; everything invites you to sink in and relax. Bedrooms are quiet with their light contemporary style, lots of light, beautifully maintained tadelakt bathrooms. Climb steeply to the terrace to sunbathe in privacy, book dinner to enjoy delicious fresh specialities such as fish pastilla and tangia marrakchia. Aim to arrive in the morning when taxis are allowed to come closer.

rooms	6: 2 doubles, 1 twin, 3 suites.
price	€100–€145. Suites €190–€225.
meals	Lunch €15–€20. Dinner €25–€30. By arrangement only.
closed	Never.
directions	From Café de France enter medina at Derb Dabachi; Derb Moulay Abdelkader along on left: small street entrance with trees in green metal pots.

	Cees & Maryk Vanderberg
tel	+212 (0)61 15 81 73
fax	+212 (0)44 38 90 91
email	info@riadazzar.com
web	www.riadazzar.com

Guest house

Map 4 Entry 59

Riyad El Cadi

87 Derb Moulay Abdelkader, Derb Dabachi, Marrakech-Medina

Ancient foundations, antique hangings, eight centuries of art from Morocco and all over the Islamic world living in eight old houses round a maze of patios in pure local style, the finest one an exuberance of citrus. Quiet, harmonious décor is a perfect backdrop for original painted woodwork, a highly personal mix of furniture – vibrant gifts of human talent from down the centuries – and no clutter. No artificial authenticity either: the local Art Nouveau copper kettles are real. Their collector, the scholar and diplomat Herwig Bartels, left his collections for ever in August 2003 but his high-class tinker's universe of "pots, pans and old rags", as he called it – a hymn to Islamic and Berber cultures – is his epitaph and his daughter Julia is a fitting heir to this treasure-house. The 'budget' Blue House – two bedrooms, salon, patio – is a dream retreat for two couples; suites are simply magnificent, all rooms revel in natural gracious taste and soft tadelakt bathrooms. The cuisine is 'international', the staff are a delight with their ready smiles and quick intelligence. A rare privilege for body and spirit.

rooms	12: 1 single, 5 doubles, 6 suites.
price	1,450Dh–2,900Dh.
meals	Lunch 150Dh. Dinner 350Dh. By arrangement.
closed	July.
directions	From Place Jemaâ El Fna, right Derb Dabachi (beyond Café de France), left Derb Moulay Abdelkader; No 87 is little low door on left.

Guest house

		Julia Bartels & Ahmed El Amrani
tel		+212 (0)44 37 86 55
fax		+212 (0)44 37 84 78
email		info@riyadelcadi.com
web		www.riyadelcadi.com

Map 4 Entry 60

Riad Magi

79 Derb Moulay Abdul Kader, Derb Dabachi, Marrakech-Medina

Magic in the oldest quarter of the medina? Yes, that's how Maggie Perry feels about her house and how she hopes you'll feel, too. A magic place to stay in colourful simplicity: she designed the interior, with her painter's feel for colour. There's a gaggle of citrus and two fountains in the graceful patio where Islamic green, white and ochre make a fresh background to antique painted doors. One of them leads to the refined Moroccan salon whose carved frieze ties white and cream walls and plum-coloured cushions into luscious, unshowy harmony. Lemonwood tables and silver teapots finish the picture; there's a silvery touch in your bedroom too. Green or yellow or white and blue, it may have a stucco ceiling, it certainly has an antique chest, super fabrics and a little tadelakt shower room. The whole place, from patio to roof terrace (those medina-to-Atlas views), has a gentle-firm personality, modern yet respectful of the fine old architecture, and is incredibly quiet. Maggie is often here and Abderrazak, the welcoming, efficient manager of house and staff, speaks fluent English. *Trips organised.*

rooms	6: 4 doubles, 1 twin, 1 single.
price	700Dh–1,000Dh.
meals	Dinner 150Dh. Lunch 100Dh. By arrangement. BYO.
closed	Never.
directions	From Place Jemaâ El Fna, right Derb Dabachi (behind Café de France); pass mosque then first left; down to bottom, right to end, house on right. Or ring for escort from Café de France.

	M. Perry & A. Sanhaji Moutiq
tel	+212 (0)44 42 66 88
mobile	+212 (0)73 25 76 42
fax	+212 (0)44 42 66 88

Guest house

Map 4 Entry 61

Ryad El Borj

63 Derb Moulay Abdelkader, Derb Dabachi, Marrakech-Medina

Ever since Pasha Glaoui built it as a lookout, the 'tower' (*borj*) has had the highest view of the medina, magic at any hour, sublime at sunset. Down below, the big leafy blue patio leads to the green first floor which leads to the red terrace – all properly dramatic. When renovating his ryad, Daniel took care to preserve the original décor: it all wears the patina of time and feels like a real Moroccan house rather than a made-for-gringos riad. Coca the dog is an essential, if ageing, presence, too. Almost all the extremely comfortable rooms have decorated ceilings while the great glass-vaulted suite is remarkable value with its big bedroom, sitting room, excellent bathroom – and extra salon onto the patio via a superb moucharabieh screen. Colours are pale and sober, materials are noble cedar and finely-wrought ironwork, doors are antique, floors are strewn with carpets and leather cushions from the Saharaoui south giving the exotic sense of a *khaima*, a nomad tent; dinner is absolutely fabulous and the ever-smiling Khaddouj is a delight. Pool, drinks and meals are just as you would wish.

Guest house

rooms	5: 4 doubles, 1 suite.
price	€60–€80. Suite €105–€120. Sole occupancy €1,700–€2,700 per week (max 8).
meals	Lunch or dinner by arrangement.
closed	Never.
directions	From Place Jemaâ El Fna take Derb Dabachi (straight on past Café de France coming from Koutoubia side); pass mosque on right, first left; house 30m on right.

	Daniel Ghio
tel	+212 (0)44 39 12 23
mobile	+212 (0)61 67 59 42
fax	+212 (0)44 39 12 23
email	ryadelborj@wanadoo.net.ma
web	www.riadelborj.com

Map 4 Entry 62

Riad Ifoulki

11 Derb Mqqadem, Rue Arset Loghzail, Marrakech-Medina

One of the oldest houses in the medina, this enormous edifice rambles through five courtyards, up to the huge roof terrace, past masses of original tiles, arches, fountains and stucco. The house remains a perfect example of the Islamic inner-sanctum ideal: inside you can hear birdsong and yet this riad is only a short stroll away from bustling Jemaâ el Fna. Quiet white walls set off the multifarious greenery and the traditional iron grilles – it feels utterly authentic. Peter is a charming, much-travelled and loquacious polyglot, Gabriele is quieter and a most talented cook. Exceptionally integrated, they have many Moroccan friends – filmmakers, writers and artists – and dining with them is a real pleasure for mind and palate. Décor is luxurious without being flashy and the rooms, varying in size, mostly have muslin-draped four-posters, carved Moroccan furniture, brass lamps, lovely bathrooms and towels with tassels. This is a cosmopolitan meeting place, and Peter is thrilled to be a catalyst igniting new friendships.

rooms	15: 11 doubles, 4 suites.
price	€80–€300.
meals	Lunch/dinner from €15.
closed	Never.
directions	From Place Jemaâ El Fna down Rue Dabachi; right Arset Loghzail, 3rd right Derb Mqqadem; or ring for escort from Jemaâ El Fna. Also accessible by car from Bab Ghemat.

	Peter Bergmann
tel	+212 (0)44 38 56 56
mobile	+212 (0)61 42 39 40
fax	+212 (0)44 38 56 56
email	riadifoulki@riadifoulki.com
web	www.riadifoulki.com

Guest house

Map 4 Entry 63

Dar Attajmil

23 rue Laksour, Bab Laksour, Marrakech-Medina

Attajmil means to make beautiful, exactly what Lucrezia has done for this small intimate medina house, with her firm, gentle youthfulness and her Italian instinct for style. You come down from the big nailed door into a dark hall then out into the red-pillared patio where proud banana plants tower to the upper floor and two black cats parade. There is just a slight trickle of water somewhere. Rooms are as natural and pleasing as this cool/warm space, there's nothing formulaic or overdone: pure white sheets, a painting, a pot, a coloured cushion on a plain wool blanket. Some fine and unusual pieces of furniture will catch your eye, giving each room its own personality, but the effect is light and human. The salon has some intriguing African stools as well as books, CDs, soft padded benches and subtle lighting. Lucrezia, who is active in local development projects, leaves the quiet delightful Brahim in charge of her excellent staff if she ever goes away but she also sets up yoga, cuisine, embroidery and even tadelakt courses. A lovely person and a beautiful house – that is also easy to find!

rooms	4 doubles.
price	700Dh–1,000Dh.
meals	Lunch 150Dh. Dinner 200Dh. By arrangement.
closed	Never.
directions	Enter medina at Bab Laksour; 2nd right 200m; on corner on left.

Guest house

	Lucrezia Mutti di Vallemuzia
tel	+212 (0)44 42 69 66
mobile	+212 (0)64 23 59 54
fax	+212 (0)44 42 69 66
email	darattajmil@menara.ma
web	www.darattajmil.com

Map 4 Entry 64

Riad Ksiba

147 Derb Kbala, Kasbah, Marrakech-Medina

The wise British owners entrusted their riad to a talented Moroccan couple: Najib the architect to restore, Nadia the powerhouse to manage. Najib wanted to say a lot with a little so he kept to black, white and pale tones for the background, to perfect muted effect. Nadia embellished it with bright voile curtains, cushions, candles and rugs, for a somewhat theatrical note. She is the life and soul of this house, a bundle of Moroccan energy bubbling with enthusiasm, giving guests masses of her time, scattering her beloved red roses everywhere. The furnishings are careful, uncluttered and quiet though, with splashes of colour, some interesting modern Moroccan art in the cool first-floor salon and a brilliant little 'pond' in the patio – just for sitting in among the rose petals. The high-ceilinged bedrooms, named after poets or philosophers, have silky curtains (some purple), brass-topped tables, lantern lamps and superb big tadelakt bathrooms full of shelving and mirrors. Stairs lead to a large terrace with mountain views. Its tented area is ideal for candle-lit dinners or for relaxing in the shade.

rooms	6: 2 doubles, 1 twin, 3 suites.
price	1,045Dh-1,815Dh. Sole occupancy 44,275Dh-56,565Dh per week.
meals	Dinner from 200Dh. Lunch from 80Dh.
closed	Never.
directions	From Bab Agnaou right at mosque Rue de la Kasbah. Pass Tombeaux Saâdiens, straight on, right to Derb Kbala.

	Nadia Tabiai
tel	+212 (0)44 38 98 38
mobile	+212 (0)61 20 15 26
fax	+212 (0)44 38 56 50
email	contact@riadksiba.com
web	www.riadksiba.com

Guest house & catered house

Map 4 Entry 65

Les Jardins de la Médina
21 Derb Chtouka, Kasbah, Marrakech-Medina

After the medina dazzle, the upside-down tree in the dark hall is a brilliant trick. Carry your graciously-preferred key through to the miracle gardens where birds rejoice and a heated infinity pool smiles smoothly. The abandoned palace where Princess Farah Diba and Egyptian singer Oum Khalsoum once stayed, its rich garden turning to jungle, was resuscitated in 2001 by a Morocco-loving family. There might be 80 people in the hotel but, apart from summer swimming bustle, you could believe it's half empty, so clever has the architect been with leafy private terraces, secret corners and jigsaw layouts. His Moroccan/Tuscan influences inform the clean, uncluttered décor, timeless in its sober fancy and luxurious detail. Every secluded room has careful individuality in rich fabrics against plain walls, well-chosen pictures and carpets, superb Moroccan-finish bathrooms. The many terraces, spray-cooled in summer, include a beauty centre; below, a brilliant chef conducts a symphony in Moroccan, Mediterranean and Thai; salons and dining rooms are fitting backgrounds for these delights.

rooms	36 singles, doubles, triples & 'Privilege' rooms.
price	1,650Dh-3,150Dh. Single 1,240Dh-2,360Dh.
meals	Lunch/dinner 75Dh-295Dh.
closed	Never.
directions	From Bab Agnaou right at mosque into Rue de la Kasbah; pass Tombeaux Saâdiens, straight on to Derb Chtouka; hotel down on right, white doorway.

Small hotel

	Franck Seguin & Michel Sautereau
tel	+212 (0)44 38 18 51
fax	+212 (0)44 38 53 85
email	info@lesjardinsdelamedina.com
web	www.lesjardinsdelamedina.com

Map 4 Entry 66

Dar Pangal

132 Derb Chtouka, Kasbah, Marrakech-Medina

Doves coo in the leafy patio of Julio's simple quiet *dar* deep inside the royal estate between the kasbah and the great Agdal Gardens but Dar Pangal's best feature is the roof: from the terrace you have a spectacular view across the palace and the looming Koutoubia to the snowy Atlas. Julio, a kindly chatty Chilean, adopted Morocco years ago, serves a simple Moroccan breakfast, can provide endless insights into country and people and is a talented designer. A light earthy wash is the background for a mass of greenery in the arcaded patio and for his own mix of Latin American, Moroccan and sub-Saharan styles in the plain, sober salon and bedrooms. It has a comforting lived-in feel, all very unpretentious with clever storage systems made of woven palm leaves and pale lemonwood, terracotta lanterns, ingenious raffia blinds to screen rooms from the patio – all his own designs. You can order yours from his showroom here. The pretty yellow and ochre shower rooms have some unusual touches – and you'll find quantities of peace and quiet in this gentle old house streaked with originality.

rooms	4 doubles.
price	600Dh.
meals	Lunch/dinner 100Dh.
	By arrangement.
closed	Never.
directions	From Bab Agnaou right at mosque into Rue de la Kasbah; pass Tombeaux Saâdiens, straight on to Derb Chtouka. Accessible by car; car park nearby.

Guest house

	Julio Miranda Thiel
tel	+212 (0)44 38 09 50
mobile	+212 (0)67 96 40 50
fax	+212 (0)44 38 69 98
email	pangal2003@yahoo.fr

Map 4 Entry 67

La Sultana

6-8-9 Derb Agadir, Kasbah - El Mechouar, Marrakech-Medina

Overwhelming: the exotic African room, a shady gallery where you sit with the latest designs; the gnu's skull presiding over an imperial silver bed; the hot humid envelopment of Roman baths (the spa); the extravagant bathrooms. It took the best contemporary craftsmen two years to transform four riads into this triumph of the copyist's art in marble, chiselled plaster, carved and painted wood: to each a different atmosphere – and exactly the same music. Between brick arches, the pearly pool mirrors the great palms; Moroccan Art Deco is next door. Vast terraces are full of flowers and views onto the Saadian tombs. Bedrooms are in luxurious keeping, all decorated on a different animal theme: antiques, works of art, more exquisite craftsmanship. La Sultana shares her treasures with you and provides stylishly white-robed human service. And their new French chef is already provoking cries of "one of the best tables in town". Come to relax and be pampered, or hold a fairytale, gastronomic, party. Real old Morocco is just outside the brass doors of this small luxury hotel.

rooms	20 + 1: 12 doubles, 8 suites, 1 apartment.
price	2,400Dh-5,800Dh. Soft drinks included. Sole occupancy possible.
meals	Lunch 200Dh. Dinner 400Dh. Visitors by arrangement.
closed	Never.
directions	Enter medina at Bab Agnaou, right at mosque, first left after Tombeaux Saâdiens into narrow alley: brass door at end.

Guest house & catered house

	Isabelle Niclot
tel	+212 (0)44 38 80 08
fax	+212 (0)44 38 77 77
email	contact@lasultanamarrakech.com
web	www.lasultanamarrakech.com

Map 4 Entry 68

La Maison Arabe

1 Derb Assehbe, Bab Doukkala, Marrakech-Medina

A small army staffs this legendary restaurant grown into small hotel, yet it has an intimate, almost guest house, atmosphere – one feels like royalty staying with friends. Pillars and sumptuous antique tables divide the big salons into quiet traditional-feel corners (the buildings are modern) lit by Berber stripes and good pictures; the fabulous painted ceiling of the big new restaurant, its raw marble floor and the gentle patio beyond frame a real Moroccan food experience. And the 'Arabian Nights' bedrooms are no let-down: the designer owner melds furniture, colours and paintings with thoughtful skill so that antique carpets and mirrors, surfaces of traditional brick, beautiful tiles or smoothly polished tadelakt, rich and varied furnishings and some excellent modern art co-exist in powerful harmony. In its lush oasis setting, the swimming pool is exceptional for Marrakech, birds sing and your dinner vegetables grow in the vast kitchen garden… it's ten minutes out of town by Maison Arabe shuttle – they have thought of everything. You can even take Moroccan cookery courses.

rooms	17: 8 doubles, 9 suites.
price	1,900Dh-2,500Dh. Suites 3,000Dh-6,000Dh.
meals	Lunch from 120Dh. Dinner from 350Dh.
closed	Never.
directions	From Rue Fatima Zohorn, opposite Bab Doukkala mosque; sign on Derb Assehbe.

Small hotel

	F. Ruspoli, T.Ghaffouli, N. Dakir
tel	+212 (0)44 38 70 10
fax	+212 (0)44 38 72 21
email	maisonarabe@iam.net.ma
web	www.lamaisonarabe.com

Map 4 Entry 69

Riad Maroc

100 Derb El Halfaoui, Bab Doukkala, Marrakech-Medina

So close to the life – and taxis – of Bab Doukkala and the old Glaoui Palace, it is an enchanting house, an unspoilt medina riad of welcoming, sober opulence, without any attempt at artificial orientalisms. Michele's second home can be yours for a spell, with the bonus of Amina to housekeep and cook fine Moroccan food, and Jalil to produce mouth-watering pasta, organise mountain or seaside trips, guide you through the souks – all in excellent English – then produces a painting or two. They are delightful talented gems. Purple bougainvillea cascades down the arches of the pretty old tiled patio, myriad plants flourish, the beautiful padded wooden bench summons you to contemplate the cool peace. Or repair to the chaises-longues of the frondy, tented roof terrace. Colours are cool light white for summer, rich red for winter with bright Moroccan cushions, of course. To each lovely bedroom its own colour scheme for silk throws or warm wool – *saison oblige*. Michele is involved in Marrakchi cultural events and has taken care to provide a well-stocked bookcase for your free moments. *Access to nearby hotel pool.*

Catered house

rooms	4: 1 double; 2 doubles sharing bath, 1 twin with private bath.
price	Sole occupancy from £350 per week for two excluding meals. Single nights can be negotiated.
meals	Breakfast 20Dh-50Dh. Half-board 150Dh p.p. Children half price. Lunch upon request.
closed	Never.
directions	From Dar Bacha pass Dar Marjane restaurant; right Derb El Halfaoui; blue door at end of street.

	Michele Cohen
tel	+44 (0)1243 551 660
mobile	+44 (0)77 485 70493
email	michele.cohen@btinternet.com

Map 4 Entry 70

Dar Doukkala

83 rue Bab Doukkala, Marrakech-Medina

Ask to see the lovingly painted doors, originally a 17th-century Berber ceiling and freed from their sheet-metal prison by the renovator who tended this 19th-century palace in the Mouassine quarter, returning it to its Glaoui glory (helped by 1930s French/Moroccan craftsmen): more ancient doors in new frames, the odd reminder of black Africa, some vastly original fireplaces. Palm trees rise from the patio past shimmering mosaic pillars, stucco marvels and darkly carved galleries; the grand yet inviting salons burst with contrasting antiques. The patio gives a foretaste of the landscaped terraces up above, one for the discreet pool and its outdoor salon, one for guests of the grand suite (and its double bath…), the largest with masses of cushioned space beneath slatted canopies – and views. Each big bedroom has a richly individual feel and an exceptional bathroom while managers Alain and Marie-Noëlle and owner Philippe create a convivial atmosphere that is as stylish and warmly human as the house. Unforgettable.
Hammam to be booked, no extra charge. Dar Aïda for 6, 2,400Dh per day.

rooms	6: 4 twins/doubles, 2 suites.
price	€130-€270. Suites €180-€330. Sole occupancy €915-€1,373 per day.
meals	Lunch 160Dh. Dinner 280Dh. By arrangement.
closed	Never.
directions	From Dar El Bacha, Rue Bab Doukkala west; door on left, 60m from taxi set-down.

	P. Bouyé, M. & A. Schenck
tel	+212 (0)44 38 34 44
fax	+212 (0)44 38 34 45
email	dardoukkala@menara.ma
web	www.dardoukkala.com

Guest house

Map 4 Entry 71

Riad 72

72 Arset Awzel, Bab Doukkala, Marrakech-Medina

Working with an Italian-trained Moroccan architect, Riad 72's strong-minded Italian owner achieved this superbly white renovation of one of the medina's highest mansions whose lofty terrace looks the Pasha's palace in the eye. In the patio, a dream of rest and clear spirit, a breathtaking white cubic fountain overflows beneath giant banana plants – the colours of serenity. In bedrooms and salons, the marriage of Moroccan decorative arts and Italian style and sobriety brings class and originality: quiet greys, shimmering dark velours, subtle sabra stripes set off clean contemporary shapes and strikingly beautiful old carved ceilings. Bedrooms have big tempting beds, some straight from design magazines, occasional bright touches, nothing flashy, masses of presence. The vast suite rises up to a century-old octagonal carved cupola whence the light filters down onto the great red bed and the grey tadelakt floor. Each bathroom is utterly original in shape and finish, every detail attended to... as you will be by Raja, Giovanna's sweet and efficient housekeeper, and her ever-helpful staff.

rooms	4: 2 doubles, 1 twin, 1 suite.
price	1,100Dh-3,300Dh.
meals	Dinner 250Dh. Lunch 30Dh-110Dh. By arrangement.
closed	2 weeks in July.
directions	In the medina, telephone from Dar El Bacha for guide to riad.

Guest house

	Giovanna Cinel
tel	+212 (0)44 38 76 29
fax	+212 (0)44 38 47 18
email	info@riad72.com
web	www.riad72.com

Map 4 Entry 72

Riad Malika

29 Arset Aouzal, Bab Doukkala, Marrakech-Medina

Let yourself be swept up in this collector's passion – and deposited luxuriously in a 1930s club sofa or a 1960s leather Saarinen. Your host is larger than life and utterly human, his wonderful house – Morocco's first ever guest house – is a living museum of 20th-century Moroccan design: at the height of their glory the Glaoui clan mixed European ideas with tradition – behind high palace walls. Malika was one of these palaces, updated in the 1920s with balconies and huge windows over the luxuriant patio. In a labyrinth of stairways and levels (the triplex suite flashes with glorious colour), Jean-Luc's designer talent and Martine's quiet presence do the rest. Every one of the multitudinous details deserves attention: six decades of clocks, mirrors, statues, paintings; deep-carved Moroccan doors, intricate lamps, hand-painted pieces from renovated mosques, beautiful zellige walls, stucco above, rugs below. And so much space. Generosity embraces every bedroom, brilliant tiled bathrooms have more antiques, meals are sybaritic delights, staff are friendly with buckets of class. It's hard to leave.

rooms	11: 8 doubles, 3 suites.
price	Half-board for two: doubles €115, suites €145.
meals	Light lunch from 100Dh. Dinner 210Dh. By arrangement.
closed	Never.
directions	From Dar El Bacha, Rue Bab Doukkala west; first left under arch labelled Riad Malika & follow signs.

	Martine Hubert & Jean-Luc Lemée
tel	+212 (0)44 38 54 51
fax	+212 (0)44 38 54 51
email	jean.luc@iam.net.ma
web	www.riadmalika.com

Guest house

Map 4 Entry 73

Tamkast

10 Derb Sidi Bou Amar, Zaouiat Lahdar, Marrakech-Medina

Pascal has taught in Morocco for many years and lived in this house for seven: it is clearly a home without any pretensions to boutiquery or décor hype. It takes its name from a Berber village and there is a country gentleness to the bejmat floors, the hand-carved wooden furniture, the plain natural-textured bedcovers. In the beautiful wafer-bricked courtyard, the four citrus beds in their fountain-fed watery basin take their geometric layout from the Saadian tombs, jasmine and orange blossom give a heady scent, the fountain sings – all your senses are stroked. And the ground-floor twin has the privilege of its own lovely cushion-strewn little patio and fountain. This, the oldest part of the medina, is almost a small village within the larger old town and Pascal knows virtually everybody. He is also the perfect consultant on what to do and see and where to eat – he feels guests should eat out and get to know this unique urban environment while they can; his knowledge of Islamic culture goes deep and warms easily to visitors' interest in the subject. A quiet, unassuming place and great value.

rooms	4 twins/doubles.
price	600Dh–880Dh. Sole occupancy 2,000Dh–3,200Dh.
meals	Lunch 80Dh. Dinner 150Dh–200Dh. BYO.
closed	July.
directions	Near Medersa Ben Youssef. Directions given on booking.

Guest house

Pascal Massat

tel	+212 (0)44 44 01 89
mobile	+212 (0)63 44 57 95
fax	+212 (0)44 42 68 12
email	info@tamkast.com
web	www.tamkast.co.ma

Map 4 Entry 74

Riad Aïda

Riad Zitoun Jdid, 59 Derb Lamouagni, Marrakech-Medina

In an unusually quiet corner of the medina, Riad Aïda flows with milk, honey and an air of tranquil history. The cultured, sophisticated Boudons have kept their well-loved second home as true to its original spirit as possible. The patio doors are 150 years old and identical to those in the Bahia Palace next door: this was the palace chamberlain's house, with a secret door into his master's domain. Rather than digging a pool, they kept the fountain and the four trees that symbolise the rivers of wine, milk, water and honey running out of Paradise. The restoration uncovered some original Essaouira thuya wood, a superb painted (*zouak*) cedar ceiling, some hidden arches. If your hosts are here, you'll enjoy hearing the stories. The décor is an intimate, friendly compromise between east and west with some gorgeous tadelakt surfaces. The salon has tiles, tadelakt and stucco – and a Russian samovar. One suite is 'Arab-Andalusian' with tiles made in Seville and a sunken bath in its cleverly arranged bathroom; another has a four-poster; all are lovely. *Free entry to Sunset Club pool in Palmeraie.*

rooms	6: 3 doubles, 3 suites.
price	530Dh-1,580Dh (3,700Dh-11,000Dh per week). Sole occupancy €3,171-€4,140 per week.
meals	Lunch 165Dh. Dinner 220Dh. By arrangement.
closed	Never.
directions	Airport transfer available or, inside medina, ring for escort from Préfecture.

Guest house

	Jean Luc & Nicole Boudon
tel	+212 (0)44 37 89 84
mobile	+212 (0)61 23 00 06
fax	+212 (0)44 37 89 84
email	info@riadaida.com
web	www.riadaida.com

Map 4 Entry 75

La Villa des Orangers
6 rue Sidi Mimoun, Marrakech-Medina

The pure white pool patio and tranquil garden are the latest expression of the Orangers' subtle mix of French refinement and Moroccan authenticity, so close to rowdy, crowdy Jemaâ El Fna yet holding soft peace behind beautiful doors, its roof terrace gazing at the incomparable Koutoubia. The Beherecs furbished their hotelier arms in Paris, then fell in love with Marrakech, whence brass and bronze, inlay and filigree, shimmering rugs and subtle stucco, the song of water at every patio turn. Featherlight breakfast crêpes are served beneath the orange trees, soft drinks in the salon where light and shade play or the fire leaps in the Luxor-style fireplace, Mediterranean or Moroccan dinner in the sleek smart restaurant. Wonderful big uncluttered bedrooms, some with their own terrace or balcony; hyper luxury in the new garden suites; lovely bathrooms, each with bath and shower; superb bedding; and no colour overload, just genuine understated luxury. The beautifully-mannered staff will serve you perfectly, as befits Morocco's first *Relais & Châteaux*. 1% of income goes to a Moroccan village project.

Small hotel

rooms	19: 5 twins/doubles, 14 suites.
price	Half-board, light lunch, 2,900Dh–6,800Dh. Includes soft drinks at bar, laundry, airport transfer.
meals	Half-board only. Dinner 480Dh–580Dh.
closed	Never.
directions	Enter medina by Bab Jdid; Houmane El Fetouaki 600m; right into Rue Sidi Mimoun.

	Véronique & Pascal Beherec
tel	+212 (0)44 38 46 38
fax	+212 (0)44 38 51 23
email	message@villadesorangers.com
web	www.villadesorangers.com

Map 4 Entry 76

Dar Tchaïkana

25 Derb El Ferrane, Azbest, Marrakech-Medina

A vibrant young Belgian couple have realised their clear and luminous dream at 'the house where one drinks tea'. A dream of simplicity, sobriety, softened Marrakech light on beige and ochre, gentle blue arcades against pure white walls and a personal, sensitive mixture of furniture: modern black easy chairs and Moroccan basketweave pouffes, tadelakt bathrooms and original batik pictures, some fascinating sub-Saharan pieces which bring Delphine's beloved nomads indoors: her knowledge is as deep as her passion, the engraved funeral urn on the staircase is a quiet wonder, the bed made of sturdy Berber tent posts, rough-hewn with the marks of their other life, an image of strength. Big rooms, huge suites, where firm, unintrusive decoration makes the shape and atmosphere of the old house palpable and each tiny detail takes its place with pride. Between the white salon and the red salon lies the green-planted, terracotta-tiled patio where water plays and meals are shared at simple black tables with hosts of intelligence and lively humour. This is quiet unusual magic, the purest of the pure.

rooms	5: 3 doubles, 2 suites.
price	700Dh-1,500Dh. Sole occupancy 25,000Dh-28,000Dh per week (max 12 people).
meals	Dinner 150Dh. By arrangement.
closed	Rarely.
directions	Airport transfer (100Dh) or meeting place arranged for escort to house.

	J. Claeys & D. Mottet
tel	+212 (0)44 38 51 50
fax	+212 (0)44 38 51 50
email	info@tchaikana.com
web	www.tchaikana.com

Guest house & catered house

Map 4 Entry 77

Riad Meriem
97 Derb El Cadi, Azbest, Marrakech-Medina

In the oldest part of the medina, the alleys get narrow, narrower… all the better to flood you with the joyousness of this house. A remarkable couple, François and Myriam came from Belgium, found this riad, bathed it in sensual tadelakt, designed their very own original lamps, chose the best trio to help them scatter petals on the little pool, cook like angels and be happy here, then opened it to privileged guests. When she is here, Myriam's powerful arty presence fills the house with exuberance. With Karima's smiling help, Malika will spoil you wonderfully with her luscious cooking; wonderful Hassan will take you to the bazaar. In cooler weather, the salon is a delight in its quiet oriental dress and its steps down to the hearth; or be private in the small patio room; otherwise, the bedouin tent or the parasols on the terrace invite you to laze between sun and shade with your mint tea and home-cured olives. And sleep at last in a generous room with its gentle décor, wide bed, big cupboards and splendiferous bathroom: candles, rose petals, oils, baths big enough for two.

rooms	5 twins/doubles.
price	850Dh-1,500Dh. Sole occupancy 3,500Dh-5,000Dh per day.
meals	Lunch from 50Dh. Dinner 180Dh-280Dh. By arrangement.
closed	Never.
directions	Directions given on booking.

Guest house & catered house

	Myriam & François Gottignies
tel	+212 (0)44 38 77 31/+32 47 386 3702
fax	+212 (0)44 37 77 62
email	contact@riadmeriem.com
web	www.riadmeriem.com

Map 4 Entry 78

Riad Maizie

95 Derb El Qadi, Azbest, Marrekech-Medina

Fruit stalls line the streets, the alley is narrow, the door is beautiful: you know you are living in real Moroccan Marrakech and the English owners of this old family house have kept it genuine, just adding good lighting and bathrooms. Finishes are fine tadelakt, delicate zellige and warm bejmat, colours are stimulating, furniture is mosaic-topped or hand-painted, beds as wide as possible in those narrow riad rooms over the citrus patio; fabrics glow with the reflected light of Morocco. There's a really good kitchen off the dining room, a fireplace in the sitting room, an amazing pink salon upstairs, a stunning painted ceiling, a nomad tent and a splendid dome to greet you as you emerge onto the plant-filled roof terrace to sing with the fountain and salute the distant Atlas mountains. The douiria, a tiny adjoining house with bedroom, bathroom and salon for a couple wanting a bit of independence, joins the big house by the roof. Nourdine manages brilliantly and will even shop for you. A lovely traditional family house for you, your family and friends.

rooms	4: 3 doubles, 1 twin.
price	£50-£70. Airport transfer included.
meals	Cook available. BYO.
closed	Never.
directions	Directions given on booking.

Miranda Innes & Nourdine Fartmizi

tel	+212 (0)44 38 59 28/+34 952 034 321
mobile	+212 (0)68 67 48 33
email	riadmaizie@menara.ma
web	www.marocandalucia.co.uk

Catered house

Map 4 Entry 79

Jnane Mogador Hôtel

116 Riad Zitoun Kedim, Derb Sidi Bouloukat, Marrakech-Medina

In the heart of the old imperial city, great expectations take you through the imposing 19th-century doorway into a glorious patio of smooth pillars, fine tiles, marble fountain and plants galore. You should not be disappointed. The friendly young owners restored the authentic riad architecture with a Marrakech-red basis and great attention to the traditional arts of chiselled stucco, sculpted stone and silky tadelakt by the best craftsmen in town. The marble staircase marches hand in foot with antique urns, doors are hand-painted wood, windows screened with moucharabieh. Most attractive. Rooms are in simple contrast with their curly wrought-iron furniture and fixtures and unfussy wide-striped bedcovers. Bedding is excellent and cupboards generous, bathrooms are snug and pretty in their tadelakt finishes, the new suite has its own terrace. There are two fine communal terraces, one open, one elegantly enclosed, for breakfast or mint tea or romantic lunch or dinner. And now there's a beautiful hammam and massage room.
A friendly, welcoming place for smaller budgets just yards from Jemaâ El Fna.

rooms	18: 6 doubles, 5 twins, 2 singles, 1 suite, 1 triple, 3 quadruples.
price	Doubles/twins 400Dh. Triple/quadruples 490Dh-640Dh. Suite 690Dh.
meals	Lunch/dinner 80Dh-115Dh.
closed	Never.
directions	From Place Jemaâ El Fna take Riad Zitoun Kedim; hotel 100 metres down on right.

Small hotel

	Mohamed Araban
tel	+212 (0)44 42 63 23/24
fax	+212 (0)44 42 63 23
email	contact@jnanemogador.com
web	www.jnanemogador.com

Map 4 Entry 80

Riad El Arsat

10 Derb Chemaâ, Arset Loughzail, Marrakech-Medina

The biggest private garden in the medina – 1600m2 of bird-filled orchard and palm trees, singing fountains, sandy paths and big pool – this was the house of a great sugar trader. Each bedroom has its own little terrace onto the magical greenery, the colonnade marches past joining winter house to summer house; it is palatial and unpretentious. In the grand salon where the family held court, Nicole's collection of photographs, paintings and drawings adds interest, the stupendous cedar ceiling demands admiration, a flurry of rich carpets softens the bejmat floor – and you may use the CD collection. Bedrooms, shared between the two houses and one little cottage, are comfortable but not enormous ("we live out of doors here") with Nicole's variously personal décor: yet more paintings, fine old brass beds, fascinating bits of furniture, draperies and regal colours, chiselled friezes and a sitting corner by the fireplace, so welcome on some winter evenings; good bathrooms, too. And your live-wire art historian hostess knows all about the city, old and new. *Also catered house for eight in same street.*

rooms	7: 5 twins/doubles, 2 suites.
price	1,750Dh-3,300Dh.
meals	Lunch/dinner 250Dh. Picnic 50Dh. By arrangement. BYO.
closed	Never.
directions	Easy directions given on booking.

Guest house

	Nicole Arbousset
tel	+212 (0)44 38 75 67
mobile	+212 (0)61 58 27 49
fax	+212 (0)44 38 76 05
email	nicolearbousset@yahoo.fr
web	www.riad-elarsat-marrakech.com

Map 4 Entry 81

Riyad El Mezouar

28 Derb El Hammam, Issebtinne, Marrakech-Medina

Glorious shock! Such serenity after the populous clanging of the old Arab alleys. One of the fine great mansions once owned by the Alaoui dynasty, El Mezouar has an angel star that fell into the patio and a sublime emerald-green pool to reflect its clear arcaded symmetry and the greenery that lines it: this long and lovely perspective breathes serenity. Exquisitely renovated by two French interior designers who have Morocco in their bones, it has the unostentatious elegance of pale backgrounds and natural cedar, perfect detailing and occasional flashes – a deep pink curtain, a glowing red vase from China. Bedrooms have space, light and a perfect mix of antiques and Michel's own designs. Bathrooms are marble and gleaming copper, tadelakt and the odd claw foot. But richest of all is their extraordinary collection of oriental paintings, prints, objects and hangings, each one so sensitively positioned. Your charming hosts and their staff adore this pure and lovely house and will do anything to convert you, including serving superb food with white-gloved style. Really special.

rooms	5: 1 twin, 1 double, 3 suites.
price	1,900Dh. Suites 2,200Dh.
meals	Lunch 200Dh. Dinner 400Dh. By arrangement. BYO.
closed	Never.
directions	Directions given on booking. Accessible by car.

Guest house

	J. Vermelin & M. Durand-Meyrier
tel	+212 (0)44 38 09 49
mobile	+212 (0)63 16 60 48
fax	+212 (0)44 38 09 43
email	info@mezouar.com
web	www.mezouar.com

Map 4 Entry 82

Dar Hanane

9 Derb Lalla Azzouna, Marrakech-Medina

So much simple beauty. So much space. Françoise approached her unusually wide, high rooms with love, respect and absolutely no frills: they reflect her intelligence and sensitivity. From the crowded streets with their little market and nearby tanneries, stop at the majestic door and prepare to fall in love, as she did in 2000. The monastic walls, deep-lobed doorways and blue-grey carved woodwork round the perfect little patio say it all: in such peace and grandeur, you can be yourself. The pale background is warmed by purple divans, mauve pouffes, red cushions and some lovely Berber rugs. Gentle bedrooms have one fine piece of furniture each, a carefully-chosen lamp, a walk-in cupboard and a pastel tadelakt bathroom; the wonderful suite extends to a latticed mezzanine; the gorgeous terrace, with its canvas tent draped stylishly over your cushions, is one of the highest in Marrakech. Soft, gentle taste is the hallmark of an unintrusive hostess and her delightful assistants Aïcha and Raja. And Aicha's 100% Moroccan cooking is not to be missed. *Free entry to pool in the Palmeraie.*

rooms	5: 4 doubles, 1 suite for 2-6.
price	€75-€140. Sole occupancy €380-€460 or €2,600-€4,300 (New Year) per week.
meals	Lunch 80Dh. Dinner 200Dh. Picnic possible. By arrangement.
closed	Never.
directions	Near Medersa Ben Youssef: directions given on booking.

	Françoise Lefebvre
tel	+212 (0)44 37 77 37
mobile	+212 (0)63 83 92 92
fax	+212 (0)44 37 70 74
email	contact@dar-hanane.com
web	www.dar-hanane.com

Guest house & catered house

Map 4 Entry 83

Dar Nadir

93 Derb Tizzougarine, Marrakech-Medina

Down a blind alley, through a brass door, a studded wooden door, a dark lamp-lit hall where a brazier glows in winter – and into the patio: on a striking old marble floor, three keyhole arches stand astride a still dark pool that glimmers in the lantern light, your eyes climb to the top of the magnificent old doors then up with the vigorous plants to the roof. Converting Dar Nadir for themselves, the architect-decorator owners, who now live in France, did the bedrooms, big and small, with panache and strong colours, silky white duvets and rich hangings, and made each bathroom an original creation to fit its odd space. Details are perfect, traditional Moroccan objects do not clutter and local contemporary art provides interesting focus in the darkly atmospheric interior. Houda's sister Amal runs the house with gentle smiles, quiet efficiency and delicious meals, be it grilled sardines and salad or the full gastronomic works, in the little salon off the patio, or the superb 'men's quarters' Moroccan dining room upstairs, or on the roof terrace. Super breakfasts, too.

rooms	5 twins/doubles.
price	1,400Dh. Sole occupancy 8,000Dh per day.
meals	Dinner 150Dh-250Dh.
closed	Never.
directions	From Dar El Bacha Glaoui ring for escort.

Guest house & catered house

Francis & Houda Mabileau

tel	+212 (0)44 42 92 61/+33 (0)1 45 85 34
fax	+212 (0)44 42 92 61/+33 (0)1 45 85 34
email	darnadir@noos.fr
web	www.ryad-nadir.com

Map 4 Entry 84

Dar Al Kounouz
54 Derb Snane, Mouassine, Marrakech-Medina

The two Michels chose to renovate their diminutive *dar* in a rich, almost Fassi style: the palm-treed patio foams with delicate chiselled plaster like a wedding veil, the salon and bedroom walls are subtly friezed, ceilings and arches are frosted – it took the best ma'allem in town two years. They then finished the job with traditional mosaics, tadelakt, painted wood – and a wealth of ornaments, paintings, unusual metal lamps, black leather pouffes. The cosy little bedrooms, each different, have trendy things to look at and smart jacuzzi bathrooms (and safe, telly and phone). Eggshell-white galleries show off the beautiful carving; the lovely, gently ochre terrace has masses of plants, blue trellises, pink-cushioned chairs and views over the treetops of the Glaoui palace where the King's guests stay: you can reach out and touch the ramparts. The owners and their team are proud of the house, will offer you mint tea and much help on living in the medina and beyond; you can watch the Moroccan cook preparing her delicious local recipes then relax in the marble hammam with a massage.

rooms	6: 5 twin/doubles, 1 family.
price	950Dh-1,200Dh.
meals	Lunch 150Dh. Dinner 200Dh.
closed	Never.
directions	From Koutoubia, Rue Fatima Zohra north to Bab Ksour; right Rue Sidi Yamami to Derb Snane (on left) & follow signs. Alternatively take taxi to Bab Ksour & call hotel.

Guest house

	Michel Arnaud & Michel Mongelard
tel	+212 (0)44 39 07 73
mobile	+212 (0)62 40 11 28
fax	+212 (0)44 39 07 74
email	info@daralkounouz.com
web	www.daralkounouz.com

Map 4 Entry 85

Angel's Riad

6 Derb Houara, Berrima, Marrakech-Medina

An unusual, highly-tuned, much-travelled woman of Greco-Armenian extraction, Claudia, who speaks seven languages, has at last come to rest in Marrakech, "thanks to her guardian angels". And a troupe of white angel cherubs came too, with a few storks and a bunch of stars. A laid-back atmosphere is Claudia's aim — she has a passion for health and happiness: there's a hammam and, up the narrow stairs, the Berber tent draped over the roof-top chill-out space is really beautiful. You will be welcomed with mint tea, fresh flowers and good, essentially organic, Moroccan food. You can watch your tagine cooking on its traditional earthen brazier on the terrace. The bedrooms, each with a sitting spot, are light for so small a riad and done with lots of Greek-style blue and white, heaps of bright little cushions, the occasional star in an iron lamp or a niche in the wall and fabrics that echo the colour theme of each room; their smooth tadelakt bathrooms are in sober good taste. Claudia came to find peace and, with the help of delightful Hassan and Sanaa, hopes you will share in her ongoing search.

rooms	5: 4 doubles, 1 suite for 4.
price	€55–€110.
meals	Lunch/dinner 150Dh.
closed	Never.
directions	Directions given on booking.

Guest house

	Claudia Koranian & Hassan Kebdani
tel	+212 (0)44 38 02 52
mobile	+212 (0)65 17 07 07
fax	+212 (0)44 38 02 52
email	kclaudia7@hotmail.com
web	www.angelsriad.com

Map 4 Entry 86

Riad l'Étoile du Sud

64 rue Touareg, Ksibt N'Hass, Marrakech

A petal-strewn bed, a pair of babouches to take you to the claw-footed copper bathtub, painted ceilings and almost Chinese-elaborate doors, a bowl of fresh fruit, a courtyard fountain to sing you to sleep: could this be the Arabian-Nights experience you thought you couldn't afford? The new French owners of the 'southern star' are eager for you to get all you hoped for and there's their utterly delightful manager Mohamed to introduce you to real Morocco. A Berber nomad for 18 years, he'll happily to take you trekking to remote corners of his beloved Atlas and a kinder person is hard to imagine. His sister Fatma is apparently a superb cook of traditional Berber dishes (her breakfast will last you the day). The house is fully dressed with candlesticks, dark furniture and bright kilims, brass-topped tables and original floor tiles, rope-covered chairs, lantern lamps, plates and daggers. There is colour in every corner – crimson ceilings, yellow vases, blue tiles – yet the place feels quiet and restful. A modest house full of heart in a superb position, it is remarkable value – and there's pampering in the hammam.

rooms	5 doubles.
price	€65-€80.
meals	Many restaurants nearby.
closed	Never.
directions	Just outside medina between Tombeaux Saâdiens & Palais El Badi: ring for escort from here.

	Martine Bernard	Guest house
tel	+33 (0)6 77 74 19 18	
mobile	+212 (0)62 10 56 00	
fax	+212 (0)44 37 81 60	
email	lagazelle@riadmaroc.com	
web	www.riadmaroc.com	

Map 4 Entry 87

Les Deux Tours

Douar Abiad, Circuit de la Palmeraie, Ain-Nakhil, Marrakech-Palmeraie

Half a dozen villas and a communal heart make up this unusual guest village where gardens exuberate in the semi-desert and you enter someone else's dream. Charles Boccara built it for friends with the textures he loves; then opened it to the world. You stay in a house or a superb luxury suite that has patio, garden, pool, salon and fireplace; the suites also have hand-painted light switches. Add a wealth of fine Moroccan craftsmanship to honour the fascinating Moroccan antiques. All different, villas and rooms may have balconies, alcoves or arches, sunset views or sunrise experiences, a bathroom in a medieval apse or a spare room in splendid solitude down an alley – the Lost Villa – or the hugest bed like a throne on a platform. But above all you will have a sense of exclusivity, with breakfast by your fire or in your garden then a spin in the luscious hammam and, at the end of the day, a stylishly served meal in the new dining space with its fairytale atmosphere of trickling water and myriad candles. A beautifully orchestrated, subtle, sybaritic indulgence.

rooms	29: 8 doubles, 16 twins, 5 suites. Sole occupancy of villas possible.
price	1,300Dh-5,500Dh.
meals	Buffet lunch 240Dh. Dinner 380Dh.
closed	Never.
directions	From Marrakech for Fez; left onto Circuit de la Palmeraie. Pass hotel Issil, right for Les 3 Golfs, left for Deux Tours. Details on booking.

Small hotel

	Charles Boccara & Jacques Abtan
tel	+212 (0)44 32 95 26
fax	+212 (0)44 32 95 23
email	contact@les-deuxtours.com
web	www.les-deux-tours.com

Map 4 Entry 88

Dar Ayniwen
Tafrata, Marrakech-Palmeraie

This house has the soul of a family home and the Abtans still live nearby. The image of the soberly grand Moorish mansion shivers down a series of formal ponds and the gardens feel like a corner of paradise, ancient palms telling their celebrity tales to giant olive trees over secluded benches. Beyond the majestic old door with its mane of bougainvillea and the oversized atrium with its stunning lattice balconies, the scale becomes human again. Jacques Abtan, who loves Morocco and its 1920s antiques with a passion, has filled the house with wonders, a remarkable collection of Protectorate period posters and an endearingly dated feel: at any minute, Hercule Poirot might step in. It is orientally, luxuriously, overly decorated and we love it for its authenticity – brocades, brasses, kilims and all. Also, wide new beds and all things IT in the splendid bedrooms, amazing bathrooms, a fine marble hammam with full spa treatments, divine food and first-class staff under the caring, professional eye of son Stéphane, who trained in America then returned to his beloved childhood home.

rooms	7 twins/doubles.
price	1,900Dh–5,400Dh. Includes airport & city transfers, hammam, sauna.
meals	Dinner 450Dh. Lunch 350Dh. By arrangement. BYO.
closed	Never.
directions	From Marrakech for Fez left onto Circuit de la Palmeraie then right for Douar Abiad; after palm in middle of track, first track right, straight on to great wooden door.

Small hotel

	Jacques & Stéphane Abtan
tel	+212 (0)44 32 96 84/85
fax	+212 (0)44 32 96 86
email	infos@dar-ayniwen.com
web	www.dar-ayniwen.com

Map 4 Entry 89

Jnane Tamsna

Douar Abiad, Circuit de la Palmeraie, Marrakech-Palmeraie

The garden (*jnane*) flowering in the oasis gives organic veg for excellent meals. There are space, light, air (and a clay tennis court) beneath the palms and colonnades, splendid rooms, the Atlas beyond the terrace. Meryanne, erstwhile barrister and an accomplished designer with Caribbean-Senegalese roots, mixes Morocco, Africa and Europe in her highly original furniture – exotic woods, peasant iron – and luscious layered fabrics. Here are columns of bone bracelets from Senegal, 'Syrian' antiques, echoes of the three Mediterranean religions, good pictures and prints artfully hung to grab your attention. These rooms, earthy or fiery or coolly limpid, are a delight. Set back beside its own pool, the Travellers' House takes you from west to east, Africa to India, in five rooms of Islam-inspired design. Gary, an ethno-botanist, works passionately for bio-diversity and village development; take one of his interesting and valuable conservation-centred tours and contribute to Moroccan development. Remarkable people in a very special house. *15 mins from town. Luxury catered villas also for rent.*

Small hotel

rooms	Main house: 10 doubles. Travellers' House: 5 doubles. Dar Ylane: 2 doubles.
price	2,600Dh-4,500Dh. Includes dinner on arrival.
meals	Lunch 140Dh-280Dh. Dinner 300Dh-450Dh. By arrangement.
closed	Never.
directions	From Marrakech for Fez onto Circuit de la Palmeraie for Douar Abiad; pass Hôtel des Deux Tours; house 500m beyond, left through arch.

	Meryanne Loum-Martin & Gary Martin
tel	+212 (0)44 32 94 23
mobile	+212 (0)61 24 27 17
fax	+212 (0)44 32 98 84
email	loummartin@aol.com
web	www.jnanetamsna.com

Map 4 Entry 90

Dar Zemora

72 rue El Andalib, Marrakech-Palmeraie

Escape the city's dust-filled pandemonium to the blessed relief of green air and cossetted seclusion in Dar Zemora's domed, buff-coloured elegance where the garden is an exuberance of white oleander and bougainvillea round the pool, fine palm and olive trees rise to decorate the eternally blue sky and birds sing their hymns. Light and taste are masters here. Cupolas add interest, the salons adapt to all seasons, the peaceful ivory tadelakt finish is in harmony with the stained woodwork and natural bejmat floors. Furniture, an attractive, personal mixture of contemporary and antique plus high-class Moroccan craftsmanship, is set off by purple High Atlas carpets and one handsome old mirror. Only the red dining room differs in its superb G'naoua pictures backed by almond green and ochre curtains. Your big, light-filled bedroom may have a four-poster bed, an antique chest, a sitting area or a private terrace; all have perfect pastel tadelakt bathrooms. You will want for nothing. Genuine and open-hearted, Valérie and Youssef head a team full of charm and smiles and put everyone at ease.

rooms	6: 3 doubles, 2 suites, 1 pavilion.
price	€220–€400.
meals	Lunch 150Dh. Dinner 300Dh.
closed	August.
directions	From Marrakech for Fez, pass Circuit de la Palmeraie turning; left at 60km speed limit sign, 1st right, bear left & follow signs to Dar Zemora.

Paul & Lindsay Kentish & Valérie

tel	+212 (0)44 32 82 00
mobile	+212 (0)61 08 07 61
fax	+212 (0)44 32 82 01
email	info@darzemora.com
web	www.darzemora.com

Guest house

Map 4 Entry 91

Villa des Palmiers

Douar Ouleg Rguig, Matrane, Marrakech-Palmeraie

A mirror for the Fabrys' cultured sensitivity, this sober, elegant house has the symmetry of a Renaissance villa – in pisé and brick – and the perspective of a classical garden, beneath the palm trees. Séverine, a refined, relaxed hostess, and Bernard, a deeply knowledgeable Morocco-lover and trek-organiser, live on the estate. They built this guest house in order to share their passion for their country with like-minded visitors. Big windows look down the abundant garden to the Atlas, the light dapples the treasures inside: a gentle décor of pure arcades and smooth tadelakt, a few gorgeous prints, paintings and 1920s posters of 'the Morocco that was' with just the right amount of furniture. Good taste and understatement producing unostentatious elegance. Bedrooms are, of course, big and in the same spirit with rich chocolate and caramel bedcovers, a sitting area each, a super bathroom and, above all, a wide balcony: you are encouraged to look outwards to the garden, the mountains and the call to relaxation. Exceptional value for the *Palmeraie* and such intelligent, interesting people.

rooms	6: 3 doubles, 3 twins.
price	1,490Dh-2,440Dh.
meals	Lunch 150Dh. Dinner 270Dh. By arrangement.
closed	Never.
directions	From Marrakech for Fez. Pass Metro supermarket then petrol station on left; first left to Hotel Palmariva/Club Coralia. Phone from here.

Guest house

	Séverine & Bernard Fabry
tel	+212 (0)44 32 91 94
mobile	+212 (0)61 40 22 90
fax	+212 (0)44 31 39 05
email	lavilladespalmiers@iam.net.ma
web	www.villadespalmiers.com

Map 4 Entry 92

Villa Chems Hamra
Douar Ben Amar, Route de Sidi Abdellah Ghiat km 10, Marrakech

Leave the Marrakech scrum, head for the Atlas, turn at the little mosque, pass a hamlet – low-slung against the backdrop of mighty Jbel Toubkal – and find your opulent kasbah entrance, just 15 minutes from the medina. A kind man of quiet manners, Jean-Pierre is an endearing host and a talented chef. This brand new building is his dream palace where France and Morocco meet, and he is still inventing his own little paradise: the newness will rub off, the gardens will grow and soften the starkness, the pool is serene. Jean-Pierre sings and teaches, has a fabulous collection of music and instruments all over the house and would love you to play his piano. He also collects modern art and minerals – rooms are named after them, books on them abound in the library – and can organise walks in the Ourika Valley. The house is all shiny squeaky new, the architecture is a singular interpretation of the authentic kasbah, the décor is Fassi-inspired, the furniture often simple pine with plain or sabra stripes, the food good. Plus loads of space and the stunning Atlas view ever with you.

rooms	6: 2 doubles, 3 suites, 1 twin.
price	500Dh-600Dh. Suites €700-€850.
meals	Lunch/dinner from 120Dh. By arrangement.
closed	Never.
directions	From Marrakech old road for Ouarzazate; pass Golf Royal; right forSidi Abdellah Ghiat. At 1st mosque on left, take small track 200m: pinktower entrance.

Guest house

	Jean-Pierre Barral
mobile	+212 (0)60 46 97 28
email	barral_villachems@hotmail.com
web	www.villachems.com

Map 4 Entry 93

Le Bled

Douar Coucou Taseltant, Route de l'Ourika - km5, Marrakech

Amazingly, these olive trees were only planted seven years ago. Indeed, the whole organic garden and orchard that cocoons this delightfully informal guest farm, where the tireless Moha grows ingredients for his famous restaurant in town, is a flourishing miracle. After 14 years in Switzerland, he returned with his young family to open an elegant eatery, his warm enthusiasm and superb cooking endearing him to all. Then he published two cookery books. Then he opened his 'country place'. The three older rooms round the gentle courtyard have a lived-in family feel, the four splendidly minimalist new rooms have glass walls onto the superb pool, a terrace each, 'designer Moroccan' furniture, lots of red rugs, and fine bathrooms with more glass onto the lily pond. Fresh, healthy, delicious meals are served outside in summer, by the conservatory fire in winter. Explore the gardens, meet the green-fingered Brahim and the animals – a refreshing convivial place filled with Moha's exuberance just 15 minutes from the medina. He supports an AIDS centre with fabulous charity barbecues for jet-setters here.

rooms	7 doubles/triples.
price	600Dh–1,200Dh for two.
meals	Lunch/dinner 180Dh–200Dh.
closed	Never.
directions	From Marrakech take Ourika Valley road. Pass r'about 4.5km, left at Dar Succar, continue to end & follow signs.

Auberge

	Moha & Alma Fedal
tel	+212 (0)44 38 59 39
mobile	+212 (0)61 33 64 66
fax	+212 (0)44 38 59 39
email	lebled-marrakech@menara.ma
web	www.lebled-marrakech.com

Map 4 Entry 94

Camping Camelote
Rue Bish, St Camelote

A thin frame of sticks with a generous covering of locally-woven cloth and lots of comforting, hand-gathered stones to secure it – this is the last word in eco-minimalism. It is a serious case of One Planet living, and respectful of a long tradition of such housing: 'Here is the body pent, / Absent from him I roam, / Yet nightly pitch my moving tent/ A day's march nearer home'. Flexibility and immediacy are built into the design. Their policy of waste re-use and recycling has been well established for centuries: just chuck it out and see what happens. There are always the right animals at hand to make short work of the stuff but you are expected to prevent them from sampling the carefully nutured flower bush that so graciously adorns your place to stay. And if the animals look right they can serve as dinner too. Meanwhile, they find shelter in the obsolete motor vehicle that is very gradually becoming a harmonious element of the landscape. The owners understood the crisis of oil and climate change far sooner than most of us. This tented oddity is way ahead of its time.

rooms	Room, more like – but not much of it.
price	Cheaper when sharing with the livestock.
meals	Plentiful, but revolting. Just take a morning stroll and whatever bites you is breakfast.
closed	Never - this place is wide open for all to admire.
directions	On leaving suburbia, turn left by camels and follow your nose...

	Madame Tara Tata
tel	+212 221 22 12 11 12 2
fax	+212 221 22 12 11 12 3
email	camelote@undercanvas.yuk
web	wwww.pile-o-pacotille.ma

Map 4 Entry 95

Auberge de Tameslohte
Douar Laaouina, Tameslohte

Intelligent and full of the simple joys of life, Jérôme, Michèle and darling little Clémence welcome you with delight to their pretty farmhouse inn and their adopted country, its rugged spaces and healthy food. You sleep in an outbuilding constructed, brick by clay brick, by Jérôme himself – big ochre-tinted rooms with beams and wicker furniture, warm Berber blankets and good kilims – or in charming bedouin style in your own space in the garden: a top-class brown camel- and goats-hair tent stretched over metre-high walls and furnished with good beds, pretty rugs, lanterns and a chest for your things. Life at Tameslohte centres on the pool area: beneath the straw huts at the bar, in the tents with their pretty embroidered tablecloths, or round the barbecue. The restaurant and salon both have open hearths for winter comfort: it all has the warm easy atmosphere of a simple country inn and your relaxed, laughing hosts, fans of 4x4 cross-country treks, can also arrange shooting expeditions (within official conservation limits). A real country holiday 15 minutes from the Koutoubia.

Auberge

rooms	6 + 4: 4 doubles, 2 triples. 4 tents for up to 10, sharing 6 showers, 4 wcs.
price	€53-€70. Tent €25.
meals	Lunch/dinner €9. Picnic by arrangement.
closed	Never.
directions	From Marrakech for Amizmiz 16km then follow signs.

	Michèle & Jérôme Royer
tel	+212 (0)44 48 38 40
mobile	+212 (0)66 64 45 80
fax	+212 (0)44 48 38 41
email	riad@wanadoo.fr
web	www.auberge-de-tamslote.com

Map 4 Entry 96

Dar Zarraba
Douar Akarra, Tassoultant

Michel conceived an early passion for Morocco's earth architecture, studied it in depth and at last built his own house with the help of the best craftsmen – and 54,000 adobe bricks. The kasbah-like cluster of little towers with terraces is charming, the great salon with its majestic fireplace, tataoui ceiling and polished-earth walls (a technique unearthed in an obscure village near Skoura) is its hub: library, world music, simple floor-level Saharoui furniture on lovely carpets and occasional G'naoua or Berber musical evenings. In the shade of the olive trees lies the fine oasis-like pool, decorated with Berber emblems. Michel, a man of gentleness and light, receives with simple generosity, bedrooms are as lovely and authentic as the rest with copper Arabic letters set in the floors, perfectly simple walnut and metal furniture and very snug, warm-hued bathrooms. Michel employs delightful villagers, is active in local development and suggests you experience real, wood-cooked Moroccan food with a lovely village family.
French-approved disabled facilities. 15 minutes from Marrakech.

rooms	9 twins/doubles.
price	490Dh.
meals	Breakfast 40Dh. Lunch, dinner, picnic. By arrangement.
closed	Never.
directions	From Marrakech take Ourika Valley road 13km; cross canal, 1st left; left over 2nd bridge over canal; 1st track right 700m to house. Signed.

Guest house

	Michel Lachaud
mobile	+212 (0)68 99 92 35
email	dar.zarraba@laposte.net
web	www.zarraba.com

Map 4 Entry 97

Le Relais du Lac

Route d'Amizmiz, Lalla Takerkoust

The lake, blue and tranquil beneath snowy Atlas, is out of this world and its Relais is great for families. They've got the lot: kayaks for exploring, a Cleopatra barge for showing off your tan, pedal-boats, shooting and archery, donkeys, quad bikes (which go over the hills and far away to play) and oodles of space, so the open-air restaurant where groups congregate (it becomes two well-furnished tents in winter), the great central hearth that cooks their pounds of flesh and the camp with immense nomad tents where they sleep, are well apart from the charming little stone and brick inn. Set in the garden near the swimming pool, it has grass, roses, wrought-iron chairs on its sheltered terrace and a simple yet elegant eggshell dining room full of light and well-designed iron furniture. Also the peaceful group of guest rooms. These pleasant, plainly furnished spaces are impeccably clean, have good bedding, a private outside area each and pretty tadelakt bathrooms. Some even have fireplaces. A place for families, action and fun where you will be well cared for by smiling professionals.

Auberge

rooms	10: 6 doubles, 1 suite for 4 (double & twin), 1 apartment for 4. Plus tents.
price	Half-board at inn 450Dh p.p.; 300Dh p.p. in Berber tent.
meals	Other meals 150Dh.
closed	Never.
directions	From Marrakech R203 for Asni 5km; fork right for Amizmiz 28km to dam; 1st left after dam 3km; signposted.

	Daniel Thebaud & Jean-Charles Puech
mobile	+212 (0)61 18 74 72
fax	+212 (0)44 48 44 69
email	contact@hotel-relaisdulac-marrakech.com
web	hotel-relaisdulac-marrakech.com

Map 4 Entry 98

La Ferme
Route d'Amizmiz - km 39, Takerkoust, Marrakech

The old pisé farmhouse, settled and definitely well-lived-in, stands in its garden at the end of an avenue of ancient olive trees with the road at the bottom. Patrick found his refuge from city life here and renovated it for country comfort without spoiling its authenticity. In the guest wing, the big bedrooms are unpretentiously designer rustic in earthy, sandy tones, traditional materials and worn country furniture – with the odd giant urn to hold the twisty sticks, a short 'hay-loft' ladder to remind you where you are, good bedding and simple, ageing bathrooms. The dining room mixes French checked tablecloths and Moroccan bamboo ceilings comfortably for a warm inn atmosphere; outside eating and sitting areas are shaded with straw and stripes and furnished with cotton-on-wood. Wherever it is served, Moumia's cooking is simply exquisite. A relaxed, restful, rough-and-ready place with something Tuscan in the tall cypresses, stocky olive trees and yards of vine-shaded walks. Patrick serves superb wines by candlelight and shares his life experiences, good and bad, with disconcerting simplicity.

rooms	7: 4 doubles, 2 twins, 1 triple.
price	€60. Half-board €84 for two.
meals	Lunch/dinner 120Dh. Picnic possible. By arrangement.
closed	1–15 August.
directions	From Marrakech for Amizmiz 39km then follow signs on right; 3km after dam.

	Patrick Morand
tel	+212 (0)44 48 41 66
mobile	+212 (0)65 43 65 88
email	champlat@yahoo.fr
web	www.lafermemarrakech.com

Guest house

Map 4 Entry 99

Dar Itrane

Douar Imelghas, Vallée des Aït Bougmez

Leave the scruffy Marrakech plain for the snaking mountain road (possibly not for the faint-hearted) that leads past majestic crumpled belts of rock and terraced riverside fields to a secret valley of such unspoilt beauty and an inn so genuine that you'd scarce believe it. Bernard Fabry knows all the secrets of the Atlas and opened this remote spot for real seekers 15 years ago. Brahim, the head man, helped build the flat-roofed pisé inn in its hillside cradle, cooks exquisite soups with mountain spices, makes a unique herb tea, knows all the muleteers and some dazzling walks. His team are smiling and ready to help. The great Berber living room, its walls white as the snowy M'Goun peak and adorned with geometric patterns, Koranic verses and candle niches, is gorgeous in its Aït Bougmez painted ceiling, bright cushions and big fireplace; bedrooms are all-white, like monks' cells, really comfortable; bathrooms are little gems. A natural, friendly inn where, in luminous simplicity, a Euro-Berber partnership really works. The riches of this exceptional place and its people deserve at least two nights.

rooms	11: 7 doubles, 4 family.
price	Half-board dinner 500Dh for two.
meals	Half-board only. BYO.
closed	Never.
directions	From Azilal 50km south on twisting mountain road; fork right into Aït Bougmez valley, through Agouti to Imelghas; inn on hillside on left.

Auberge

	Bernard Fabry
tel	+212 (0)44 31 39 01
fax	+212 (0)44 31 39 05
email	atlassaharatrek@iam.net.ma
web	www.atlas-sahara-trek.com

Map 4 Entry 100

Dar Al Abir
Douar Asni, Asni

Jean-Jacques left consumerism to dig more authentically into the High Atlas with his Berber wife, the young, light-spirited, laughing Saïda: at the house of the passer-by (*abir*) European and Berber meet, it is a staging post for cultural exchange. Park the car, pick your way up into the poor, peasant village and find Dar Al Abir among the other earth buildings. It is a house of almost monastic simplicity with a rose-hung, rug-strewn patio, a salon warmed by dark local wood furniture, restful whitewashed rough-beamed Berber bedrooms, few mod cons. The monastery feel comes from the total simplicity of basic accommodation with shared showers (bring your own soap) and no plastic anythings. The colour comes from warm rugs and bright cushions. All against the breathtaking backdrop of the Atlas mountains (ask Jean-Jacques for a good guide). Saïda's food, a creative mix of Arab and Berber, comes with local ingredients and inspiration: these people care about uncanned pleasures and Jean-Jacques is something of a fire-and-brimstone preacher of ecology and conservation. *Outdoor smoking only.*

rooms	4: 1 double, 1 single, 2 family, sharing 4 showers, 2 wcs.
price	Half-board 400Dh for two. Sole occupancy 11,000Dh per week.
meals	Half-board only. Other meals 80Dh-130Dh. BYO.
closed	Never.
directions	From Marrakech for Taroudannt to Asni; continue for Imlil 2km; right following signs. Last section of approach on foot.

	Jean-Jacques Gérard & Saïda Aït Sakel	Guest house
tel	+212 (0)44 48 47 57	
email	alarkam2000@yahoo.fr	
web	www.al-abir.com	

Map 4 Entry 101

Espace Al Arkam
Douar Asni, Asni

A remarkable place for those seeking a deeper, less commercial experience of Morocco and its people, Al Arkam is Jean-Jacques' mountain retreat, 45 minutes' walk from his 'base camp' at Dar Al Abir. The zigzag path trudges you up and up through the dust then suddenly offers the extraordinary gift of Talabzerg, a gorgeous flat-bottomed valley spreading through neat fields to a stone tower, your destination, and the Atlas crags beyond. Come to star- and nature-watch, visit remote Berbers in Jean-Jacques' beloved Atlas, renew your life's energy, possibly with his guidance, or simply be quiet and contemplate. Two rooms in the tower, two small houses for 6-7, furnished like Berber tents with rugs and cushions on sitting/sleeping mattresses, low tables and candles. All materials are local, all transport is by mule, washrooms are in their own building, water is solar heated: total simplicity. You will have real interaction with the villagers working here, eat delicious wholesome food cooked by Saïda's mother, breathe and sleep in beauty. An exceptional centre for eco and personal development.

Auberge

rooms	4 rooms for 2-5.
price	Half-board 240Dh p.p. Sole occupancy 17,000Dh per week. Includes staff & mule treks.
meals	Breakfast 20Dh. Lunch/dinner 80Dh.
closed	Never.
directions	From Marrakech for Taroudannt to Asni; continue for Imlil 2km; right for Douar Asni & Dar Al Abir. Al Arkam 45min walk over low pass from Al Abir; luggage can be carried by mule.

	Jean-Jacques Gérard & Saïda Aït Sakel
tel	+212 (0)44 48 47 57
mobile	+212 (0)61 41 30 56
email	alarkam2000@yahoo.fr
web	www.al-abir.com

Map 4 Entry 102

La Bergerie

Marigha, Route de Taroudannt - km 59 par Marrakech, Ouirgane

From the south, come over the spectacular Tizi n'Test pass then down the little track to the old sheepfold: it's unforgettable. From majestic Morocco you arrive at rosemary and juniper hillsides, mimosa gardens serenaded by bees, sheep and donkeys, and… a Provençal inn with stone walls, beams, gingham cloths and copper kettles. This is Françoise and Christian's baby, their refuge from the consumer culture. Make it yours too, for a spell. Your lively attentive hosts cultivate a warmly civilised *auberge* atmosphere. Given time, they will tell you the tale of creating a new life here. Several low buildings cling to the slopes, respecting the shape of the land and guests' privacy; stone is local, earth walls traditional, furniture gleaned at auction or made by nearby craftsmen, the excellent food sourced locally (one old chap brings frogs' legs and wild asparagus down from the hills and streams by Tizi n'Test). The sober bedrooms and fine suites, soft-coloured and attractive, have pretty fabrics and Moroccan rugs, earthenware lights and, oh luxury, a private garden each.

rooms	16: 10 doubles, 4 suites.
price	510Dh. Suites 820Dh-900Dh. Half-board 930Dh-1,320Dh for two.
meals	Lunch/dinner 170Dh. By arrangement.
closed	Never.
directions	From Marrakech for Taroudannt 59km; at sign 'Marigha', right to inn.

	Françoise & Christian Oliari
tel	+212 (0)44 48 57 16/17
fax	+212 (0)44 48 57 18
email	h.bergerie@menara.ma
web	www.passionmaroc.com

Small hotel

Map 4 Entry 103

Chez Momo

Route de Taroudannt - km 61, Douia Derb Ouirgane, Ouirgane

One of the most beautiful roads south of Marrakech brings you to this sweet little country inn. Momo's place is infused with his natural dynamic gaiety and as he was born in the village all his helpers are family – a genuine Berber atmosphere nourished by centuries of simple mountain hospitality. The snug pisé house has all the shape and style of High Atlas country architecture, the food is made to real Berber recipes – how about dill-flavoured chicken baked in olive purée? – and the bread, real Berber *tanourt* cooked in a handmade earth oven, arrives hot at your table; it's all excellent, served in the pink dining room or under the nomad tent, by the pool or on the terrace. Then wander through the olive groves. Momo has decorated his house with simple rustic taste: lots of ironwork, locally crafted lamps, ornaments, rugs and bedcovers, some lovely old doors put to new uses, charming bedrooms. Outside, the generous terraces look over the olive grove growing by the Ouirgane river and the great Atlas peaks seem to protect the whole place. Peaceful, pretty and remarkable value.

Auberge

rooms	7: 3 doubles, 4 suites.
price	Half-board 550Dh-884Dh for two.
meals	Half-board only. Other meals 120Dh.
closed	Never.
directions	After Ouirgane village, on right near 61km mark. Follow signs to inn; park in village.

	Mohamed Idlmoudn
tel	+212 (0)44 48 57 04
mobile	+212 (0)61 58 22 95
fax	+212 (0)44 48 57 27
email	chezmomo@menara.ma
web	www.aubergemomo.com

Map 4 Entry 104

Kasbah du Toubkal

BP 31, Imlil, Asni

Below North Africa's highest peak the valley soars away on wings of fertile terraces and red villages. This exceptional mountain retreat is a Berber-European union born of the desire to share Jbel Toubkal's splendours with like-minded visitors without destroying them. Painstakingly rebuilt by tireless Haj Maurice, run by his wife Arkia, the feudal stronghold provides two-budget sleeping: Berber salons (cushioned sitting/sleeping benches round double-height rooms) or good double rooms with bathrooms plus one superb cliff-hanging apartment. Hospitality is a Berber talent: big open smiles, intelligent local knowledge, deep respect for people and animals. Get fascinating glimpses of their culture while walking and mule-trekking; arrange an unforgettable seminar. Only 90 minutes from Marrakech, it's another world and day trips are easy. The Kasbah supports the local valley community in education and health; 5% is added to your bill to help fund projects. "Leave the world more beautiful than you find it" is their motto. *Day trips from Marrakech. Sole occupancy possible.*

rooms	14: 11 doubles (3 in one house); 3 Berber salons for 3-10, sharing bathrooms. €700
price	€140-€400; salons €110-€140 for 3-4.
meals	Lunch €15. Dinner €20. BYO.
closed	Rarely.
directions	From Marrakech for Asni then Imlil (65km). Park in village (guarded); 500-metre walk or mule ride.

	Mike McHugo & Omar Maurice Aït Bahmed
tel	+212 (0)44 48 56 11
fax	+212 (0)44 48 56 36
email	kasbah@discover.ltd.uk
web	www.kasbahdutoubkal.com

Auberge

Map 4 Entry 105

fez, meknès
& the middle atlas

The peaceful 'alpine' pastures, the lakes, forests and orchards of the Middle Atlas have preserved an astoundingly authentic Berber pastoral culture and there are umpteen opportunities for hikes and mule treks. Throughout the Atlas, the visitor may find places to stay that are simple, even basic, but touchingly typical. This is where the Amazigh culture finds its most genuine expression.

Fez, the intellectual, cultural and religious centre of the kingdom, hides, in its medina, the real palaces of Morocco and the historical base of the old aristocracy. The buildings are higher, richer, and far more expensive to maintain, the renewal of the glories of Fez comes at a price, partly covered by the visitor. Fez-lovers feel that the magnificence and refinement of these old palaces amply justify that price. If your budget is limited, stay 45 minutes away in quiet, reasonable Meknès and make the trip to Fez each day.

Meknès joined the select clan of 'imperial cities' when Moulay Idriss, unloved by Fez or Marrakech, chose it as the strategic heart of his sultanate, which lasted for half a century. The ruins of his city, much of it destroyed in the 1775 earthquake, testify to his lust for pomp and grandeur. Today it is a calmer, more relaxed town than Fez, its medina is a manageable size with good souks, little hassle - even a golf course. Moulay Ismaïl's mausoleum is open to non-Muslims - a rarity in Morocco - and Meknès is an ideal base for excursions to the Roman ruins of Volubilis and other sights.

Photo: Jose Navarro

Riad Fès

5 Derb Ben Slimane, Zerbtana, Fès-Medina

The stupefying great brass lamp suspended above the patio sets the scene for this smart little hotel; fountains and palm trees, plasterwork and myriad mosaics, Moroccan velvet divans and 1930s armchairs in neat corners testify to your architect host's knowledge of Morocco's arts and his taste for accuracy. It is the Moroccan-minimalist child of the marriage of 14th-century Andalucian designs to ideas brought by Fassis from Europe 130 years ago. Bedrooms are seriously big, solidly luxurious (hand-embroidered quilts, handsome antiques); the Royal Suite reaches summits of uncluttered splendour over a vast bed; smaller rooms (still big) harbour such treasures as an ancient carved bedhead; there's a private terrace here, a split level there, quirks of all sorts; each bathroom is a copper-tinted work of art. And now Riad Fès is expanding to create more rooms round a fairytale Alhambra-style patio where water and fire will vie for supremacy when night falls. It's expensive – but what a treat! The gastronomic restaurant is the final flourish. *Office services and lift to all floors.*

Small hotel

rooms	20: 9 doubles, 10 suites, 1 Royal Suite.
price	1,700Dh-3,000Dh. Royal Suite 6,000Dh.
meals	Lunch/dinner 260Dh-380Dh (non-residents: 420Dh-500Dh).
closed	Never.
directions	From Place Sidi El Khayat, Batha district, telephone for escort to house.

	Chakir Sefrioui
tel	+212 (0)55 74 12 06/10 12
fax	+212 (0)55 74 11 43
email	riad.fes@iam.net.ma
web	www.riadfes.com

Map 2 Entry 106

Dar El Ghalia
13-15 Ross Rhi, Ras Jnane, Fès-Medina

Omar Lebbar receives with the relaxed ease of the heir to a great Fassi family whose art, culture and traditions meet in their old palace. It also houses Dar Tajine, one of the best restaurants in town and Omar's first idea for his family house: he is a busy, interesting man. The dark narrow hall, rich in mosaics and promise, projects you into the light of an enormous patio where an intricate old floor carries columns, eclectic European and Moroccan furniture, antique silk kaftans and clocks, and luxurious salons open their hand-painted doors to more cushions, carvings and etched brass. In bedrooms and suites – some fit for royalty, some pretty modest, all with CD and radio set – beneath arches and hangings or rich quilts, is a splendid mix of 19th-century European beds, carved armoires, elegant daybeds and Moroccan paintings. You may find a fireplace or a mezzanine, a jacuzzi or a four-poster, and always a beautiful bathroom. In this display of authentic and traditional Moroccan decorative arts, the poised and helpful staff are perfect. *Lift to all floors. Solarium and gym on terrace.*

rooms	13: 4 doubles, 8 suites for 2-3, 1 Royal Suite.
price	1,300Dh-2,800Dh. Suites 2,80Dh-5,700Dh.
meals	Lunch 220Dh. Dinner 350Dh, or à la carte. By arrangement.
closed	Never.
directions	From Bab Jdid (south-west gate), follow signs.

Guest house

	Omar Lebbar
tel	+212 (0)55 63 41 67
fax	+212 (0)55 63 63 93
email	darelghalia@hotmail.com
web	www.maisonshotes.co.ma

Map 2 Entry 107

Riad Louna

21 Derb Serraj - Talaâ Sghira, Bab Boujloud, Fès-Medina

Jean-Pierre is a character with strong opinions on many subjects, Moroccan, European and other, and he doesn't mince his words. He and his wife moved here from Belgium to be near their daughter then found it too big for two and opened the door to visitors. The basis of their pretty house is genuine traditional Fez: sunburst tile patterns and high carved wooden doors with shiny brass fittings set in fine riad architecture round an ever-musical fountain. Night-time lanterns throw the deep-chiselled plasterwork into impressive relief. They have done it up in plain, unfussy, modern style: divan beds, pretty cotton prints, the occasional four-poster draped in white; with nods to Moroccan decorative ideas: brocade cushions scattered on long benches, local ceramic stoves for those cool winter evenings, some fine great vases. White walls are hung with modern paintings and Moroccan prints. Two terraces onto the patio, one with the excellent glass-fronted dining room, one open, give ample space for daytime sunning or evening tea-drinking while you wait for the gentle staff to serve dinner.

rooms	6: 2 doubles, 1 twin, 3 suites. Also 2 overflow rooms & 3 rooms in nearby house, Dar Baraka.
price	650Dh–1,050Dh. Sole occupancy 4,500Dh.
meals	Dinner 150Dh. By arrangement.
closed	Never.
directions	By Batha post office, telephone for escort.

Guest house & catered house

	Jean-Pierre & Janine
tel	+212 (0)55 74 19 85
fax	+212 (0)55 74 19 85
email	riadlouna@menara.ma
web	www.riadlouna.com

Map 2 Entry 108

Dar Al Andalous

14 Derb Bennani, Douh - Batha, Fès-Medina

The two big white patios, one green-tiled for eating, one blue-tiled for sitting (like the famous two-faced Bab Boujloud), each with a little fountain, draw down serenity and sparrows as night falls. Time stands still in this magnificent space created 100 years ago by a great Fassi family and restored with all proper respect for its sophisticated, intricate decorative origins (mosaics repaired with old tiles, for example). The suites have the formality of crimson crushed velvet or grey-green draperies, rich stained glass, heavy dark four-poster beds. Their dazzlingly carved and painted cedar ceilings are almost playful in contrast. Elsewhere, there are mementoes of the Moroccan 1930s, pretty modern colours such as taupe and lime green, lower ceilings, a private terrace here, a little staircase to a blue tadelakt bathroom there, big firm beds and lots of cushions. Mohammed Kadiri the quiet, gentle owner and Zahra his dynamic smiling manager run the house with friendly attention; you can hear the relaxed chatter and smell the delicious aromas of dinner preparations: relax and enjoy your palace.

rooms	12: 4 doubles, 8 suites.
price	1,200Dh-2,200Dh.
meals	Lunch/dinner 250Dh-300Dh.
closed	Never.
directions	From Place Batha car park, take Derb Douh eastward; 2nd right Derb Bennani; house on right.

	Monsieur & Madame M. Kadiri
tel	+212 (0)55 74 07 00
mobile	+212 (0)61 06 26 54
fax	+212 (0)55 74 07 12
email	dar.alandalous@menara.ma
web	www.daralandalous.com

Guest house

Map 2 Entry 109

Riad Lune et Soleil

3 Derb Skallia, Douh - Batha, Fez-Medina

Not only are they clearly happy in their new house and life, not only have they turned a simple little house into the warmest, friendliest possible place to stay, but Pauline also indulges in masses of fresh flowers and Jürgen has his own superbly subtle take on Mediterranean food. Meals are served in the peaceful patio with its fountain and leafy orange and lemon trees, or in the adjacent salon. The big ground-floor suites were designed as salons and the two long thin upstairs rooms should have space for all you need. Lovely bathrooms have hand-made tiles and jacuzzis "because there's no pool". You learn much about real old Fez here: ranks of curvy urns salute you in the hall, antique studded doors and giant bolts line the patio, bedroom walls display collections of artefacts, farm implements, tools (for making clothes, rugs, shoes, music, sugar), even house deeds. Jürgen is an encyclopædia on the subject and a great conversationalist, in fluent English. Despite custom-made china, it's the reverse of an intimidating palace. And the Möllers are such good company.

Guest house

rooms	5: 2 doubles, 3 suites for 3.
price	650Dh-1,250Dh.
meals	Dinner 200Dh.
closed	Never.
directions	Directions given on booking or consult web site.

	Pauline et Jürgen Möller
tel	+212 (0)55 63 45 23
mobile	+212 (0)70 78 33 43
fax	+212 (0)55 74 02 52
email	luneetsoleil@iam.net.ma
web	www.luneetsoleil.com

Map 2 Entry 110

Riad Zamane

12 Derb Skalia, Douh - Batha, Fès-Medina

Having lived for years in France, Sakina returned to her native Fez, bravely all alone, to restore this 1860s riad right by populous Place Batha and open a guest house where the blue mosaics shimmer, the little fountain sparkles and simple elegance is the style. She uses misty matching organzas and cottons against white walls (each suite has a rich base colour: sapphire blue, solemn crimson, feminine pink), good wooden furniture (a little desk, a carved table, a padded stool), excellent beds and linen and lots of cushions. The highest room, clear and maidenly in green and white, has a white iron bed, soft armchairs and its own latticed-sheltered terrace. The smaller double is a delight of soft browns and beiges. Newly-fitted bathrooms, big or small, are both pretty and practical. Sakina is a thoughtful hostess (flowers at all times), her mixed-cultural experiences make her a most interesting companion and she cooks beautifully: traditional Fassi cooking of last-minute marvels rather than long-stewing tagines, served in the uncluttered patio or the dining room, to peaceful classical lute music.

rooms	5: 1 double, 4 suites for 4.
price	1,200Dh-1,500Dh.
meals	Dinner 250Dh.
closed	Never.
directions	From Place Istiqlal-Batha, park at entrance to medina and ring for escort.

	Sakina Belcadi
tel	+212 (0)55 74 04 40
mobile	+212 (0)61 10 04 41
fax	+212 (0)55 74 04 41
email	contact@riadzamane.com
web	www.riadzamane.com

Guest house

Map 2 Entry 111

La Maison Bleue

2 Place de l'Istiqlal, Batha, Fès-Medina

If the rest of Fez vanished, this house, the city's first guest house, would bear witness to the glory of her great families, the proud vision of her architects, the refinement of her craftsmen (intricately carved doors, lace-like stucco, exquisite mosaic tiling), the learning of her intellectuals (grandfather left a libary of rare manuscripts), and the taste of her women (Rabati embroideries, Venetian mirrors, Italian draperies). The whole place, including the amazing antique bathrooms, is a romantic journey back to the 19th century. It is steeped in Moroccan history and Mehdi willingly tells tales of his childhood here. Your big four-poster suite, as beautifully, richly furnished with massive antiques and voluptuous damasks as the rest, may have belonged to one of his judge/astrologer grandfather's three wives and shares the patio with one of the most renowned restaurants in town – a place for true gourmets run by sister Kenza. Three suites have private terraces, the panoramic roof terrace plunges into the heart of historic Karouiyne University – and the breakfast pancakes are divine.

rooms	9: 4 doubles, 5 suites.
price	1,800Dh-2,800Dh.
meals	Lunch/dinner: gastronomic menu 380Dh or à la carte. By arrangement for non-residents.
closed	Never.
directions	Near Bab Boujloud, on central square Place de l'Istiqlal, Batha district.

Small hotel

	Mehdi & Kenza El Abbadi
tel	+212 (0)55 74 18 43
mobile	+212 (0)61 19 68 51
fax	+212 (0)55 74 06 86
email	resa@maisonbleue.com
web	www.maisonbleue.com

Map 2 Entry 112

Riad La Maison Bleue

33 Derb El Miter, Talaâ El Kbira - Aïn Azliten, Fès-Medina

Same name, same family, different feel from the original Maison Bleue: more intimate, despite having more rooms, the Riad is Mehdi's own brainchild. Charming and chatty, he follows his late father's model of Fassi hospitality and business sense. The little pool is a blessing in summer, the tree-shaded salons are perfect for a quiet read, the marble hammam breathes thyme-scented air. In the roof-top dining room, family cooking is served in proper Abbadi style by candlelight before the floodlit medina; or treat yourself to the Maison Bleue experience, five minutes away. The suites have romantic gauze and striking dark quilts, good paintings and handsome old carpets, some superb 19th-century Spanish four-posters and Venetian mirrors, a wealth of Portuguese, English and French antiques — Fez was ever open to other influences and fashions, though gun slits were built into the outer walls to try and keep the French out. Well modernised bathrooms have lovely zelliges and burnished copper basins. And this civilised house is expanding to tempt you even more: spa, fitness, wifi....

rooms	13: 2 doubles, 11 suites.
price	1,900Dh-2,800Dh.
meals	Lunch/dinner 380Dh.
closed	Never.
directions	From Aïn Azliten car park (guarded), telephone for escort.

	Mehdi El Abbadi
tel	+212 (0)55 74 18 73
mobile	+212 (0)61 19 68 51
fax	+212 (0)55 74 06 86
email	resa@maisonbleue.com
web	www.maisonbleue.com

Small hotel

Map 2 Entry 113

Ryad Mabrouka

25 Derb El Miter, Talaâ K'bira, Fès-Medina

The walk up to the end of the alley at the top of the medina is worth every minute: in this tall secluded house you are shielded from the souk bustle below, the emerald pool reflects the old citrus trees in Michel's luxuriant garden, peace reigns. The house is typical Fez: white pillared patio, mosaics, antique doors, intricate stucco and carved ceilings to cap it all. There's a luminous veranda for tea at sunset when the medina catches fire; a terrace where soft divans in low-slung tents invite you to be orientally lazy; attractive, muted bedrooms, some on two levels, where an eclectic mixture of French and Moroccan antiques and pictures give a style and charm all their own and Michel's taste shows rich, subtle variety – harmonies of brown and palest yellow, a flash of zebra, silks, wools and embroidery. Great bathrooms, too. Michel's love of Morocco informs the whole house, including the morning music; his books and advice are ever available, his charm and easy manner make this one of the most restful places to stay in the country and his staff are, naturally, perfect.

Guest house

rooms	8: 2 doubles, 5 suites for 2, 1 suite for 3.
price	900Dh-2,000Dh. Extra bed 350Dh.
meals	Dinner 250Dh. By arrangement.
closed	Never.
directions	From Bab Bou Jeloud walk down Talaâ Kabira 300m to Aïn Azliten car park, cross car park into lane leading up hill. By car, reach Aïn Azliten car park from Borj Nord then walk up lane.

	Michel Trezzy
tel	+212 (0)55 63 63 45
mobile	+212 (0)61 10 25 21
fax	+212 (0)55 63 63 10
email	ryadmabrouka@iam.net.ma
web	www.ryadmabrouka.com

Map 2 Entry 114

Pasha Baghdadi Massriya
Talaâ Kbira, Fès-Medina

Feel like a pasha – on a slimmer budget – in your own authentically ornate, miniature, 19th-century Fassi hideaway. A *massriya* was a separate guest house for male guests: their quarters were finely elaborate small spaces. Up two steep flights you will find the splendid salon, its lovely plaster panels at eye level (rare in their height and untouched original crispness of beehive chiselwork and pigment), arches and stars overhead, old floor tiles under your toes. Through the tiled arch is a good light bedroom with a view of the Merinides tombs way out on the hill. Furnishing is simple, bedding excellent, jellabahs on loan. At the other end of your little apartment is the lovely hammam alcove and the tiniest 'cooking cupboard' ever. Up another flight (also shared with the two Moroccan families living in the building) is the eye-boggling *menzeh*, an extraordinary double room onto the terrace with not an unpatterned inch in it: original tiled floor and walls, stucco frieze, a breathtaking painted ceiling: go to bed in another civilisation – and walk down to the bathroom. Incomparably atmospheric.

rooms	Apartment for 2 with bathroom; extra double one floor higher sharing same bathroom.
price	$125 for 2. $150 for 4.
meals	Self-catering, or cook available.
closed	Never.
directions	From Bab Boujloud, Talaâ Kbira to Place Qantrat Bourous/Ferrane Kouicha. House along on left.

Self-catering

	Lori Wood
tel	+1 831 724 5835
mobile	+1 425 940 9506
email	reservations@fesmedina.com
web	www.fesmedina.com

Map 2 Entry 115

L'Arabesque

20 Derb El Miter, Bab Guissa - Zenjefour, Fès-Medina

It's wall-to-wall, floor-to-ceiling furniture and fabrics but never overpowering, rich but not grand, a feast for the senses – eyes, nose, fingers – and a totally Moroccan experience for those who don't need constant minimalism or dustless sterility. Khalid, the sparkling, sociable owner, is an antique collector of taste and learning and he loves entertaining, as does his quietly delightful wife Amina. Dinner in the jungly candlelit patio garden at one of the best tables in town feels like a fairytale with a sweet singer and lute player to charm the air. Sumptuous is the word for the Fassi salons – the house bristles with precious things in carved wood, etched brass, embroidered silks, a grand piano if you care to perform – but the bowls of fruit and the wonderful staff make you feel totally at home. Deep in the tangle of corridors and corners, bedrooms are all different, be it draped beds made with embroidered linen or antique iron with sabra silk, all standing on original mosaic floors, all, surprisingly, with synthetic blankets. And the bathrooms have antique porcelain basins and brass fittings.

rooms	7 suites for 2-4.
price	1,400Dh-3,500Dh; 3 nights 900Dh-1,500Dh per night; incl. soft drinks, airport transfers, guided tour.
meals	Lunch/dinner 350Dh. By arrangement.
closed	Never.
directions	Telephone from Palais Jamaï car park for escort to hotel.

Small hotel

	Khalid Ben Amor
tel	+212 (0)55 63 53 21
mobile	+212 (0)61 16 29 06
fax	+212 (0)55 63 45 90
email	arabesque@iam.net.ma
web	www.arabesquehotel.com

Map 2 Entry 116

Riad Les Oudayas
4 Derb El Hamiya, Quartier Ziat, Fès-Medina

Fouad's elfin vitality and designer humour combined perfectly with his sister Houda's quiet pragmatism for the riad's two-year restoration. Now, once a month he leaves Paris for a week in his beloved native city: Les Oudayas is his contribution to saving the precious medina architecture. A miraculously silent fountain flits beneath a sculptural orange tree in the cool green patio; the skyscraper fireplace reminds us of towering Fassi proportions; apart from the *menzeh* suite, the first floor is new, including the columned gallery that ends in a truncated joke ("imitation is fine but don't take me too seriously"); the brand new roof space with thick cushions under horizontal sailcloth and the two top rooms with their own private terraces feel as authentic as the patio – and are great spots for star-gazing or breakfast. Lovely rooms and simple, high-quality furnishings: white beds, plum or pink wool seating, wonderful floors, pretty, practical beige tadelakt bathrooms, good lighting and plenty of space. It's a brilliant modern take on traditional interiors – with the prettiest hammam ever.

rooms	7 suites.
price	1,045Dh-1,120Dh.
meals	Lunch/dinner 200Dh.
closed	Never.
directions	From Place Batha car park (5 minutes walk): Derb Douh; 2nd left tiny Derb Sqalia, through double right angle; 1st right, house with cedar plinth 50m on left.

	Fouad & Houda Loudiyi
tel	+212 (0)55 63 63 03
mobile	+212 (0)61 19 81 89
fax	+212 (0)55 63 63 03
email	contact@lesoudayas.com
web	www.lesoudayas.com

Guest house

Map 2 Entry 117

Riad Norma
16 Derb Sornas, Ziat, Fès-Medina

A fine house, a sparkling opera-loving owner who lives on the spot with her grey-plush amber-eyed cat and serves exceptional breakfasts – Riad Norma is a great place. Built in the thirties, it has the look and refinement of a classic old Fassi house with modern dimensions – wider rooms and bigger windows onto the lovely tiled patio – and touches of Provence. Unusually, the embroidered arches let you out into a pretty, intelligently designed garden with shady trees, lots of flowers and a plunge pool – summer's delight. Monique fell in love with this place and moved from Paris to give it all her creative energy. Very French, she is formal yet dynamic with a subtle flair for décor: good colour mixes against pale walls but nothing ostentatious, lots of Moroccan fabrics and crafts but no clutter, the latest fittings in spotless bathrooms. Harmony and comfort are her aims. The two smaller, cheaper rooms are just as good as the biggest suite with its warm wooden furniture and sheeny sabra fabrics. Great attention is paid to food too: exquisite dinners and glorious breakfasts. *Hammam 200Dh.*

rooms	6: 4 twins/doubles, 1 single, 1 suite.
price	900Dh–1,800Dh.
meals	Dinner 250Dh. By arrangement.
closed	Never.
directions	Enter at Bab Ziat; 1st left Rue Sornas; 3rd impasse on right, house on left.

Guest house

	Monique Devaux
tel	+212 (0)55 63 47 81
fax	+212 (0)55 63 47 48
email	monique@riadnorma.com
web	www.riadnorma.com

Map 2 Entry 118

Riad Al Bartal

21 rue Sornas, Ziat, Fès-Medina

After exploring Africa, your charming, intelligent hosts found their haven in 1999, here on the edge of the medina, though the travel bug still bites them every year. Despite neglect, a wealth of stucco, woodwork and zellige had survived to be returned to glory and serve as a venerable frame for Mireille and Christian's great show of contemporary Moroccan artists. Prepare your whole trip here: they have absolutely all the books. Read them by the wood-burner in the big quiet salon, on the white-canvas roof terrace while the sun sets over ancient Fez, in your room where colours and textures from Berber villages and Fassi souks make for variety and quiet interest, or in the peace of the cool tiled courtyard where craftsmanship, creepers and myriad potted plants flourish and orange cushions sparkle. Carved furniture, modern art, jellabas or weavings on the walls, more eye-boggling tiles, pretty tadelakt bathrooms (a giant copper tanning vat serves as the tub in one) – it's superb. And the mezzanine suites are ideal for families. A perfect balance and utterly caring hosts. *Free use of garage.*

rooms	7: 4 doubles, 3 suites.
price	800Dh-1,300Dh.
meals	Dinner 190Dh. By arrangement.
closed	Never.
directions	Enter at Bab Ziat heading north; first left Rue Sornas, house on left.

	Mireille & Christian Laroche
tel	+212 (0)55 63 70 53
fax	+212 (0)55 63 70 53
email	riadalbartal@menara.ma
web	www.riadalbartal.com

Guest house

Map 2 Entry 119

Dar Bennis
Talaâ Sghira, Fès-Medina

Dreaming of your own 18th-century house deep in the fascinating medina of ancient Fez? Delicious Dar Bennis, a doll's house compared to grander old houses, is ideal for two to four. David has restored it with loving knowledge, natural materials and fine craftsmen using antique zellige to replace the irretrievably lost pieces. You enter the domestic space of a modest Moroccan family of 200 years ago, though beneath their beams the big kitchen and neat bathroom are thoroughly modern. The first-floor patio is as authentic as can be, a cool quiet space to relax in. Bedrooms open off it on two floors: space and simple comfortable furnishings – antiques, old fabrics, new mattresses; the terrace view will keep you intrigued for hours. Hafid, the perfect anchor, will bring you breakfast, bright smiles and advice on all things Fassi, in excellent English; Layla will cook for you – you'll like that – and David may let you into the secrets of living and building here, a journey into a passion for these intricate arts, æons away from mass-produced modernities. Part of your rent goes to a community restoration project.

rooms	House for 2-5 (2 doubles, 1 single).
price	880Dh p.p. Extra person 220Dh.
meals	Breakfast included; other meals self-catering, or cook available.
closed	Never.
directions	Directions given on booking.

Self-catering

	David Amster
mobile	+212 (0)61 56 43 64
email	alcfes@menara.ma
web	www.houseinfez.com

Map 2 Entry 120

Dar Seffarine

14 Derb Sbaâ Louyati, Seffarine, Fès-Medina

A poem of a palace, a simple, soaring, labyrinthine poem that needs only itself to tell the story of this ancient religious quarter. No-one knows its age nor the reason for all those outside windows, so unusual here, but the light filters in past dungeon-thick walls and delicate iron grilles, down from the 32-metre terrace to show off clustered columns, great hand-painted doors and shutters, fabulous zellige floors, some exceptional painted cedar ceilings, acres of white space – and an absolute minimum of added decoration. Alaâ the architect, an ex-Iraqi with a tale or two to tell, and Kate the serious clear-eyed graphic designer, came from Norway two years ago and are still restoring. It's a vast project undertaken with tender loving care. To preserve the living shapes and details of the house they have made neat, discreet bathrooms, put in low white-quilted beds, a chest and a hanging rack per room and laid a few gentle Moroccan rugs. Not a crumb of clutter, a guest kitchen on the glorious high wide terrace and good family dinners (Alaâ loves cooking as well as rebuilding antique doors).

rooms	7: 5 twins/doubles, 2 suites.
price	600Dh-1,400Dh; 2,800Dh-7,000Dh per week.
meals	Dinner 200Dh. By arrangement.
closed	Never.
directions	Given on booking or telephone from Bab R'Cif for escort.

	Alaâ Saïd & Kate Kvalvik
tel	+212 (0)55 63 52 05
mobile	+212 (0)71 11 35 28
fax	+212 (0)55 635205
email	info@darseffarine.com
web	www.darseffarine.com

Guest house

Map 2 Entry 121

Palais de Fès-Dar Tazi

15 rue Mokhfia, R'Cif, Fès-Medina

At the base of a soaring near-blank façade, the door to Palais de Fès is the door to a small empire of which the guest house is just one part. Amazingly, this genuine century-old Fassi courtyard house is enclaved inside the huge building, between the first floor and the great terrace, the vast carpet shop and what is arguably the best restaurant in Fez this year. These are all expressions of Azzedine Tazi's towering energy and generosity – he is a powerhouse of ideas and action. Rooms are nicely done in classic Fez style – beams, mosaic tiling, lush plush bedcovers on antique beds and brick-patterned tadelakt bathrooms in subtle harmonious colours. The two patio suites, each with its own bathroom, are ideal for a family or two couples because they share the central sitting area where you can live with and breathe in the glorious architecture and craftsmanship. The two top-floor rooms give directly onto the terrace while the big library/salon is light and comfortable. And you simply must eat in the restaurant. *"We will send a driver to collect you from anywhere in Fez free of charge!"*

rooms	7: 2 doubles, 2 twins, 3 family rooms for 3 or 4.
price	600Dh-1,500Dh. Children under 12 free, meals included. Half-board option.
meals	Lunch/dinner 280Dh-350Dh.
closed	Never.
directions	On east side of medina, at Bab R'Cif, next to Cinema Amal.

Guest house

	Azzedine Tazi
tel	+212 (0)55 76 15 90
mobile	+212 (0)61 14 72 68
fax	+212 (0)55 64 98 56
email	dartazi@menara.ma
web	www.palaisdefes.com

Map 2 Entry 122

Riad Saâda

4 rue Siage, Fès-Medina

Not only is Riad Saâda an opportunity to have a real old, proud old Fassi mansion to yourselves, be you two or ten, it is also an unmissable chance to experience Bahia, her embracing, laughing smile and her much-sung cooking, and to hear from Si Mohamed the story of this loving year-long restoration. Bahia cleans and makes those delicious Moroccan meals if you wish, Si Mohamed is the essential handyman who helped bring this medina house back to life. A deeply respectful resuscitation. But if you just want to do your own thing, that's all right too. The big patio carries its age with light grace, high cedar doors and fine plaster. The old tiles, stained glass and ironwork are authentically there and the Franco-Moroccan owners have kept their contemporary presence as quiet as possible for these beauties to shine forth: low beds, Berber covers, local rugs and the timeless medina atmosphere. The terrace room may be a bit far from the 'facilities' but it has the privilege of sky contact and isolation: star-gaze all night, step out of bed to watch the sun rise over the craggy hills. Great value.

rooms	House for 2-10 (2 doubles, 2 twins, 2 singles, 2 bathrooms).
price	1,050Dh-2,090Dh per day, depending on numbers.
meals	Breakfast included. Self-catering, or cook available.
closed	Never.
directions	Directions given on booking.

Catered house

	Rabia & Pierre Muré
tel	+33 (0)5 56 70 29 56
mobile	+212 (0)64 48 64 41
email	info@riadsaada.com
web	www.riadsaada.com

Map 2 Entry 123

Dar Roumana

30 Derb El Amer, Zqaq Roumane, Fès-Medina

Dare we say it? Roumana's belvedere probably does have the very best view of Fez: a huge plane tree to one side, the minarets waving over the twisting medina below, the craggy hills and monuments all around – and none of the uglies. Indeed, this fine old *dar*, loaded with class, zellige, cedarwood and stucco, is beautiful from bottom to top, from majestic, ornate patio up past the stupendous royal suite with its three arched windows on either side and four-poster in the centre and the simpler but lovely smaller rooms, the library and games room, out onto the brick, rush and canvas terrace. All materials feel just right, natural, quiet and carefully chosen to give centre-stage to the house and its classic features. Jennifer, young, beautiful and dynamic, learnt Arabic in America, banking and cookery in London and... architectural restoration in Fez. She has finished her house with tailormade carved furniture, white cotton and a few lustrous sabra throws or Berber blankets. Grandiose bones, impeccably simple furnishings, modern fittings and delicious dinners – that's Roumana.

rooms	5: 1 double, 3 suites, 1 Royal Suite.
price	800Dh-1,500Dh.
meals	Picnic lunch 100Dh. Dinner 280Dh. By arrangement.
closed	Never.
directions	Directions given on booking.

Guest house

	Jennifer Smith
tel	+212 (0)55 74 16 37
mobile	+212 (0)60 29 04 04
fax	+212 (0)55 63 55 24
email	info@darroumana.com
web	www.darroumana.com

Map 2 Entry 124

Dar Ziryab

2 rue Ibn Badis, Fès-Ville Nouvelle

If you prefer the bland avenues of the security-minded 'new' town to the sensual experiences and authenticity of the medina, then this 1980s house is the thing. Your host used to be an official national guide: he can talk Moroccan culture, history and music for hours, in five languages – and has reproduced here all the decorative elements of the old Fassi house without the enclosing architecture, then filled it with antiques and contemporary Moroccan art; Dar Ziryab is also an informal art gallery. It is all extremely interesting and his mother's refined, subtle cooking will transform your idea of Moroccan food. He chose the best ma'allems to decorate his big house in beautiful style with the best materials, including a splendid 'Moroccan' salon for all the gourmets wanting to dine here. Colours are soft, bedrooms have space and touches of drama, be it a carved or painted bedhead, niche or fireplace, draperies or cushions; bathrooms are masterpieces of shape and decoration. With Jalil as your guide, you will enter a new-old Morocco – and his wife can teach you cookery.

rooms	8: 2 doubles, 2 twins, 1 single, 2 suites, 1 apartment for 4.
price	€120–€180. Apartment €240.
meals	Lunch/dinner 350Dh. By arrangement.
closed	Never.
directions	In new town, behind Royal Mirage Hotel.

	Jalil El Hayar
tel	+212 (0)55 62 15 61/61 17 39 97
fax	+212 (0)55 62 31 67
email	darziryab@wanadoo.net.ma
web	www.darziryab.com

Guest house

Map 2 Entry 125

Ryad Bahia
13 rue Tiberbarine, Ancienne Médina, Meknès

Two ancient houses – the antique floors in the colourful little 'old' house, reached by going up and down two staircases, may be 11th century – with a fresh young spirit. Recently married, Abdellatif and Bouchra have transformed his childhood home into a generous, airy guest house; they even spent a month in Rajasthan learning how to cook refined vegetarian food. Both tourist guides, they are quietly delightful and have a wealth of insider knowledge to share with you, while their wonderful first-floor sitting area is rich in Morocco books (novels, too) for reading by the fire, ensconced in a Meknès armchair or on a soft embroidered cushion. The ground floor – patio and salons – is organised for eating, sitting, music or telly, all in relaxed mood with colour, cushions and traditional hangings. Bedrooms, big and light in the main house (*Bahia*: brilliant, favourite), small and atmospheric in the old house (*Harem*: sacred space), are done with originality, colour, touches of India alongside Moroccan fabrics, chests, rugs, antique carved panels – pretty, youthful and comfortable.

rooms	7: 3 doubles, 2 twins, 2 family for 3.
price	500Dh-800Dh. Sole occupancy 19,000Dh per week.
meals	Lunch/dinner 110Dh-160Dh, or à la carte. BYO. By arrangement.
closed	Never.
directions	From Place Kdim, take top right-hand entrance and follow signs to Ryad Bahia (200m).

Guest house

	Bouchra Jamaï & Abdellatif Hassani
tel	+212 (0)55 55 45 41
mobile	+212 (0)61 81 52 37
fax	+212 (0)55 55 44 68
email	contact@ryad-bahia.com
web	www.ryad-bahia.com

Map 2 Entry 126

Palais Didi

30 avenue Moulay Ismaïl, Meknès

The rough-looking outside has little to do with the delights hiding inside. This 18th-century medina palace has been in Ismaïli's family since it was built by a descendent of Sultan Moulay Ismaïl. The magnificent patio brings light and elegance, ground-floor rooms have proper grand proportions (this is where the suites are, of course), the harmonious blue and cream colour scheme is peaceful though upper-floor rooms have smaller windows and therefore less light. Within this framework, Ismaïli's renovation aims for typical Moroccan palace style with quantities of stucco, kilims, carpets, lamps and hubble-bubbles that struggle to match their aristocratic surroundings. But the Didi is in a stunning position, right next to the Alaouite mausoleum, while up on the terrace you discover the wonderful Meknès roofscape and… the royal golf course, quite a surprise in a medina. Bedrooms have great new style, bathrooms are thoroughly, newly tiled and equipped and the first-floor restaurant is warmly done in painted wafer brick while the little second-floor pool is most tempting. Lovely staff.

rooms	12: 3 doubles, 2 twins. 2 singles, 1 family, 4 suites.
price	1,200Dh–1,500Dh.
meals	Dinner 150Dh–200Dh.
closed	Never.
directions	In Meknès: hotel behind Moulay Ismaïl mausoleum (Dar El Kbira car park).

	Ismaïli Mohamed Raouf & Zaki Alaoui
tel	+212 (0)55 55 85 90
mobile	+212 (0)61 20 73 97
fax	+212 (0)55 55 86 53
email	reservation@palaisdidi.com
web	www.palaisdidi.com

Small hotel

Map 2 Entry 127

Ryad Dar Lakbira

79 Ksar Chaâcha, Dar Lakbira, Meknès

This eager owner, young, charming and enthusiastic, now has two mansions, about five minutes walk apart, with which to please all tastes, all budgets. Lakbira was the first. A snug little multi-level place with great personality, it huddles up to the 17th-century ramparts which are spectacularly floodlit at night. No number of tourists can dilute its authenticity. The patio restaurant is the heart of this big house: quiet, intimate, lots of rambling greenery, mosaic tables, old carved doors and the compulsory fountain, exclusively yours in the evenings. There is also a vast and very Moroccan salon, a collection of old radios at the end of a dark corridor, some superb antique doors. Bedrooms, on second and third floors, vary from big and exuberant with lattice, stucco and ornaments, to small, cosy and unusual (there's even a padded-feel 'tented' room) and some have private terraces. It's an intriguing labyrinth of corridors, levels, blind alleys and decorative surprises. At either house you will be welcomed with zeal.

rooms	6: 2 doubles, 2 twins, 2 suites.
price	500Dh-750Dh. Extra bed 300Dh.
meals	Lunch 60Dh-150Dh. Dinner 110Dh-160Dh.
closed	Never.
directions	In Meknès: riad near Bab El Mansour gate (Sidi Amar car park).

Guest house

	Ismaïli Mohamed Raouf
tel	+212 (0)55 53 05 42
mobile	+212 (0)61 20 73 97
fax	+212 (0)55 53 13 20
email	riad@menara.ma
web	www.riadmeknes.com

Map 2 Entry 128

Auberge Restaurant Chalet du Lac

Dayèt Aoua, Près Ifrane

A simple inn from olden times (1950s). The guardian of this lakeside timewarp also watches over the fires whence emerges its excellent Franco-Moroccan food. Mademoiselle inherited both inn and culinary art from her mother and grandmother and is as atmospherically brooding as her old-fashioned country inn. Her assistant Véronique, milder and more voluble, has taught herself Arabic to converse with the staff. The cat is young and playful. Proper principles still hold here: the food comes first, in the big light lake-view restaurant; the thoroughly Moroccan-rural setting provides the right background of bleating flocks, colourful horses and winging waterbirds; bedrooms are a definite last. They are utterly plain and simple, spotlessly clean with good bedding and one washbasin each. Shared facilities – one half-bath/shower and one loo per five rooms, are down the passage. You can swim in or pedal-boat across the lake, when drought has not taken it away; walk, cross-country bike or ride round its 7km circumference – and return for another superb meal.

rooms	20: 7 doubles, 6 twins, 7 family, all sharing 4 bathrooms, 6 wcs.
price	Half-board 217Dh for two.
meals	Lunch/dinner 195Dh, or à la carte.
closed	Ramadan & Monday-Thursday in September-June.
directions	From Immouzzer-Kandar for Ifrane 7km; left for Dayèt Aoua; inn on right: big ochre building at top end of lake.

Auberge

	Régine Beccari
tel	+212 (0)55 66 31 97/56 32 70
fax	+212 (0)55 66 31 97
email	chaletdulac2000@yahoo.fr

Map 2 Entry 129

Gîte Dayèt Aoua
Route d'Immouzer à Ifrane - km 7, Ifrane

Down by the cedar-ringed lake (*dayèt*), Abdelhamid, an interior decorator from Fez, first cultivated an apple orchard; then he built his comfortable inn with its clean sober lines and intimate rural atmosphere created by the natural feel of wool, copper, leather and wood; then he became a luminary in country tourism – and also wrote a book on wrought-ironwork. When not in Fez, Abdelhamid is a charming, compelling host and his *gîte* gives a taste of the Berber sense of spontaneous hospitality. It is run by a team of warm, courteous, intelligent villagers who also cook the simple delicious food: the inn is part of a local development project. They have horses, donkeys, guides and advice on hiking, biking and bivouacs as well as the cultural things and peacocks. It's carefully rustic with beams, Berber blankets, some super decorative plates, low-lying wool mattresses and good solid furniture. Bedrooms are clean and comfortable, simple and pretty, suites are one double room and one Moroccan salon with bench beds. People have great fun here, far from the pressures of the city.

Auberge

rooms	5: 1 double, 1 triple, 2 suites for 4, 1 suite for 5.
price	300Dh for two-three. Suite for four 400Dh. Half-board 270Dh-350Dh p.p.
meals	Lunch/dinner 100Dh-250Dh. By arrangement.
closed	Never.
directions	From Immouzer for Ifrane 7km; left for Dayèt Aoua following lake round on right; signs.

	Abdelhamid & Fouzia Ghandi
tel	+212 (0)55 60 48 80
fax	+212 (0)55 60 48 52
email	aouagite@yahoo.com
web	www.gite-dayetaoua.com

Map 2 Entry 130

Auberge Berbère
Route d'Ifrane-Ougmès-Azrou - km 5, BP 138 Ougmès, Azrou

The ultimate success story: village boy becomes boxer, champion, international star, and settles in Nice. But he doesn't forget his home or his family in the Middle Atlas and builds a fine Riviera villa – on a hill in deepest Morocco – for brother and cousin to run as a rural inn. The lovely countryside rolls below it, the sheep, goats and donkeys graze, the cedar forest rises to the famous 800-year-old giants. The inn, all shiny spanking new, is as mixed as it looks, its colonnade outside rather than in, its floor tiles more garden-suburb than Maroc-tradition, its fabrics more city slick than rural weave – but the sweep of glass round the salons is phenomenal, you could watch the pace of timeless pastoral life for days. This is the big red-rugged convivial space where everyone meets for good home cooking – if not outside under the warm woolly spread of the Berber tent. Your hosts are utterly delightful, without much English: so eager and willing, so full of smiles: Mohamed the young charmer and decorater, Hamid the wise talker and adviser. They do mountain biking and donkey treks, too.

rooms	6: 5 doubles, 1 suite.
price	360Dh. Suite 600 Dh. Half-board 250Dh p.p.
meals	Lunch or dinner 90Dh. BYO.
closed	Never.
directions	From Azrou for Ifrane N8 for 5km. Right for Le Cèdre Gouraud 1.2km then follow signs for Auberge Berbère.

Auberge

	Famille M'Rabti
tel	+212 (0)55 56 20 31
fax	+212 (0)55 56 47 41
email	aubergeberbere@hotmail.com
web	www.aubergeberbere.com

Map 2 Entry 131

Riad Cascades d'Ouzoud
Ouzoud, Tanant-Azilal

Patrick's careful renovation of this gentle old building in its incomparable waterfall position is a perfect match for the local style: earth walls, authentically simple ornamentation, the proper quiet, centred riad atmosphere. A lover of nature and solitude, he really enjoys his guests and their differences. His light touch is felt in every room: white walls, ochre-washed floors, rugs and hangings, a fireplace and some furniture from Marrakech are all you need to fall for the charm of the place. The one decorative flourish that brings it out of the 'charmingly plain' bracket of woven woollen blankets, mosaic tables and Berber cushions is his set of wonderful doors painted with Islamic designs. Otherwise there are red-ochre tadelakt bathrooms with burnished copper basins, clay pots and plants everywhere, views to watch for hours from the terrace, an orange tree to sit under in the cool patio while you contemplate the swallows at their nests. Patrick has time for his house and time for his guests – an interesting, unusual host in a calm, well-loved and harmonious house serving good honest food.

rooms	6: 2 doubles, 1 twin, 1 triple, 1 mini-suite.
price	580Dh-810Dh. Half-board 820Dh-1050Dh for two.
meals	Lunch/dinner 130Dh-150Dh. By arrangement.
closed	Never.
directions	From Marrakech P24 for Beni Mellal 175km; right for Azilal, right for Ouzoud. Hotel at end of tiny village.

Guest house

	Patrick Lamerie
tel	+212 (0)23 42 91 73
fax	+212 (0)23 42 91 75
email	patricklamerie@yahoo.fr
web	www.ouzoud.com

Map 4 Entry 132

the south

Between the High Atlas and the great western Erg of the Sahara that edges into Morocco lies a vast territory dotted with oases and imposing kasbahs, bordered by the Anti Atlas. Here people here live with little (especially water) yet share what they have with the traveller - originally the caravaneer, then the colonial, now the tourist. One is happy to swap luxury for their conviviality, charm and authenticity.

Between the river-fed palm groves of the Draâ, Todra, Dadès and Ziz valleys are swathes of arid stoniness sculpted into a terrifying rugged beauty. Northwards lie the thrilling gorges of the Anti Atlas. Forever farmers and traders, these Berber families are multi-skilled. Some are nomads driving caravans of laden camels to market, others grow cereals and dates in the oases, others herd sheep and goats from pasture to mountain pasture with their thick tents, the women and children staying in the villages to spin and weave.

In the towns, you will be offered desert and mountain treks almost as often as carpets. At desert inns, you will be given bottles of iced water when leaving to confront the dusty track.

Zagora is a lively place, its modern centre a creation of surpassing ugliness, its *palmeraie* a delightful shady maze of walled alleys, gardens and houses. Erfoud or the desert market town of Rissani are essential if you want to visit the dunes at Merzouga, the first reaches of the Sahara's 3000km. The famous sunrise-viewing spot can be reached with any standard car: 4 x 4 is not essential, but a guide is – avoid the false ones if possible and don't go during a sandstorm.

Photo: Jose Navarro

Desert oases

Kanz Erremal
Touz Haci El Bide, BP 12, Merzouga

Guarding the feet of the rolling sand dunes, the kasbah, the highest building in
the area, is a marvel of old-new design. Its great interior courtyard, open to the
skies and looking east right into the dunes, acts as a natural cooling system: you
can hardly believe there's no air conditioning here and the lofty, airy space fully
makes up for the lack of garden. Bedrooms, nearly all with desert-gazing
windows, are arranged round the first floor of this, the hub of the elemental earth
building, and upstairs in the four corner towers. The terrace is up there, too, a
place where only sky, sand and peace exist. Tower-room guests may sleep under
the stars. There is a relaxed air about the whole place in its minimalist, earth-
coloured, almost bohemian décor, as if it were the work of a totally un-pompous
designer. Separations in bedrooms are done with fine fluttering curtains,
bathrooms are simple but carefully done in local hand-made tiles and smooth
plaster. And all infused with the soothing personality of friendly, soft-spoken
Brahim who provides that elusive combination of privacy and attention.

rooms	14 doubles.
price	€42.
meals	Breakfast €3.
	Lunch/dinner €9-€11.
closed	Never.
directions	From Rissani for Merzouga 33.5km, left at sign then 2.5km of track.

Small hotel

	Brahim Aït Ali
tel	+212 (0)55 57 72 65
mobile	+212 (0)66 03 91 78
fax	+212 (0)55 57 72 65
email	info@kanzerremal.com
web	www.kanzerremal.com

Map 5 Entry 133

Kasbah Mohayut
Ksar Hassi Labiad, BP 8, Merzouga

What makes this dune-side inn so special? The people, ten times over. Moha took a degree in English then, realising that tourism had become the only source of livelihood for his friends and relatives here, returned to turn his family house into a delightful place to stay. He has natural charm, exceptional integrity, loves contact with others and puts all his energy into making your stay unforgettable. Indeed, the whole family works together with welcoming smiles and caring attention. Moha also supports the local crafts cooperative and is fighting the spread of quad bikes here. After all the dryness outside, you find two garden courtyards with flourishes of greenery and fountains, a cool contrast that fills one with gratitude. The traditional earth building is a rambling single-storey complex where palm and eucalyptus beams hold the roof, old Berber doors are carved with ancient symbols, walls are encrusted with lettering. It has warm inviting bedrooms, good little shower rooms, wrought iron furniture standing on Berber carpets. Lovely people, great value – and high-class overnight camel excursions.

rooms	14: 6 doubles, 4 suites, 2 twins, 2 triples.
price	Half-board 400Dh–600Dh for two.
meals	Lunch/dinner 90Dh. Picnic 40Dh. By arrangement. BYO.
closed	Never.
directions	From Rissani for Merzouga, after 33km left at sign then 2.5km of track.

Auberge

	Mohammed Oubadi
tel	+212 (0)66 03 91 85
mobile	+212 (0)66 03 91 85
fax	+212 (0)55 57 84 28
email	mohamezan@yahoo.fr

Map 5 Entry 134

Desert oases

Auberge Ksar Sania
BP 4, Merzouga

Forge on through the swarm of false guides at the town gates: Ksar Sania is worth fighting for. At the foot of a towering dune (you could scarcely be closer), it's in a spectacular position with a superb approach. And the inn is a perfect combination of natural Moroccan flair with delightful Françoise's refined French style. She also wears a relaxed and unfading smile. Behind the imposing gates lies a multitude of small kasbah-type buildings arranged round the pool in an extravaganza of oleander and mature shrubs: a haven. First, you discover the heart-space that is the elegant hall and sitting area: with its tadelakt dome and beautiful original works by Moroccan and European artists, it feels like an art gallery; there's a fantastic pink tadelakt lounge and an ochre dinng room, too. Bedrooms are all different in lovely subtle colours and textures, a terrace here, a spiral stair to the children's room there, lots of wrought-iron partitions, silky bedcovers and handicrafts. Bathrooms are just a bit less special, the tents are good value for smaller budgets. Now launch desertwards on foot, quad bike or dromedary.

Auberge

rooms	29: 13 doubles, 2 suites, 8 family; 6 tents for 10.
price	Half-board 600Dh-900Dh for two. Tent 175Dh p.p. half-board.
meals	Half-board only. Lunch 100Dh.
closed	Never.
directions	Through gate at Merzouga, right, immediately left & follow signs 800m.

	Françoise Thomazo-Crocq
tel	+212 (0)55 57 74 14
mobile	+212 (0)61 35 99 10
fax	+212 (0)55 57 72 30
email	ksarsania@yahoo.fr
web	www.ksarsania.com

Map 5 Entry 135

Maison Merzouga
Hassi Labiad, BP 24, Merzouga

In the sleepy and blessedly untouristy village of Hassi Labiad, this sweet and friendly house does Berber homestay so don't expect high-level hotel service – or maddening touts when you walk in the dunes, which are a stone's throw from the door. The Seggaoui family also have the vast and colourful carpet shop next door: with its good selection, this could well be the place for you to buy yours. Theirs is a modest family house, all wonderfully neat, clean and tidy, with simple welcoming rooms. The use of colour is rich yet restrained and there is, of course, a wealth of carpets on floors, walls and even tables. The slightly bare living area is for night-time conviviality when the lamps come on, guests gather, and the plentiful, wholesome home cooking of the women of the household comes into its own. Beds are good under their Berber blankets and classic bedcovers and the good-sized shower rooms, with their wrought-iron fixtures, better than many one finds in more expensive places. The brothers run their combined business with knowledge and pride and can advise on desert excursions.

rooms	8 doubles.
price	Half-board 360Dh–540Dh for two.
meals	Half-board only. Lunch 90Dh.
closed	Never.
directions	4km before Merzouga left onto track 2.5km. House signposted at village entrance.

Guest house

	Ali et Lahcen Seggaoui
tel	+212 (0)55 57 72 99
mobile	+212 (0)61 25 46 58
fax	+212 (0)55 57 84 28
email	mdmerzouga@yahoo.fr
web	www.merzouga-guesthouse.com

Map 5 Entry 136

Auberge Chez Tihri
BP 5, Merzouga

What a welcome! All those colourful, mysterious, Amazigh wall motifs (one represents the Amazigh ideal of the 'true man', free and fearless), the great dune at your back door, no false guides as in town, and strikingly beautiful people offering genuine, unaffected desert hospitality. Before settling in 1975 they were nomads living under canvas: true, proud Amazighs. The heart of their simple inn is the dining room where a conversation can usually be started at one of the tables dressed in its hand-embroidered cloth. Superb food is served here, too, mouth-watering *kalia* and lush, generous salads. The windowless front bedrooms, rough-painted like the rest with Tataoui ceilings, local lamps and bits of pottery, may get rather hot; the even simpler back bedrooms are airier. The garden grows, the dromedaries and 4x4s stand by for outings. Omar can talk to you about local activites such as a nursery school where Tamasheq-speaking children can learn some Arabic and French, a women's weaving co-op, and the talented traditional music group he belongs to (you may be lucky and hear them play).

rooms	16: 6 doubles, 8 triples, 2 family; 2 doubles sharing bathroom.
price	240Dh-500Dh half-board for two.
meals	Half-board only.
closed	Never.
directions	Coming from Enfound, 2km before Merzouga left at electricity pole & inn sign. Follow track 2km towards dunes & Tihri.

Guest house

	Omar Tihri
mobile	+212 (0)61 38 18 43
fax	+212 (0)55 57 65 77
email	cheztihri@yahoo.fr
web	www.tuaregexpeditions.com

Map 5 Entry 137

Auberge Kasbah Derkaoua - The Desert Inn

Route de Rissani-Merzouga - km 21, Erfoud

After the mesmerising desert, the entrance arch announces civilisation, the trees peeping over the wall suggest oasis. And oasis it is, with all that implies of gentle hospitality. A wiry old enthusiast, Michel is remarkable: desert-struck from childhood, he has lived his life within reach of the Sahara. He resuscitated Derkaoua, a ruined Sufi *zaouia* founded in the 1800s by holy man Kaoua. It is now a virtually self-sufficient inn with two wells, two giant generators, a vegetable garden, an orchard, a farm full of goats, hens, sheep – all struggling to survive in the enduring drought. Horses and camels stand by for desert treks; the big pool lies apart from the shady gardens with their lounging and eating spaces (expect really good Moroccan food); simple, attractive bedrooms in soft desert colours with Berber blankets and hangings have excellent bathrooms. A dry, dusty, deserty inn whose extraordinary atmosphere of sand-filtered peace brings you back to essentials, a sense of adventure and, perhaps, monastic contemplation. Their 'luxury' overnight bivouacs in the dunes are exceptional – do book.

rooms	21: 10 doubles, 1 duplex, 6 bungalows, 3 apartments, 2 tents.
price	Half-board 500Dh p.p. Overnight bivouac 600Dh p.p. incl. dinner, 4x4 transfer, dromedary.
meals	Half-board only. Other meals 185Dh.
closed	January & June-August.
directions	From Erfoud for Taouz 17km; left at sign, follow excellent track 5km (green & white markers).

Guest house

	Michel Auzat
tel	+212 (0)55 57 71 40
mobile	+212 (0)61 34 36 77
fax	+212 (0)55 57 86 79
email	aubergederkaoua@hotmail.com
web	www.aubergederkaoua.com

Map 5 Entry 138

Kasbah Oasis de Fezna

Ksar Jallal, Oasis de Fezna, Erfoud, Caidat de Jorf

An oasis indeed. After living in Morocco for years and organising desert bivouacs, Hélène was smitten with a need for that desert purity and dry air that feed the soul. And her dream came true. In the charming village at the end of the little oued, in an oasis of palm trees with mountain views, she built a group of buildings, part-riad, part-kasbah, in a big green garden. There are terraces for all with private corners, pretty bedroom suites in different colours with comfortable rich-cushioned beds, storage alcoves and lots of space among four or five houses, including a real suite for disabled guests with its own terrace. The décor is subtly exotic, a careful, personal mix of Asian and Moroccan that respects the traditional architecture and spartan customs of the desert. Abderrazak is a manager with long experience of the inns and bivouacs of the south and Fezna is also a trekking centre: bivouac, dromedary, 4x4 or hiking, all the adventures from your front door. This fine new place to stay is just the mixture of comfort and authenticity that Merzouga needed.

rooms	8: 1 double, 1 twin, 6 suites.
price	1,250Dh–1,800Dh.
meals	Dinner 240Dh. Lunch 180Dh. Picnic 120Dh. By arrangement.
closed	Never.
directions	From Erfoud for Jorf, right at sign in palm grove.

Guest house

	Hélène Viant-Bénard
tel	+212 (0)55 78 95 07
mobile	+212 (0)61 08 16 49
fax	+212 (0)55 78 95 18
email	fezna@menara.ma

Map 5 Entry 139

Ksar Jenna

Aït Ouzzine, BP 70, N'Koob

Fifty old kasbahs stand in this amazing oasis village where southern traditions are fiercely upheld but Ksar Jenna is brand new. Its deeply committed owners, Youssef a son of the south, Stella who came from Italy and couldn't leave, have created a big restaurant serving convivial meals beneath a splendid great carved and painted dome and, separately, six excellent guest rooms done with flair in solid wood and the best in uncluttered traditional décor. This means high beamed ceilings, smooth tadelakt walls, Berber carpets on softly pale floors and, the modern touch, good big beds: building a new kasbah has made it possible to have wider rooms than the old norm. Shower rooms are also big and light with super bright tiling and decent towels. Outside, the wonderful cool garden greets you with arcades, all sorts of southern trees and swathes of lawn. Youssef and Stella want you to remember your stay for ever: they arrange excursions that reproduce the caravan trek along the old Dra Valley route and luxury desert bivouacs. Wonderful people, exquisitely simple elegance, superb value.

rooms	6 doubles.
price	800Dh.
meals	Lunch 150Dh. Dinner 200Dh.
closed	Never.
directions	From Ouarzazate for Erfoud via Adgz; ksar 2km before N'Koob on left.

	Youssef Amiri & Stella Mischiatti
tel	+212 (0)44 83 97 90
mobile	+212 (0)67 96 32 48
fax	+212 (0)44 83 97 91
email	info@ksarjenna.com
web	www.ksarjenna.com

Small hotel

Map 4 Entry 140

Desert oases

Maison d'Hôte El Khorbat
Tinejdad

After arriving through the drought-stricken, rubbish-strewn palm grove, you enter a genuine, unadulterated *ksar*, a fortified pisé village, a film-set grid of alleyways designed by the nomads of the day as their best defence system, where people still live as they did generations ago – in a state of unusual innocence. The guest house is part of the *ksar*, brilliantly restored by Roger Mimó to keep the magical austerity of a medieval house. It is dim, labyrinthine, minimalistic and beautiful in its earthy ochre colours and moving simplicity. The urns and jars are pure art, the beds, bathrooms and functional furniture are modern and good. Plus there's a remarkable museum of Berber life past and present: to visit it is an educational journey in itself. An amazing man manages all this: Ahmed Ben Amar provides excellent food, including vegetarian dishes, but also actively encourages guests to dine with local families, an exceptional experience, and is deeply committed to the El Khorbat development projects (literacy, women's weaving cooperative, *khettara* restoration).

rooms	8: 6 doubles, 2 suites.
price	800Dh-1,200Dh.
meals	Lunch/dinner 60Dh-100Dh.
closed	Never.
directions	From Tinerhir for Er Rachidia. 6km before Tinejdad right at sign, 500m to ksar, just over oued.

Guest house

	Ahmed Ben Amar
tel	+212 (0)55 88 03 55
fax	+212 (0)55 88 03 57
web	www.elkhorbat.com

Map 5 Entry 141

Dar Azawad

Douar Ouled Driss, BP 16, M'Hamid

The desert sand flows seamlessly up the solid walls of this very civilised base for exploring the barren lands and fabulous dunes that lie beyond M'Hamid, the southernmost village of Morocco. Vincent, a charming, energetic Arab-speaking art collector, has fulfilled his dream of creating a high-class trekking centre in a tiny palm grove. He has done it with true French refinement: sober, local style outside, some zinging colours on tiles, sabra-silk bedcovers, bright Berber rugs and remarkably original bathrooms inside. You sleep either in an individual miniature kasbah or in a bright-doored cabin with a camel-hair roof (they can get very hot). Each room is different, full of personality, yet calm and comfortable with a fascinating tadelakt bathroom. The tent corral washroom is unbelievably smart – tadelakt basins topped with copper taps and brass-framed mirrors; the dining room is a mass of fabulous pieces from Vincent's collection; the lovely pool is in the centre of the 'hamlet'. Come to discover the desert – on foot, dromedary or 4x4. It may seem expensive but there's none other like it.

rooms	6 + 7: 5 doubles, 1 suite. 7 tents for up to 4.
price	Half-board 1,000Dh–1,200Dh for two. 700Dh per tent for two half-board.
meals	Half-board only. Lunch 110Dh.
closed	Never.
directions	From Zagora south to M'Hamid 86km. House on right 900m after Ouled Driss sign.

	Vincent Jacquet	Small hotel
tel	+212 (0)44 84 87 30	
mobile	+212 (0)61 24 70 18	
fax	+212 (0)44 84 87 30	
email	vincent@darazawad.com	
web	www.darazawad.com	

Map 5 Entry 142

Desert oases

Kasbah Hôtel Porte au Sahara

Dunes de Tinfou, Tamegroute

The one and only star-gazing kasbah hotel in the country. The staggeringly clear night skies of Tinfou persuaded businessman Koring to build an astronomical guest house here (though he failed in his attempt to buy the famous Dune of Tinfou outright: it is a national monument) and his two-telescope observatory on the vast roof terrace is the reason for coming here (you may bring your own, too); gaze all night or even practise your astrophotography. The building is a peculiar mix of Teutonic castle and Moroccan kasbah, the dunes push against every part of the perimeter wall, inside and out, sand gets everywhere: the owner calls it total integration with the desert... And it is real desert that gets really hot in summer, until the whole empty plateau feels like a furnace. There's no more shade in the grounds of the hotel than out in the furnace so your refuge is the inevitably sandy, plain and functional interior – and the good Berber food. Or choose a desert excursion: dromedaries and Land Rovers are available with good guides. You come to experience the power of nature not a luxury hotel.

rooms	14: 13 doubles, 1 suite.
price	440Dh-580Dh. Half-board 660Dh-800Dh for two.
meals	Lunch/dinner, 3 courses, 120Dh.
closed	Never.
directions	25km south of Zagora on M'Hamid road (RN 9); signposted.

Small hotel

	Fritz Gerd Koring
tel	+212 (0)44 84 85 62
mobile	+212 (0)61 17 28 66
fax	+212 (0)44 84 70 02
email	hotelsahara@menara.ma
web	www.saharasky.com

Map 5 Entry 143

Dar Raha
Hay Amezrou, BP 142, Zagora

The real riches of Morocco are here: these thoughtful, creative, committed owners have made Dar Raha ('house of rest') into a place for encounters. Under their guidance, discover local history, architecture and culture, meet craftsmen and families, glimpse their gentle, traditional lifestyle, take mountain, valley or desert treks with seriously knowledgeable guides in partnership with a local association. In the heart of dusty red Amzrou where the flourishing palm grove keeps the desert at bay, their big old family house sits proud and cool beneath a protecting kasbah. Its long dark corridor leads past the dining platform to a dramatic patio whose four huge pillars rise pale and unadorned to the light. Sober pisé architecture, minimal decoration, simple comforts. Rooms have their own or shared terraces, colourful Moroccan fabrics to match their spice labels, ingenious 'clothes ladders', shared washrooms. From the terrace, way up above, you can watch 5,000 years of history melting into the palm grove as earth bricks give way to cement. Your interest can help save some of it.

rooms	9: 7 doubles, 1 single, 1 triple, all sharing 5 showers, 5 wcs.
price	375Dh. Half-board 500Dh for two.
meals	Lunch/dinner 100Dh-150Dh. By arrangement. BYO.
closed	Mid-June–mid-August.
directions	From Zagora centre for M'Hamid; over bridge 500m to Amzrou entrance; right at Maison Toudra & follow signs.

Guest house

	Josiane Morillon & Antoine Bouillon
tel	+212 (0)44 84 69 93
fax	+212 (0)44 84 61 80
email	darraha_zagora@yahoo.fr
web	darraha.free.fr/

Map 4 Entry 144

Villa Zagora
La Palmeraie d'Amzrou, BP 130, Zagora

Set in the green peace of the palm grove, Michèle Arnaud's personal version of the Moroccan house is a fine mix of old and modern, æsthetic and practical, secret and open. You arrive to the freshness of the multi-level garden and the pool among giant old palm trees (shade all day) and a great veg patch for the kitchen — the food is delicious. Next is the inner courtyard up to the sky and a cool central focus; its modern décor, subdued lighting and explosively colourful paintings are a breath of fresh air beneath traditional tataoui ceilings. Bedrooms are simply perfect with loads of storage, mosquito nets, interesting things on the walls, soft colours and textures and lots of windows. Finally, the roof terrace with its tent has space for overflow and a brilliant view of the sunset. After that, the seductive little pool with its inside illumination becomes the focus for long atmospheric evenings. You can walk straight out into the palmeraie with Mohamed who gives his all to make you comfortable and happy: nothing is too much trouble. Be you an individual traveller or a group of friends, it's wonderful.

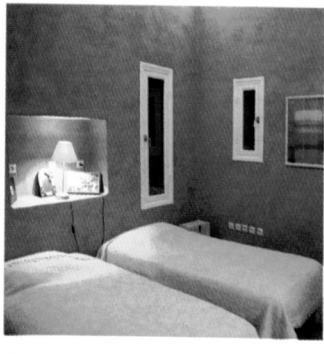

Guest house

rooms	7: 1 twin with separate bathroom; 2 doubles, 2 twins, 1 suite. 1 tent for 7.
price	450Dh-600Dh. Suite 850Dh. Tent 150Dh B&B. Sole occupancy 10,000Dh-15,000Dh per week.
meals	Lunch/dinner 120Dh.
closed	Never.
directions	From Zagora centre for M'Hamid, cross River Dra, pass Kasbah Asmaâ; house on left before right bend, behind Caravane du Sud; sign.

	Michèle Arnaud
tel	+212 (0)44 84 60 93
email	michele@mavillaausahara.com
web	www.mavillaausahara.com

Map 4 Entry 145

Chez Pierre

Douar Aït Oufi, Gorges du Dadès, Boumalne Dadès

Pierre bought a hillside and built upon it a vertical poem in brick and stone. From the road, his little inn climbs the slope; you follow – up the steps and out of the tunnel into the light of a leafy terrace-salon, the only general sitting space (in cool weather you just have your room). Fabulous food is served here by solemn staff in a big white cliff-hanging restaurant, one of the best in southern Morocco, where you sit in low rustic string-backed chairs. Above, there are apple blossom terraces, rosemary among the dry-stone walls, creepers and succulents, the beautiful blue mosaic pool with its stripey chaises-longues. And the guest rooms, each with a bit of terrace, all separately dotted among the terraced gardens that look up the magnificent gorge. They are very simple with lots of space, good shapes, arches, restful colouring – white and sand with flashes of rugs and curtains against terracotta floors, fittings of raw, twirly wrought iron, arched hangings and shelf alcoves. Bathrooms are simply sweet, the apartment is palatial, it's all new yet you feel it has belonged here for ever.

rooms	10: 4 doubles, 2 triples, 3 quadruples, 1 apartment for 8-9.
price	650Dh. Half-board dinner 550Dh p.p.
meals	Breakfast 60Dh. Lunch 45Dh-200Dh. Picnic possible 55Dh.
closed	10 Nov-20 Dec; 10 Jan-10 Feb; 6 June-31 July.
directions	From Boumalne Dadès, slow potholed track along north bank of Oued Dadès 26km; inn on right.

	Pierre Delaude	Auberge
tel	+212 (0)44 83 02 67	
fax	+212 (0)44 83 02 67	
email	chezpierre@menara.ma	
web	www.morocco-travel.com/h/ChezPierre	

Map 4 Entry 146

Kasbah Itran

Route de Tourbiste, BP 124, El Kelaâ M'Gouna

Lots of sharing, lots of humanity, the genuine simplicity of a Berber family in their age-old fortress. The Kasbah of the Star (*itran*) is run by five brothers of a young (some of them very young) dynamic tribe; others living in the luxuriant valley willingly receive foreign families for the day, children, women, men, each with their own: you might gather roses for rosewater, steam in the village hammam, wander in the fertile gardens. Or join an expedition to remoter Berber desert or mountain villages: you will see places, meet people you could never have found on your own and possibly create enduring friendships. Rooms here are as simple and unsophisticated as the people: ochre-washed cement floors, thick blankets and rugs, minimal handmade furniture, pretty mirrors over Berber washbasins (urn with tap over china bowl, plughole to bucket). Some have stupendous views of valley and sky, some just have internal windows, all have the right feel. They are planning Berber pottery workshops in mountain villages and are passionate about preserving their people's rich culture.

Guest house

rooms	9 doubles, 5 sharing bathrooms.
price	Half-board dinner 350Dh-500Dh for two.
meals	Half-board only. Lunch 90Dh. By arrangement.
closed	Rarely.
directions	From Ouarzazate for Er Rachidia, enter El Kelaâ M'Gouna; left at fork in centre, follow track 4km; kasbah on hill on left.

	Mohamed & Lahcen Taghda
tel	+212 (0)44 83 71 03
mobile	+212 (0)62 62 22 03
fax	+212 (0)44 83 71 03
email	mohamed@kasbahitran.com
web	www.kasbahitran.com

Map 4 Entry 147

Sawadi

Douar Tajanate, BP 28, Skoura

Deep in the palm grove, Bernard's guest farm, the fruit of his remarkable vision, is a finely finished miniature kasbah with an immaculate pool and a real farm – a haven of lushness and peace seized from the barren wasteland. He came to Skoura for lunch, stayed three nights, and bought this site. Self-sufficient in water, poultry, lamb and fodder, pomegranates and apricots, olive oil and coriander (fresh farm produce and the track make complete, and delicious, sense of compulsory half-board), Sawadi looks as exquisitely authentic as any other kasbah along this famous route and takes no more than 19 guests so there's room for all to find their own space: it's a garden round a group of houses rather than houses with a bit of garden. The houses are simply, functionally, pleasingly furnished and plumbing is European quality: Bernard and his welcoming manager know what travellers need. There's off-road biking for the energetic, boules for the slothful, all bathed in seductive Moroccan cooking smells. Brilliant for families, despite unfenced pool. *20-30 minutes from town; take 7km rough track with great care.*

rooms	Tamaris: 2 twins/doubles; Oliviers: 2 twins/doubles; Palmiers: 1 twin/double, 1 triple, 2 singles.
price	Half-board €115 for 2, €385 for 7.
meals	Half-board only.
closed	Never.
directions	From Ouarzazate left at fork into town centre; at end of tarmac sharp left onto rough track 7km, cross oued, follow green/yellow signs & white arrows/green dots to Sawadi.

Catered house

Bernard Ribet

tel	+212 (0)44 85 23 41
mobile	+212 (0)66 91 79 29
email	info@sawadi.ma
web	www.sawadi.ma

Map 4 Entry 148

Kasbah Ellouze
Tamdaght, Aït Benhaddou

Here is rural Berber Morocco at its best and most genuine – but cross that oued with care. Loaded with history, the kasbah used to be Pasha Glaoui's workers' residence. Colette, stylish, welcoming and very chattily French, restores buildings and has done a splendid job here: it's all clean lines, smooth earth walls, strategic openings and shady terraces overlooking the palm grove. Fine brass lanterns hang just where they should, birds sing, cranes rattle their beaks, the fountain hums and you relax. Traditional and modern blend seamlessly, colours are natural earthy ochres, ceilings tataoui, bedding excellent; (peculiarly) doorless tadelakt bathrooms are being renovated in 2005. A decent distance from tourist-stuffed Aït Benhaddou, a real old kasbah in a glorious palm grove that also grows almonds, pomegranates and olives, with troglodyte villages to walk to, endless photo opportunities… The whole area deserves two or three days and half-board is the right choice: high-quality ingredients, delicious homemade dishes, superb puddings: Michel is a trained French chef, a marvellous bonus.

Guest house

rooms	9: 3 doubles, 3 triples; 3 twins sharing shower & separate wc.
price	€36–€60. Half-board €56–€80 for two.
meals	Lunch/dinner 120Dh.
closed	End June to first week August.
directions	From Ouarzazate for Taroudannt 25km; left to Aït Benhaddou; continue 5km (ford over oued is passable without 4x4). Follow signs to car park then walk to house (arrows on walls).

	Michel & Colette Guillen
tel	+212 (0)44 89 04 59
mobile	+212 (0)67 96 54 83
fax	+212 (0)44 89 04 59
email	m.guillen@wanadoo.fr
web	www.kasbahellouze.com

Map 4 Entry 149

Dar Mouna
Aït Benhaddou

One of the four original families of the legendary, UNESCO-listed kasbah of Aït Benhaddou, the Mounas built their 'new' family house, the first ever on this side of the oued, in 1949. Although Dar Mouna is now surrounded by various eye-sores, its breathtaking position is revealed the moment you step into an east-facing room or onto the terrace. Far from being yet another stylish restoration, this house allows visitors a glimpse of its personal past. The elegant restaurant, cool inside its thick earth walls, is bright and petal-strewn and smells of incense; surrounding the patio, air-conditioned bedrooms are slightly tireder in their rustic Berber finish and air freshener, though Grandmother's room has its own wonderful viewing terrace. You cannot match these views anywhere else in town. Effervescent and energetic, 'Mouna' is proud of his Berber origins, has decorated the rooms with colourful Berber blankets, rugs and fabrics and is the ideal, knowledgeable host. And he recycles all waste (including those plastic bags that others leave for the wind to play with), some of it to heat the hammam.

rooms	12: 10 doubles, 2 family.
price	Half-board 650Dh-800Dh for two.
meals	Half-board only. Lunch from 100Dh. By arrangement.
closed	Never.
directions	Entering Aït Benhaddou right on unpaved lane just behind Hôtel Kasbah; house & car park 50m, at end of lane.

Guest house

	Abdellah Mouna
tel	+212 (0)48 84 30 54
mobile	+212 (0)61 38 57 20
fax	+212 (0)48 82 30 80
email	info@darmouna.com
web	www.darmouna.com

Map 4 Entry 150

I Roccha
Tisseldei

The welcome is as genuine as you'd expect from a happy, harmonious couple doing what they love. Smiling and diplomatic, Ahmed brought his bright, artistic Catherine from France to the tiny mountainside village where he was born. They built a stone and earth house then opened it to guests, also providing valuable jobs for a few local people. With a courtyard garden at its heart, the house faces spectacularly south across a picture of a sweeping landscape – you could sit all day on the shady terrace, noticing a new detail at every moment. Rooms, simple but not basic in their sandy rough-plastered frames, are done with solid wooden furniture, unusual bits of art, variegated fabrics and neat little shower rooms. The big Berber-style sitting/dining room has generous windows to those views, laughter in the air and a fine tataoui ceiling. In the little salon is Catherine's brilliant modern version of a painted ceiling – geometric shapes in strong dark colours like a child's building bricks. Good honest food, too. *A no-smoking house. Unlit track to house: better to arrive in daylight the first time.*

Guest house

rooms	5 twins/doubles.
price	Half-board dinner 400Dh p.p.
meals	Half-board only. Lunch 120Dh, by arrangement.
closed	Never.
directions	From Marrakech for Fez 9km; right for Ouarzazate 150km to Tisseldei; sign in village on left, follow track round to right (50km from Ouarzazate).

	Ahmed Agouni & Catherine Rophé
mobile	+212 (0)67 73 70 02
email	asifatlas@hotmail.com
web	www.terremaroc.com

Map 4 Entry 151

Dar Infiane
Douar Infiane, Tata

Tata, fascinating in its desert-edge austerity, its 20,000-strong palm grove the finest in the south, has given its name to those sensual ceilings of woven palm and oleander. A superb old stone kasbah, Dar Infiane is an explosion of colour after the dry barren approach – and a brilliant use of space. Ducking and shrugging, up and down, through the convoluted layout and small openings (mind your head!), you discover four leafy patios, amazing painted woven ceilings, lofty spaces and a heart-stopping view from the panoramic terrace. The house is naturally old in its bones, modern in its services: besides the soberly respectful Berber salon with its painted plaster ceiling, there are rooms for computing, television and reading, an ethnography museum, a small bar (yes) and big comfortable bedrooms where you are greeted by lovely stripey Rif fabrics against earthy walls, antique tataoui chests, minimalistic shower rooms. Patrick Simon works to rehabilitate the southern palm groves, the only viable basis for life in these regions; Latifa keeps an impeccable, well-designed house and cooks memorable meals.

rooms	6: 2 doubles, 4 twins.
price	900Dh.
meals	Lunch/dinner 200Dh. Picnic 120Dh. By arrangement.
closed	August.
directions	Leave Tata for Akka, i.e. right 350m after twin towers at town outskirts; track into palmeraie 250m, over earth embankment, bear right 50m, park in square. Steep steps from square to house.

Patrick Simon & Latifa Maali

tel	+212 (0)44 43 72 92
mobile	+212 (0)61 61 01 70
fax	+212 (0)44 43 73 68
email	darinfiane@wanadoo.net.ma
web	www.darinfiane.com

Guest house

Map 4 Entry 152

Riad Maryam

Avenue Mohamed V/Derb Maalen Mohamed, 140 Bab Targhount, Taroudant

Wind through the "prettiest old town in the south", push the door and enter the rug-strewn fine-tiled garden where birds sing in the lemon trees. This proper family house has thick earth walls, a cool garden courtyard and five simple rooms where zany colours contrast with soft old tiling. Not in the least luxurious, it's wonderfully cheerful, Habib and his family can't do enough to help you, their wild kitschy décor of mixed colours, shapes and patterns is just right. Also, you'd be mad to eat anywhere else, the food is exceptional and hugely generous; Latifa should be teaching others. Guests can use the kitchen, too – a rare privilege: it's a family-run guest house with no staff to stake territorial claims. Wherever you are, you're aware of opening onto the calm of the garden, the cool and pleasant salon has restful couches for quiet reading and one bedroom clutches a finely lacquered and carved set of wardrobe doors. The whole simple place is spotlessly clean, the family's sense of hospitality is generous and genuine and dinner beneath the greenery the best treat after a long hot day.

rooms	5: 1 double; 1 double, 2 twins, 1 quadruple, sharing two bathrooms.
price	350Dh–800Dh.
meals	Dinner about 150Dh. By arrangement.
closed	Never.
directions	Instructions given on booking.

Guest house

	Habib Moultazim
tel	+212 (0)66 12 72 85
mobile	+212 (0)65 48 54 52
email	ryadmaryamtaroudannt@yahoo.fr
web	www.riadmaryam.fr.fm

Map 3 Entry 153

Hôtel Palais Salam

Boulevard Moulay Ismail, BP 258, Taroudannt

Just inside the ancient medina walls, the former pasha's palace has bloody glory in its bones, romance in its crenellations, peace and civilisation in its Andalucian courts; the extraordinary gardens make it really special – brick paths shaded by palms, bougainvillea and butterflies, sitting and dining corners among the fountains, the pasha's wives' quarters rustling their banana skirts round a charming tiled square. The old wing oozes nostalgic colonial romance in its sculpted walls, vaulted ceilings and birdsong at dinner, brass lanterns with the finesse of antiquity and near-Venetian gold sofas. The new wing has no garden of its own but much modern sophistication: designer Morocco at its best mixing old and new in a wealth of split-level style, comfort and equipment (massage, sauna and fitness rooms as well as two swimming pools). Everywhere, light filters through stained glass onto the finest of carpets. It's a really big place, sometimes taking groups of 80 to 100, but organised in small enclaves (everyone can feel private), a chain hotel with personality and history.

rooms	140 twins/doubles.
price	650Dh–2400Dh.
meals	Lunch/dinner 150Dh.
closed	Never.
directions	From Agadir to Ouarzazate; through town (walls on left); at double r'bout by Hôtel de Ville bear left for old ramparts (palm trees) & hotel entrance.

	Khalid Aït El Hachmi	Hotel
tel	+212 (0)48 85 21 30/25 01	
mobile	+212 (0)61 28 39 41	
fax	+212 (0)48 85 26 54	
email	palsalam@menara.ma	
web	www.groupesalam.com	

Map 3 Entry 154

Festivals

Planning where to go in Morocco, particularly if this is your first visit, can be difficult. For those with limited time, choosing from the country's amazing list of attractions, from imperial cities to deep desert to 10,000-foot mountains, may prove daunting. However, one of the many festivals and *moussems* that take place between May and September may be just what you need to point your compass at a particular destination. The energy, passion and *joie de vivre* in the festivals we list below is exceptional - and highly contagious. Moroccan festivals are like Moroccan daily life on overdrive: endless stimuli for your senses. Come prepared and enjoy them.

Fête des Roses (May)

An explosion of colour in the town of El Kelâa des M'Gouna, in the Dadès Valley, celebrating the rose harvest – rosewater is the area's main product.

There are traditional dances by men and women wearing the most beautiful costumes and an array of arts and crafts for sale. This has to be one of the most joyous and idiosyncratic events in the country.

Fez Sacred Music Festival (end-May-early June)

www.fesfestival.com
From Sufi music to Christian Gospels: your chance to discover an extraordinary variety of entrancing religious music from all over the world.

Tan-Tan Moussem – Sheikh Sidi Mohammed Ma El Ainin's *moussem* (end-May-early June)

Tribes and nomads from the Moroccan Sahara and beyond gather in Tan-Tan in remembrance of holy man Sidi Mohammed Ma El Ainin. Touaregs, camel caravans, nomads' tents on the dunes: this event is as fascinating and exotic as festivals go. Banned by the late King Hassan II, the festival has undergone a revival thanks to Mohammed VI and the support of UNESCO.

Essaouira G'naoua & World Music Festival (June)

www.festival-gnaoua.co.ma
An opportunity to enjoy not only the hypnotic G'naoua music of Morocco but also a plethora of musical styles from all over the world. A must for world music lovers.

Marrakech Festival of Popular Arts (June)

www.ucam.ac.ma/fnap.aga

A showcase for the cultural microcosm that is Morocco. There are over 250 tribal groups in Morocco and many of them are represented at this celebration of Morocco's cultural diversity, including G'naoua, Arab & Amazigh dance & music groups from all corners of the country, from the Rif to the Sahara.

Moussem Moulay Abdellah – El Jadida (August)

If you want to see the most spectacular *fantasias* (traditional, cavalry charges) in Morocco, this is the place to go. The Atlantic beaches of El Jadida are the perfect setting for these daring displays.

Imilchil Wedding Festival (September)

More than 25,000 people from the High Atlas gather at one of the most emblematic Berber events, during which young women of the Aït-Haddidou tribe engage in a boastful display of beauty and grace in their search for a husband. At an altitude of 2,600 metres, the vast plateau around Imilchil teems with life and tradition in a meeting which, however touristy it may have become, still enthralls locals and visitors alike.

Photo Jose Navarro

Moussem de Meknès – Moussem de Moulay Idriss Zerhoun (September)

Folklore and religious fervour in remembrance of the founder of the Idrissid dynasty. This festival doesn't enjoy the same international publicity as events in Essaouira or Fez but it is undoubtedly the most significant religious gathering in the country. Fantasias, music, arts and crafts complement this highly recommended festival.

Agadir Festival of Popular Music (September)

The strong emphasis on Morocco's oral tradition makes this an exceptional festival. Griots from the far south, poet-musicians of the Souss and Anti-Atlas, G'naoua singers: here is a chance to learn about some of the less-well-known Moroccan music.

Reading list

The following list contains an eclectic mix of authoritative and impassioned books, from autobiographies of Moroccan authors to evocative novels by non-Moroccan writers. We don't list many travelogues - they can be prone to shallowness; nor do we suggest dense reference books on architecture, history or the arts. Instead we invite you to allow our recommended authors to guide you through the complexities of their culture by peeling off the many layers of this fascinating country. We strongly suggest that you include books by Moroccan writers in your reading list; their insights can be illuminating, thought-provoking, even shocking at times.

Fatima Mernissi

An influential Moroccan feminist concerned about the role of women in Islamic societies. Her passionate writing challenges preconceptions about women in Muslim countries.

Dreams of Trespass: Tales of a Harem Girlhood

Mernissi's autobiographical account of her upbringing in a riad in Fez is a beautifully written book. It opens a window on the secret world of Fassi harems during the French Protectorate, a world which was as alien to people outside Morocco as Morocco was to the women of the harem.

Beyond the Veil

A contemporary exploration of women's issues in the Muslim tradition and their status in male-dominated Arab countries.

Doing Daily Battle

A series of interviews with Moroccan women across a wide social spectrum.

Sheherazade Goes West

Mernissi's experiences travelling alone in western societies. This book is a chance to see ourselves reflected in the mirror of a different culture.

Paul Bowles (1910-1999)

An American composer turned writer, a modern nomad who left his base in New York for Tangier and wrote some of the most evocative novels ever set in North Africa.

The Sheltering Sky

The North African deserts are the backdrop for a couple's travels and attempts to reconcile their estranged relationship. The hardships of travelling in the barreness and emotional tension are the essential ingredients for an exploration of the meaning of life and love.

The Spyder's House

Set in Fez during the 1954 uprising against the French Protectorate, this novel is poignantly relevant to today's troubled relationship between western and Islamic societies. Again, Bowles explores the meaning of life, the chasm between the West and the Arab world, the isolation of the traveller in alien cultures.

Tahar Ben Jelloun

A prolific Fassi writer who chose to write in French rather than Arabic, his mother tongue. He has produced a plethora of novels dealing with cultural taboos, frequently personified in his characters. His essays go from the disconcerting and the surreal to the outright alienating.

The Sand Child

A politically charged novel that challenges established Islamic traditions, it tells the story of a father of seven girls. Cursed by the lack of a son and the birth of yet another baby girl, he finds a drastic solution to his social ostracism: he will raise the newborn girl as a boy.

The Sacred Night

A continuation of the life of Mohammed Ahmed, the girl raised as a boy in The Sand Child.

Mohammed Choukri (1935-2003)
For Bread Only

The blunt autobiography of a controversial Arab author. Born in the Rif mountains in a time of famine, he led a semi-nomadic life before settling in Tangier. Illiterate until the age of 20, he decided to learn to read and write Arabic, a decision that would radically change his life. The book gravitates around Choukri's dysfunctional upbringing and touches on sensitive issues such as sexuality, prostitution and drugs. These themes and language, labelled as blasphemous by many Arab scholars, resulted in the book being banned from bookshops until 2000.

Gavin Maxwell (1914-1969)
Lords of the Atlas: The rise and Fall of the House of Glaoua 1893-1956

The story of one of the greatest dynasties of modern Morocco. Unfettered history and adventure in the warrior-tribe-cum-dynasty, a tale of feudal fiefdoms which still reverberates today.

Walter Harris (1886-1933)
The Morocco That Was

An exploration of the last years of the Sultanate, before the French Protectorate, first published in 1921, this book has both the gripping narrative of a good traveller's tale and the authoritative approach of an insider who lived in Morocco for nearly 30 years.

Antoine de Saint-Exupéry (1900-1944)
Wind, Sand and Stars

A true classic from the famous pilot and author of The Little Prince. Saint-Exupéry describes his adventures

Reading list

flying postal routes in primitive aircraft and precarious conditions in South America, Europe and Africa. A crash landing in the Libyan Sahara provides the setting for a philosophical and lyrical account of the life and beauty that he found there.

Jeffrey Tayler
Valley of the Casbahs
Written in classic travelogue style, it tells of the author's adventures crossing the arid plateaux and valleys of the Moroccan south on foot and camel. Tayler discovers a microcosm of life in the far south, well beyond Morocco's best known destinations.

Culture Shock!
Culture Shock! Morocco: A Guide to Customs and Etiquette.
Unless you are planning to cocoon yourself in the comfort of your hotel for the whole of your stay, you will need this book. It's a practical and informative guide to social interaction and the subtle yet powerful rules of engagement in Moroccan culture. It makes the traveller aware of the stark differences to be encountered in a

country which is geographically so close, yet culturally so different from Europe. An absolute must.

Marrakech, the Red City
A delightful collection of writings about Marrakech full of insights and personal experiences.
Ed. Barnaby Rogerson & Stephen Lavington

Marrakech - Voyage du Haut Atlas à Essaouira
A beautiful mixture of photographs and drawings, articles, itineraries and maps to guide you into the secrets of Marrakech, Essaouira and the High Atlas. *Published by Bab Sabaa, Marrakech*

Maps
The Éditions Gauthey city maps are useful for detailed exploration of Tangier, Essaouira, Marrakech or Fez.

Fez: Fez from Bab to Bab
(PM Editions, Casablanca) is a book of guided walks with an excellent map of the medina; the names are transcribed so you can ask your way in North Africa's biggest medina.

Marrakech: Bab Sabaa in Marrakech publish a new guide to the medina with the latest detailed map. www.babsabaa.com.

Essaouira: Jack's Kiosk on Place Moulay Ismail has good town maps.

Photo Harriet Richardson

Conservation & development

Desert, water & environmental awareness

Desert landscapes have fascinated us for centuries and since Victorian times desert regions have been used to escape from our cluttered lives. The allure of remote environments, the sensuality of their sand and rock formations, the enigmatic, fearsome and romantic peoples who inhabit them: the desert has fuelled the European imagination. Morocco is no exception. With more than 80% of the country statistically arid or semi-arid, Morocco has places to fulfil the most demanding visitor's expectations. From the palm groves and oases of the Draâ Valley to the sinuous dunes of Merzouga, Morocco's desert landscapes will surely be one of the highlights of your trip.

This romantic vision of the desert, exacerbated by the excitement of going away, makes us oblivious to the obvious: deserts are deserts because of lack of water. This is where romanticism ends and the reality of an arid environment begins. Some areas of the Moroccan Sahara and Saharan Atlas receive less than 100mm of rain per year (less than 1/10th of the average annual rainfall in south-west Britain), and more than 75% of that is lost to evaporation, leaving a meagre amount to replenish man-made reservoirs and the underground water table.

Any traveller to the Moroccan south should understand the environmental pressure weighing on the people there, particularly in rural areas, and the delicate ecosystems of the region. And an awareness of how one can help reduce the environmental impact of one's visit is an essential pre-requisite for the environmentally-conscious traveller.

A delicate balance

Desert oases are the natural setting for life, something we have probably known since childhood, but we will be mistaken if we think that oases, left unassisted, have an inexhaustible capacity to support life. Oasis towns and villages along the Draâ and Dadès valleys or the Tafilalet in the remote south-east, for example, are delicate symbiotic units where the environment depends on the inhabitants as much as they depend on it. Not only do the palm and olive trees of palmeraies contribute to the local

Photos Jose Navarro

economy with export crops, they also provide a shady environment for the cultivation of a variety of other crops, from cereal to alfalfa to beans and fruit. The diversification of the palm groves is essential in a subsistence economy – the situation of many remote villages in the south. Cultivation of the fields between the palm trees contributes, in its turn, to a healthy palm grove, guaranteeing irrigation of the trees, preventing soil erosion and keeping shifting sands at bay.

When the balance is altered

This subtle but important symbiosis of Moroccan palm groves is easily upset by both natural and human causes. Date palms are particularly vulnerable to fungal disease called Fusarium Wilt. More than 12% of palm groves in Morocco have been lost to this unwelcome guest in recent years.

The death of a palm grove, regrettable in itself, has major side-effects. People stop cultivating a palmeraie when it no longer offers the right conditions for healthy crops. Untended, the now-empty space is rapidly taken over by sand, which further prevents the regeneration of the palmeraie and its suitability for cultivation. The vicious circle of desertification begins. On a socio-economic level, the lack of prospects of good crops

and the availability of more profitable activities such as tourism discourage the young from continuing this subsistence lifestyle, which is all but disappearing.

Whose water is it?

The small quantities and the unpredictability of rainfall in Morocco's arid and semi-arid regions mean that the underground water reservoirs are their lifeline. Traditionally, water for irrigation and consumption in an oasis did not always come from the oasis itself. Water was brought from distant natural underground reservoirs – located in seemingly impossible places such as the middle of sand dunes – using *foggaras* (or *khettaras*), a system of underground galleries, now protected by UNESCO,

Conservation & development

which taps into the water table and takes the water to the oasis. Such underground canals can be as long as 20km; each one consists of a horizontal channel, slightly inclined so that water flows by gravity, and a series of access wells on the surface for ventilation and maintenance. The beauty of the *foggara* system is that it reduces loss by evaporation to a minimum. This clever irrigation system provides about 10 to 15 litres per second at the oasis, just one more example of the ingenuity of desert dwellers.

There is magic in seeing water pouring out of the end of a *foggara*, feeding the small irrigation channels. This resource is still traditionally managed in many oases. In the Tafilalet, the village Sheikh usually allocates a share of the water to every family in the village, who irrigate their fields in turns. A whole family may have no more than five hours of *foggara* water per week. It is also everyone's responsibility to inform the next person on the irrigation rota when their turn is. Failure to follow this rule results in a penalty of one hour on the following week's rota. This system ensures that no water is wasted.

However, the *foggaras* are gradually falling into disrepair and oblivion. On the one hand, the severe drought that has affected the south of Morocco in recent years and subsequent lack of use mean the foggaras are drying up or subsiding. It is estimated that by 2020 the current water table will have fallen by 50%, which will disable many existing *foggaras*. So desert residents are digging more and more wells in the oases, thus lowering the local water table even further.

On the other hand, the burgeoning tourist industry has put extra pressure on limited desert water resources. Local rural populations have a natural ability to use water sparingly: the average daily needs of an oasis dweller are a mere 20 litres whereas a minimum of 120 litres per person per day is used in towns. We town-dwelling tourists often bring a total disregard for the need to save water, or indeed a voracious demand for it. One of the most controversial issues is the automatic installation of swimming pools in tourist hotels. However soothing it may be to dip in a cool pool after a day in the south, we mustn't forget the cost of that luxury. Few people realise how much is lost to evaporation due to hours of hot sun and low humidity. A modest 18'x12' swimming pool, will lose between 30 and 50 litres of per day – even before counting splashes and leaks.

Photo Jose Navarro

What you can do to avoid wasting water

Consider following these suggestions on your trip to the south:

• Have only one shower a day, preferably in the evening to relax after a day in the heat – it makes more sense than having a shower in the morning.

• Spend a minimum length of time in the shower. As a rule of thumb you use 5 litres of water every minute you are in the shower, which means that a 4-minute shower uses as much water as the average rural inhabitant needs for a whole day.

• Apply the Olde-English water-shortage rule of No pull for a pee – unless you happen to find a dual-flow flush in your bathroom. If you dislike this thought, remember that the average lavatory cistern holds more than 10 litres of water, half a desert dweller's daily requirement.

• Bring your dirty clothes home rather than having them washed.

• Ask the hotel not to change your sheets and towels every day.

• Don't clean your teeth, wash your hands or shave under a running tap.

• Drink plenty of natural fruit juice from locally-grown oranges and grapefruit, not just bottled water or fizzy drinks which contain water from the country's underground reservoirs.

The country needs its tourist trade, vitally, but it also needs ever more intelligent use of water to support development for so many people. So bring your eyes and your ears and your taste buds, experience the mind-boggling differences that Morocco offers – and remember the villagers next door, go easy on their precious water.

Jose Navarro

Conservation & development

Some projects:

• Argan Biosphere Reserve in the Essaouira region; to protect, encourage and research further uses of argan oil (cookery, cosmetics, medicinal).

• Southern Oasis Biosphere Reserve between Ouarzazate and Skoura; to protect the fragile pre-Saharan ecology.

• The Akhiam Association in Amzrou, a community in the Zagora palm grove, works for the concerted development of the neighbourhood by:

- preserving the local heritage, recording the memories of the older inhabitants, recruiting and training local youth as tour guides;

- setting up cultural activities designed to help the young to develop and grow in their own district;

- cooperating on communication of the association's aims and activities to all potentially interested groups. Dar Raha of Amzrou is a founding and active partner of the Akhiam movement.

• ABDBO Education project for Berber village girls to learn contemporary skills alongside cultivation and use of traditional herbal remedies in a mixed environment of weekly boarding school and home village. A year's sponsorship of one student costs only $650. Donations to: Association de Bienfaisance et de Developpement du Bassin de l'Ourika, BP16, 42350 Ourika.

• Association des Bassins d'Imlil for the protection and sustainable development of the valley populations around Imlil and the

Photo Jose Navarro

Toubkal National Park. There's a donation box in the hall of Kasbah du Toubkal or donations can be sent to: Wafa Bank, Agence Médina, Marrakech.

• Agence de Développement Local (ADL) works primarily in Chefchaoun province and the nearby Rif areas, promoting and coordinating projects in conservation, sustainable development, education and training, focusing mainly on forestry, farming, tourism and communications.

Illegal wildlife trade in Morocco

There is a growing list of endangered Moroccan species that it is illegal to capture, buy, sell or export. The Global Diversity Foundation are well under way with their National Geographic-funded wildlife trade survey carried out with the Marrakech Musuem of Natural History. They have made over 1000 collections of plants and animals and interviewed over 100 vendors.

The diversity of wildlife in Morocco is still remarkable. To help save a frighteningly dwindling resource, do take note of the banned exports list which includes:

Tortoises or land turtles
Snakes
Chameleons
Spiny-tailed lizards
Leopard and other wild-animal skins
All the indigenous butterflies of the Atlas mountains
Numbers of indigenous snails (mixed with farmed edible snails)
Hirudo medicinalis leeches

It is also worth pointing out that the thuya tree is becoming an 'endangered species': Moroccan craftsmen have traditionally made their carved and inlaid tables and chests from this strong characterful wood but the trees take years to reach maturity and the developing tourist trade has so increased demand that the forests are being depleted faster than they can replenish.

World Heritage Sites of Morocco

The medina of Marrakech has been a UNESCO World Heritage Site since 1985 and Place Jemaâ El Fna was designated the first UNESCO Oral Heritage Site in 2001.

Medina of Fez
Medina of Essaouira
Medina of Tetouan (formerly Titawin)
Historic city of Meknès
Portuguese city of Mazagan, the modern-day El Jadida
Roman arcchæological site of Volubilis
Ksar of Aït Benhaddou

History of Morocco

Prehistory

Mankind emerged from East Africa and moved into North Africa where, ultimately, the drifting groups of hunter-gatherers settled. The indigenous people of North Africa can henceforth be described as Berbers, a word of Greek origin, and the earliest historical records speak of their devotion to war, to polygamy, to their chariots and to their herds of sheep and goats.

The Phoenicians and Romans

It was the Phoenician merchants of the coast of Syria who first introduced the higher arts of the Near East to Morocco. They were the fairy godmothers of ancient Morocco, though their motives were entirely mercenary. By 1,000BC they had established a permanent settlement at Tangier, soon followed by other colonies down the Atlantic coast. From these centres the skills of metal-working, stone-carving, weaving, pottery and improved agriculture were disseminated. Carthage emerged as the leader of all the Phoenician colonies in the Western Mediterranean during the sixth century BC when they all felt threatened by the expansion of Greek colonial settlements. From this period comes a description of the Carthaginian admiral Hanno's voyage down the coast to West Africa and the techniques of silent barter with the natives for gold.

After the destruction of Carthage in 146BC, Rome assumed the 'protection' of the Phoenician colonies. The interior of North Africa was ruled by native Berber kings whose territories were slowly annexed by Rome over two centuries. Juba II, who ruled over northern Morocco and central Algeria from the inland capital of Volubilis, was a noted scholar who had been educated in the household of the Emperor Augustus, where he had met and married the princess Silene, the daughter of Mark Anthony and Cleopatra. His Moroccan kingdom resisted annexation but was finally conquered in AD44, during the reign of the Emperor Claudius.

This new Roman province of Mauretania Tingitania consisted of just the fertile northwestern coastal plain and was not even connected by road to Roman Algeria. When the Baquates tribe overran the defences at the end of the third century the Empire decided hold onto the strategic city ports of Tangier and Ceuta only. Later powers like the Vandals and Byzantines followed their example, leaving the fierce Berber tribes of the interior to their own devices.

The spread of Islam and the Arab conquest

This was all to be changed by a theocratic state that had been established in the Arabian peninsula. The Prophet Muhammad died in 632 but the cavalry armies of his successors soon conquered an enormous empire. In 682 Oqba ben Nafi made his legendary raid into Morocco, riding out into the Atlantic surf to prove that there was no land any further west to be conquered for Islam - before returning to his base in Algeria. Next, between 705 and 710 Musa ben Noussir established garrisons at Tangier and the Tafilalt but it was soon made clear that his real objective had been to conquer Spain and secure the desert trade route. The only value Morocco held for the Arab governors was as a source of slaves and recruits for their army.

Photo Ann Cooke-Yarborough

In 740 the disillusioned Berber soldiers in the Tangier garrison assassinated their Arab governor and revolted. They adopted a rigorous puritanism in order to make a clear distinction between their passionate support of Islam and their rejection of their Arab overlords.

The Idrissid Monarchy, 789–828

Berber enthusiasm for the new religion was further demonstrated in 789. Moulay Idriss, great-great-grandson of Muhammad, had fled to Morocco to escape the vengeance of Harun al Rashid, the great Caliph of Baghdad. He was acclaimed ruler by the Berber tribes around Meknès but was poisoned by an agent of the Caliph two years later. Fortunately his Berber mistress was pregnant and gave birth to a son who later reigned as Idriss II, ruling central Morocco and establishing Fès as a great bastion of Arab and Islamic culture. After his death in 828 his kingdom

History of Morocco

was divided among nine sons who have attained legendary status as missionary princes who brought the faith to far-flung provinces. Though the power of the Idrissids soon waned, their spiritual prestige remains a strong and continual feature of Moroccan history.

Unity under the Almoravids, 1042–1147

By the 11th century Morocco had deteriorated into a patchwork of petty states and feuding tribes with many of the chief ports and towns under the control of foreign powers - albeit Muslim ones. In the far reaches of the Western Sahara a native scholar, Ibn Yaasin, had returned from Mecca determined to create a true Islamic state. His vision and discipline, allied to the ferocity of the Saharan tribes, created a powerful force of warriors. The *al-murabitun* "the men of the fortress of faith", would become known to Europe as the Almoravids. These warriors emerged out of the desert in 1042 and conquered an enormous desert empire that stretched south to the Niger river and north towards the High Atlas mountains of Morocco. This was to be further extended by Youssef ben Tachfine, an Almoravid general who crossed the mountains and established Marrakech as his base camp in 1071. Within 20 years Youssef had conquered not only

Morocco but also the sophisticated city-states of Muslim Spain. Skilled Andalucian craftsmen, secretaries and architects were employed by the Almoravid court and began to introduce the higher civilisation of Moorish Spain into Morocco.

The Empire of the Almohads, 1147–1248

At the height of the Almoravid Empire, Ibn Tumert, another native scholar, returned from Mecca full of schemes to establish an even more rigorous Islamic state. Rejected there, he fled the city and established himself at Tin-Mal in the High Atlas where he created an obedient army from the Berber highland tribes. Victory over the Almoravids was only eventually achieved by his successor, Abdel Moumen; his empire stretched over Spain, Algeria, Tunisia and part of Libya. It is the golden period of Moroccan history, when Almohad fleets dominated the Western Mediterranean and great philosophers like Averroës received the full support of the sultan's court. Some of that glory is still reflected in the magnificent buildings that adorn Rabat and Marrakech: the Koutoubia and El Hassan minarets and the formal gates of Oudaya and Aguenaou. In 1213 a military defeat in Spain rocked imperial authority and the sultans were faced with a series of revolts. In 1248 the

Photo Jose Navarro

Almohad sultan died while on campaign on the Algerian border and his leaderless army was massacred by the powerful Beni Merin tribe as it struggled home. The tribal chiefs of the Beni Merin established their capital at Fès but it took another 21 years of war before they could destroy the last Almohad army that defended Marrakech.

The Merenid dynasty, 1248–1554
The reigns of Sultan Abou Hassan, 1331-51, and his son Abou Inan, 1351-58, are the zenith of the centuries of Merenid rule. In this period, Merenid armies twice occupied Tunis and seemed at the point of restoring the unity of the Almohad Empire. The Merenid architecture of the 14th century, particularly the medersas (schools for Koranic studies) in Fès, Meknès and Salé, testify to the exquisite taste of the sultans and their patronage of religious learning. The works of Ibn Battuta, 'the Muslim Marco Polo', and Ibn Khaldoun, one of the world's greatest historians, are proof of the lively intellectual life of the period. Wealth poured into the state coffers from the enormously profitable trans-Saharan caravan trade in gold, precious oils and ivory. The period finished in 1358 when Sultan Abou Inan was smothered with a pillow by his vizier. This royal murder is a parable for the gradual decline of the state. The

sultans became mere figureheads as real power fell into the hands of a corrupt coterie of viziers, financiers and generals. In the 15th century the Portuguese began to seize control of Moroccan ports which the Merenids proved powerless to hold. By the mid-16th-century the Portuguese were in almost complete control of the coastline and in 1578 the boy king Sebastian attempted outright conquest.

The Saadian Sultans, 1554–1668
The inability of the Merenid rulers to oppose the Portuguese allowed for the rise of a number of local war leaders. The most effective of these were the Saadians, from the oasis valley of the Draâ in southern Morocco, who organised the siege of Agadir in 1510. This Portuguese fort finally fell in 1542, by which time the Saadians were already established in Marrakech as the rulers of southern Morocco. Seven years later they captured the Merenid capital of Fès. In 1578 the Saadian dynasty won eternal fame with the crushing defeat of the Portuguese invasion at Ksar-el-Kebir. Sultan Abdel Malik died in the hour of victory. His brother Ahmed inherited the throne, took the title El Mansour - 'the victorious' – then gained additional fame by the conquest of Timbuctoo whose treasure gave him another epithet - El Dhabbi, 'the golden'. Surviving

memorials of his reign include the glittering Saadian tombs and the ruins of the palace of El Badia in Marrakech. His sons destroyed their inheritance in a furious war of succession and discredited the dynasty by selling the port of Larache to the Christians in 1610. Though a number of Saadian princes lived on in splendour at Marrakech, real authority was exercised elsewhere. A three-cornered fight developed between petty dynasties based on the Rif, Anti-Atlas and Middle Atlas mountains.

However, after 40 years of warfare, power fell into the hands of Moulay Rachid, a young prince of holy lineage whose Alaouite family came from the oasis of Tafilalt. Within four years of raising his standard at Taza he had seized control of the country. He ruled for four years and was succeeded by his younger brother, Moulay Ismaïl.

Moulay Ismaïl, 1672–1727
Certain monarchs breed legends and the reign of Moulay Ismaïl has always been in danger of being overwhelmed by stories of his cruelty and sexual prowess. He was undoubtedly fertile and tyrannical but his long reign was also a period of great achievement. He reformed the nation's cult-ridden religious life, disciplined the Berber mountain tribes, liberated Tangier from the English and Larache, Asilah and Mehdiya from the Spanish.

The imperial city at Meknès was built in this period but there are many other testaments to his energy: the bridges, kasbahs and markets that he built throughout the country and the numerous mosques, palaces and walls that he had restored. It was the proud boast of his reign that the roads were safe enough for a woman or a Jew to travel across the breadth of the country without being troubled. This unaccustomed order was only achieved by an authoritarian regime backed by a standing army of 150,000 Negro slaves. His failure, and it was a great one, was not to delegate authority to any of his many sons. His death was followed by a 20-year war as his regiments and heirs struggled for dominance.

Photo Jose Navarro

History of Morocco

Decline in the 18th and 19th centuries

None of the immediate descendants of Moulay Ismaïl was to match the great sultan's power. Their authority was in practice restricted to the coastal plains and river valleys, the area which was known as the Bled-el-Makhzen, the land of government, while the mountainous areas of tribal power were known as the Bled-es-Siba, the land of dissidence. Sidi Mohammed, who reigned from 1757 to 1790, was one of the most astute sultans of this period, reforming the customs service, building new ports and quietly suppressing the Barbary corsairs whose ancient profitability was declining against the growing technical superiority of the European fleets.

The 19th century was a period of increasing European Power, graphically demonstrated by the French invasion of Algeria in 1830. After 1856, European merchants in Morocco were running their own law courts while their coinages began to displace the native currency. By the turn of the century the two chief ports of Tangier and Casablanca were effectively under the control of the foreign consuls. Despite the reforms attempted by Sultan Moulay Hassan the country slipped ever more into debt and European influence.

Photo Jose Navarro

The French Protectorate

The rivalry between the European powers over Morocco was settled by secret negotiations at the 1906 conference of Algeciras. France was given central Morocco while Spain received the poorer areas in the extreme south and north. The next year French troops landed at Casablanca. Several years of confused fighting and diplomacy were resolved in 1912 when the sultan signed away sovereignty through the treaty of Fès. Later that year the tribal army of El Hiba, the Blue Sultan of the desert, was destroyed outside Marrakech. The French immediately began work on the colonial transformation of Le Maroc Utile - 'useful Morocco'. The less rewarding mountain regions were not completely pacified until 1934 while the 1921-1926 Rif rebellion nearly succeeded in expelling the Spanish from the north of the country.

The technical achievements of the 44 years of colonial rule were impressive. A complete road and rail network was established and ports, airfields, dams, irrigation projects and new administrative centres were created. The rewards of this new society - the hotels, hospitals and schools - were reserved for the 300,000 European settlers and the traditional Moroccan ruling class.

History of Morocco

Independent Morocco

By 1947 the uglier aspects of French colonial rule were being questioned by Sultan Mohammed V and the Istiqlal, a small independence party. By 1951, both the Sultan and the rapidly expanding Istiqlal were working to awaken the political life of the nation. This was dramatically achieved in 1953 when the French deposed Mohammed V and sent him into exile in Madagascar. In 1955, the mass demonstrations for his return had begun to escalate into a guerrilla war. The French government, which was then faced with a revolution in Algeria, decided to quit Morocco with grace. Mohammed V returned and by March 1956 had formally negotiated independence. He changed his title from sultan to king while his popularity helped him outmanoeuvre the party bosses and remain the dominant political figure.

He was succeeded in 1961 by his son Hassan II. In the following three decades parties, constitutions, crises, coups and cabinets challenged the system but the king remained very much in charge. Such key figures as the Minister of the Interior and the Minister of Defence always remained the personal appointees of the king. Successes like the nationalisation of foreign businesses in 1965 and the Maghrebi Union treaty of 1989 are eclipsed by the Green March of 1975 which was by far the most popular achievement of his reign. As General Franco of Spain lay dying, the king led 350,000 unarmed Moroccans across the southern frontier to lay claim to the Spanish-held Western Sahara. This enormous territory is now integrated into Morocco, though the irredentist Saharan nationalist Polisario movement sought independence through a guerrilla war. An armistice has led to a permanent UN presence and an agreement to determine the future of the province in a referendum, though agreement on the qualifications to vote remains a contentious issue.

In July 1999, the old king died and was succeeded by his young son. Mohammad VI, known affectionately by his people as 'M6', dismissed his father's unpopular minister of the interior and has presided over an increasingly democratic and liberal regime. Morocco is a constitutional monarchy with a free press and free and open elections. It also faces great challenges: to feed and find employment for its burgeoning population of 27 million and also to remain a shining example of a Muslim nation - all the more devout because of its tolerance, individual freedoms and intellectual diversity.

Barnaby Rogerson 2003

لا إله إلا الله محمد رسول الله

ILa ilaha ill'Allah, Muhammad rasul Allah.

(There is no divinity but God, and Muhammad is his Prophet.)

With this short creed, all Muslims profess the basic tenets of their faith. Islam literally means 'submission' and implies the offering up to God of total faith and trust. The will of God was directly passed to the Prophet Muhammad through the medium of the Archangel Gabriel. Muhammad's principal task as Prophet was the recitation of this divine message. It is these recitations of the word of God that are collected in the Qu'ran, the holy book of Islam.

To Muhammad, Islam was not a new religion, it was intended to be a reformation of the ancient monotheistic tradition taught in the Old and New Testaments, the holy books of Jews and Christians. In both the Qu'ran and Muhammad's private conversations there are repeated references to the various prophets who had brought the message of God to mankind before him. Muhammad was proud to be numbered in the long line of prophets which stretched back through Issa (Jesus), Yahya (John the Baptist), Sulaiman (Solomon), Davud (David), Musa (Moses), Harun (Aaron), Idris (Enoch), Yakub (Jacob),

Yunus (Jonah), Noah and right back to Abraham and to the first man, Adam. The Qu'ran was intended to present an opportunity for the various squabbling Christian and Jewish sects to unite beneath a new definitive revelation.

However, the task of converting all the Christians and Jews in central Arabia proved impossible and towards the end of his life Muhammad realized that Islam must stand alone. Muslims began to pray facing Mecca rather than Jerusalem and Friday became the Muslim holy day as opposed to the Saturday and

Sunday celebrations of the Jews and Christians. Some festivals, such as Achoura (based on the Jewish Day of Atonement) remained like stranded bridges stretching between the faiths. The Prophet ordered all Muslims to respect the 'peoples of the Book', as Christians and Jews are called. Muhammad's tolerant attitude can be heard in his answer to a theological squabble with his neighbours, 'Will you dispute with us about God? When he is our Lord and your Lord! We have our words and you have your words but we are sincerely his.'

The Prophet Muhammad

The Prophet Muhammad was born in AD 570. The young Muhammad was to be thrice orphaned before the age of eight by the death of father Abdallah (before he was born), mother Amina and grandfather Abdul Muttalib. He grew up in the household of his paternal uncle, Abu Talib, who was the sheikh of one of the most prestigious clans within the Quraysh tribe which dominated the oasis city of Mecca. Although of noble blood, Muhammad was not rich and had to earn his keep as a shepherd-boy before being trained to work on the camel caravans that plied the routes that crossed the Arabian desert from Yemen to Syria. As a young man he was known as Amin, 'the trusty one', for his honesty and dignified bearing. This led him to be trusted with the goods of Khadijah, a wealthy widow whom he later married. Mecca was the centre of pagan Arab spiritual life and Muhammad and his wife joined the circle of Hanif who sought enlightenment through some form of monotheism and were familiar with Jewish, Christian and Persian doctrines.

Muhammad received his first revelation in AD 610 when he was 40 years old. The Archangel Gabriel appeared to him in a cave, which he frequently used for prayer and meditation, outside Mecca. Doubtful at first about these revelations but encouraged by his wife, he risked ridicule and shared the word of God. His ardent monotheism and criticism of the pagan worship in Mecca won him some followers but even more enemies. Eventually, the protection of his clan proved inadequate and, to avoid assassination, he moved to

Photo Jose Navarro

the oasis of Yathrib (renamed Medina) where he was welcomed and honoured as the Prophet of God on 15 June AD 622.

This date marks the beginning of the Muslim era, known as the Hegira. Muhammad refused any royal or military power and accepted only an official role as mediator. From these modest foundations he established a theocratic state and perfected the daily ritual of prayer and the annual festivals which still dominate the life of a Muslim. He also developed a body of moral and legal codes to cover the practical problems that a Muslim might face. His personal example, his innate modesty, easy approachability and hospitality set an additional example to his followers alongside his teaching. From Medina he waged war on the Meccan caravans and, having survived a number of testing battles and sieges, his authority was gradually accepted by all the surrounding Arab tribes which included those of Jewish and Christian faith alongside the pagan majority. By AD 630, two years before his death, his authority extended over all Arabia and the first Arab cavalry armies had been sent into Syria.

The question of Muhammad's successor, the Caliph, rends the Muslim world to the present day.

The first four successors contributed important aspects to the developing body of Muslim faith and are accepted as the 'Rightly Guided' by the majority of Muslims, known as Sunni. Most of North Africa and practically all Moroccans are Sunni. However, an important minority, the Shiites, believe that Ali, who was Muhammad's cousin, his most devoted disciple, son-in-law and spiritual confidant, should have been the first Caliph. Lesser sects like the Ismaili, Druze and Kharijites are divided by their own interpretations of the rightful succession.

Religious Life
The Qu'ran sets out the five pillars of Islam, the pre-requisites of Muslim life. These are the profession of faith, prayer five times a day, the giving of alms, fasting during Ramadan and pilgrimage to Mecca.

History of Islam

The Muslim profession of faith, "La ilaha ill'Allah, Muhammad rasul Allah" (There is no divinity but God, and Muhammad is his Prophet), is a simple enough matter, though the Prophet himself recognized that there was an enormous difference between submission and real faith. He also recognized that even among that first community of believers in Medina there were hypocrites motivated by fame, wealth and ambition.

The first prayer of the day, known as Moghreb, is held four minutes after sunset, Eshe when it is quite dark, Soobh Fegr at dawn, Dooh at noon (or just after the sun has passed its zenith), and Asr at the end of the siesta but officially calculated as halfway between noon and sunset. At each mosque the muezzin announces prayers by calling "God is great. I testify that there is no God but God. I testify that Muhammad is his prophet. Come to prayer, come to security. God is great." Before the morning prayer an extra inducement, "Prayer is better than sleep," is added. Before prayer all believers ritually purify themselves by washing with water or, in arid areas, with clean sand. Facing Mecca, they stand with hands held up and open to proclaim God's greatness. With hands by their sides they recite the opening verse of the Qu'ran, the fatiha, before bowing with hands on

knees and then fully prostrating themselves. Kneeling again, they recite the *chahada*, a prayer for the prophet. The three positions of prayer, standing, bowing and prostrate, symbolise the superiority of man's rational rather than his animal nature, a servant before his master and submission to the sovereign will of God. Friday is the chief day of prayer, when the community gathers for noon prayers at the most important local mosque, followed by a sermon, *khutha*.

Almsgiving was enshrined in the ascetic example of the Prophet who throughout his life scorned the accumulation of possessions. It later became a pivotal definition of membership of the Muslim community which he led from Mecca. All who professed to be Muslim were to offer an annual tithe from their crops and herds to the head of the Muslim community who distributed them to the needy, the deserving poor, widows and orphans as well as feeding travellers, ransoming captives, freeing slaves and relieving debtors. It became enshrined as the *zakat*, the only legitimate tax an orthodox Muslim leader could collect, which was often assessed at a fortieth of wealth. Nowadays tax and alms are usually separate and the practice is purely voluntary.

Photo Jose Navarro

History of Islam

The fast of Ramadan proscribes sex, smoking, drinking and eating during the daylight hours of the ninth month of the Muslim year. Only children, the sick, nursing or pregnant mothers, old people and travellers are exempt. The fast commemorates the month in which Muhammad received his first revelation but is also based on pre-existing Christian and Jewish spiritual practices.

Pilgrimage to the Kaâba at Mecca, revered as the altar of Abraham, takes place between the seventh and tenth days of the last month of the Islamic year (Dhu al-Hajja). It is governed by a strict set of rules and observances involving fasting and long treks between the holy sites in the desert heat. For a poor man it may be the journey of a lifetime, partly paid for by friends who will receive merit by their contribution. He will return to his community with the proud title of 'Haj'. The distance of Mecca from Morocco and the dangers of the route (from both bedouin tribes and Christian corsairs) made it especially arduous. This gave rise to the hope that seven visits to such local pilgrimage centres as Moulay Idris and Moulay Brahim might equal the journey to Arabia, a pious hope without any doctrinal backing.

The Qu'ran

Qu'ran means 'recitation', for the Prophet Muhammad was enjoined by the Archangel Gabriel to recite the word of God as it was dictated to him. It was orally delivered by Muhammad to his followers between AD 610 and 632, memorized and often recited. It was first collected into a definitive written version 18 years after his death in AD 650. The Qu'ran is divided into 114 unequal chapters or suras, arranged in order of length starting with the longest. Each sura is known by a name, such as the cow, the bee, the ant, generally believed to have no other significance than as a memory aid - for Muslims are taught to recite the Qu'ran by heart. The very beauty of the language of the Qu'ran is taken as proof of its divine inspiration: "you will never understand... until

Photo Jose Navarro

you can feel in your heart the poetry and music of the noble Qu'ran." No passionate Muslim can accept that a translation from Arabic is adequate as a holy text, though translations are accepted as a useful commentary for non-Arabs if placed side by side with the Arabic text.

In content, the Qu'ran divides roughly into four themes: the worship of Allah, the Day of Judgement, stories of earlier prophets, and social laws, though it is a feature of the Qu'ran that each sura can stand alone, like a miniature summary of the faith. It is also, at times, like receiving only one half of a dialogue, as if it were a collection of divine answers to Muhammad's prayers, though these original petitions have been lost. Although some sura can be identified with a given incident in the Prophet's life, the Qu'ran cannot be read as a consistent narrative (like the Gospels) but is rather a series of exhortations that develop and embroider the same themes of calling mankind to God. Western critics who talk disparagingly of repetition have merely 'read' a book that was designed to be lived. Sura 17:22-39 contains a set of commands similar to the Ten Commandments encouraging kindness, charity, sobriety and humility and prohibiting murder, adultery, idolatry and meanness.

A secondary source, known as the hadith, is also available to Muslims. This is a collection of the memorized sayings, actions, judgements and traditions of the Prophet Muhammad. It is the Hadith (but never the Qu'ran) which is open to interpretation and to arguments about the validity of the source. A single authoritative edition has never been agreed upon, although Al-Bukhari's multi-volume collection has become the most respected single source.

From the Qu'ran and the Hadith a legal system, known as sharia, was created. Traditional Islamic countries have no civil code and criminal acts as well as spiritual sins are judged according to sharia. In Morocco and a handful of the more progressive states, such as Iraq, Syria, Tunisia and Turkey, civil codes have also been introduced in the 20th century. The difference in legal systems is not as large as may be thought, for most of the so-called secular codes are merely an addition to, not a substitution of, sharia. At the forefront of most fundamentalist campaigns is an official recognition of sharia as the foundation of all law. Although this might seem mere window-dressing, it is acutely relevant as to where sovereignty lies: with a secular assembly, by royal decree or with the scholars of religious law?

Sufism

The spread of Islam was greatly assisted by the Sufi brotherhoods who set up religious centres, known as zaouia, throughout the Muslim world. The term Sufi may derive from 'suf', meaning wool and, by inference, the coarse woollen cloth worn by ascetics. Sufis are not satisfied merely to worship God by obeying Islamic law, they aspire to direct spiritual experience through additional devotions. The Prophet Muhammad's celebrated night journey to Jerusalem serves as the orthodox role model for such aspirations.

In addition, it is believed by many Muslims that, aside from his public declarations on faith, the Prophet Muhammad taught Ali and Fatima various private practices of prayer

and meditation which were too confusing and physically demanding for the main body of believers. It is these oral traditions that Ali taught to his own followers, who passed the spiritual heritage on down the generations of believers. Each Sufi brotherhood can trace this spiritual line of descent in the same manner in which the Pope looks back across the centuries to his apostolic succession from St Peter. The various Sufi brotherhoods (who are often compared with Christian monastic orders) each established a set of rituals and prayers to achieve the desired union with God. Most Sufi regimes are simple and ascetic and include outward features such as charity and teaching as well as the inner search for wajd, the ecstatic experience of the divine. They often prescribe a repetitive physical action, such as recitation, music or dancing, as a tool in their quest (for instance, the whirling dervishes). To outsiders, the best-known Sufi trait is indifference to worldly concerns which sometimes led to the practice of self-mutilation to show indifference to pain.

Christianity and Islam

Muslims see their religion as a reformation of Christianity which, with the evidence of the cult of the Virgin, the sacrifice of the Cross, odd doctrines on celibacy and confusing doctrines about the Trinity, they see

Photos Jose Navarro

as a corrupted version of monotheism. Christianity for its part has always found it difficult to venerate Muhammad whose long life, many wives and battles seem to be in sharp contrast with the poor, miracle-working Jesus nailed up on a cross aged 33. This contrast is partly about the availability of source material. We know an enormous amount about Muhammad from a number of near-contemporary biographies, as well as thousands and thousands of hadith. For the life of Jesus, the chief sources are the four gospels and the epistles, which were written down 30 years or more after his death, while all rival accounts and the trivial human details of his existence were lost during the Roman suppression of the Judaean revolt followed by the destruction of Jerusalem.

Photos Jose Navarro

The alarming antagonism between these two religions, however, stems as much from their proximity and continual history of conflict as from actual doctrine. Early struggles in the Middle East between Byzantium and Islam were institutionalized by the Crusades, which continued seamlessly into the Hapsburg-Ottoman War, prolonged by the Corsair Wars of the 16th-18th centuries. In the 19th and 20th centuries, the political dominance of Christian European nations over every Muslim country (except Saudi Arabia and Turkey) has compounded the mutual mistrust. Just when the post-war independence movement and oil discoveries seemed to be establishing a new equality of relationship, the creation of the state of Israel, fostered by the USA, prolongs the tension. Daily, the newspapers carry proof that the age-old ignorance and antagonism that exists between the two faiths continues largely unabated.

Islamic Celebrations

The main religious event of the Muslim year is the fast of Ramadan which is still adhered to, in public at least, by the whole Moroccan population. For the entire month, productivity drops and a sense of lassitude descends during the day. When Ramadan falls in the summer, tempers are notoriously frayed, but everything is forgotten at the setting of the sun, when cafés fill with hungry customers who traditionally break the fast with a bowl of steaming soup. Deep into the night towns reverberate to the sound of revelling as families take to the streets after their communal meal. Musicians, storytellers and puppet-shows monopolise the pavements. After a few hours' sleep and a nourishing breakfast before sunrise, the fast begins again. The feast of Aïd es Seghir at the end of Ramadan is a time for new clothes and sumptuous banquets.

Most of the popular rites of passage that are celebrated by Christians in a church (such as baptism, confirmation and marriage) do not take place within a mosque in Morocco. The mosque is just for prayer and the study and recitation of the Qu'ran and does not act as a ceremonial stage. The Moroccan equivalent of baptism usually occurs on the seventh day after birth, when children are named and presented to the family, adorned with amulets for good luck and to chase away the 'evil eye'. Following the tradition of the Prophet Muhammad, the name of the child is formally announced by the eldest male member of family (normally the grandfather) who may also whisper the call to prayer in the ear of the newborn. The mother will be the hero of the day and showered with presents and congratulations from her family and neighbours.

Circumcision is an ancient Semitic rite that predates the teaching of the Prophet Muhammad by thousands of years. It is believed to have been instituted by the Prophet Abraham as a substitute sacrifice after the intended sacrifice of his child Ishmael (the ancestor of the Arabs and half-brother to Jewish Isaac) was halted by angels. A popular tale recounts that the Prophet Abraham was about to use an axe on himself for the 'operation' when once again an angel interceded and suggested a sharpened razor blade. It is now usually performed between the ages of five and seven and begins with the young boy's first visit to the mosque accompanied by his male relations. He will be dressed up in the finest traditional robes (including a fez), possibly allowed to ride a horse hired

for the day and much will be made of him and his bravery. The surgery is now usually performed by doctors but the local barber still plays his traditional role in country areas. At the moment of circumcision, other older children may break a jar of sweets on the ground, to distract the *jinn* - the spirits - from entering the child through the wound and to add a distracting element of fun and laughter to drown any moans of pain.

Weddings are often signalled by a cavalcade of hooting, decorated cars or, in the countryside, by a hired lorry or two complete with young drummers. Preparations begin some weeks before with a visit to the lawyer's office where the marriage contract, concerned with dowries and the terms of both marriage and divorce, is drawn up and signed by bride and groom. The old week-long festivities are nowadays often packed into a couple of days. The bride's body hair is all waxed off and the palms of her hands and soles of her feet covered with temporary henna tattoo. Sumptuously dressed, she is shown off to family and friends sitting on a dais, before men and women separate to eat the marriage dinner. Traditionally the bride then walks seven times around her home, bidding farewell, before being taken to her marriage bed. The husband returns from the town with a group of friends who leave him at the door. The last to bless him as he enters the bedroom is his mother. Though it is rare for the bloody sheet to be displayed (as graphic proof that the bride came to marriage a virgin) the concept is still a very valid expectation.

Death is greeted with frenzied ululations from female relatives and friends, though men are traditionally

supposed to hold back from passionate expressions of grief. In the words of the Prophet, "what comes from the heart and eye - that is from God, what comes from the hand and tongue - that is from Satan". Muslims are buried quickly (normally within a day or two of death, though the requirements of state funerals override these traditions). The body is washed and scented before being wrapped in the simple white clothing of a pilgrim. It is carried to the cemetery on a bier, supported by male friends and relatives and followed by a cortège of male mourners often headed by a man reciting the Qu'ran. There is no solemn funeral march in Islam, in fact, the more religious believe that the dead should be carried at a slow trot to speed them on their way to meet their Maker. The body is often buried on its side facing towards Mecca. For the most pious, the grave should be decorated with no stone memorial though it is common to plant a pair of stones so that the ground is not inadvertently dug up. On the first night two terrifying angels, Munkar and Nakir, are believed to descend into the tomb to question the dead and chastise the wicked. After this severe night, the long sleep of the grave will only be broken by the calling together of the last great Assembly, a time when all mortals shall stand dumbfounded before the divine presence and watch the publishing of the pages of their past life while their very limbs will stand witness against them. They will have to cross the bridge over the fires of Hell to reach the gardens of Paradise, filled with "what the eye hath not seen, nor the ear heard, nor hath ever been thought of by mankind".

Barnaby Rogerson 2003

Glossary

Adrar Mountains/Mountainous area

Aïd Islamic holy day or feast such as Aïd es Seghir, the end of Ramadan, or Aïd el Kebir, the feast of the sheep which commemorates Abraham's sacrifice of a ram instead of his son Isaac (their Arabic names are Ibrahim and Ismaël)

Aït Tribal group

Amazigh The 'true man'. Singular of Imazighen, original inhabitants of Morocco (also known as Berbers, a term disliked by many Amazigh people)

Argan Tree Species native to southern Morocco; its fruit is used to make argan oil

Bab Gate or door

Baraka Blessing, obtained through saints, or marabouts (holy men)

Bejmat Unglazed terracotta tiles

Beldi From *bled*, countryside: rustic, indigenous, hence traditional Berber style

Berber/nomad tent A sweep of strips of goat and camel hair sewn together and slung low over two or three poles

Bir Well

Bohou/Bhou Small salon opening directly onto the patio of a traditional house

Caidal tent Tall rectangular 'formal' tent of heavy white canvas with dark purple or black 'kasbah tower' designs sewn on at regular intervals. Interior often lined with wide bands in red and green - the national colours

Dar Traditional Moroccan house with a patio that has a water feature but not necessarily a garden. Also 'residence of' as in Dar Bacha, the Pasha's residence

Dayet Lake

Derb Street or neighbourhood, usually in an old town or medina, with one entry from a main street and any number of dead ends within its own system

Dess or tadelakt-dess, uses the same materials as tadelakt but with more stone chips; traditionally used for flooring, it requires many hours of hard regular tamping, done in teams, led by the rhythmic chanting of the m'aallem to which the workers respond in unison with their movements; a labour-intensive craft that is less often used nowadays despite its wonderful effect

Douar Village

Douiria Small part of mansion with its own patio where guests or staff were lodged or where the women retired for privacy when strangers were visiting

Erg Large dune field (e.g. Erg Chebbi)

Fantasia Colourful horse-riding spectacle, simulating military exercises

Fassi Of Fez or Fès

Foggara Underground water canal. also known as *khettara*

Fondouk Former traders town inn

G'naoua Originally a brotherhood of negro slaves, now used for the music and whirling dances in tribal costume performed by Moroccans of G'naoua descent; their presence is said to be bring good luck.

Gebs/djibs Plaster; sometimes used as another word for stucco

Haïk Large cloth wrap made of wool from Essaouira and used by women to cover themselves in public

Hammada Stony plateau

Kasbah Citadel or countryside stronghold

Kalia A speciality of Erfoud. A meaty dish in a spicy red sauce (about 40 spices), slowly stewed and served with a fried egg on top.

Khettara Underground water canal. also known as *foggara*

Kif Hashish

Kilim Woven carpet

Ksar (plural *Ksour*) Probably derived from 'Caesar' – a fortified village that many contain a number of kasbahs

Ma'allem Master builder or craftsman

Maghreb Arabic for Western lands, i.e. North Africa, as opposed to Eastern lands, i.e. the Near East. (Al-Maghrib = Morocco)

Maillechort Moroccan silver.

Marabout Holy man or saint of Islam; by extension, a holy-man's tomb, often domed.

Marrakchi Of Marrakech

Medersa Koranic school: institution dating from the 12th century where residents study the Koran and Islamic law

Medina Originally 'town', nowadays the old, often walled quarter of a city where most streets are high narrow lanes without pavements and virtually impassable to motors (the Moroccans are endlessly skilled at getting through despite women with baskets, children playing or running errands, men sharpening knives or building furniture, overloaded donkey carts being urged on with blows and jabs to get through the maelstrom and reach their delivery point, all this all over the 'street')

Mellah Jewish quarter

Menzeh In mansion or palace, a loggia or pavilion where one may eat, generally on a terrace or rooftop with a view

Moroccan salon or dining room: room lined with upholstered benches along the walls for lounging or sitting at table, low or lowish tables for eating at

Moucharabieh Wood panels carved in intricate filigree pattern to allow women to see out but no-on to see in. Also name for bay windows fitted with these panels

Moussem Festival of a religious nature or to celebrate annual harvest

Oued River or, more frequently, dry river bed

Palmeraie French for palm grove, sometimes translated as palmery

Pastilla A savoury flaky-pastry dish with various fillings.

Pisé Earth architecture: a form is erected then filled, layer by layer, with a wet mixture of earth and clay that is rammed and packed before

Glossary

the next layer is started. The structure then bakes dry in the sun. Adobe (from the Arabic *t'bud*, brick) is the sun-dried earthen brick method.

Potager French word for kitchen garden

Ramadan Month of fasting during the ninth month of the Islamic calendar

Riad Properly, an enclosed, watered garden, presumed to imitate the earthly paradise; by extension, a mansion house with a patio of at least 100m² and a real garden, arcades on all four sides and galleries above; by further extension, any good-sized house with a central courtyard that is not always very big, is generally arcaded but does not always qualify as a garden

Rabati Of Rabat.

Sabra Shimmering fabric with wide or narrow coloured stripes proper made of cactus fibre or 'silk', nowadays often synthetic.

Saharaoui Of the western Sahara region (also Sahraoui).

Souiri Of Essaouira.

Tadelakt A waterproof plaster made of a fine mix of lime, ground stone and pigment, carefully smoothed then polished with black soap for an incomparably smooth silky finish; originally used for hammams, has become a favourite with interior decorators for shower cubicles, bathrooms, even living rooms, in contemporary restorations.

Tataoui Coffered ceiling made of reeds or palm or oleander stems and leaves. Originated in Tata, the southern oasis town on the river Tata

Tamazigh Language

Zelliges Geometric tiling patterns of endless variety made with shapes cut from multi-coloured enamelled tiles and repeated ad infinitum. The style originated in Fès.

Zouak Hand-painting with vegetable pigments on wood (ceilings, doors, furniture).

Names of houses

Abir Passer-by, ferryman, taste.

Arsat Orchard or kitchen garden.

Assad Lion

Assafir Birds

Ayniwen Palm trees

Bahar By the sea

Bartal Bird

Bled Countryside, home town or village

Borj Tower

Cadi Judge of Muslim law

Ifilkou Flower

Itran(e) Star

Jdid/Jedid Young, new

Jnane Garden (of paradise)

Malik(a) Sovereign (one of the Arabic names of God)

Nour Light

Ouarda/Warda Roses

Qdima/Qedim/Kdim/Kedim Old

Raha Rest

Soukaina A Berber tribe

Tchaikana The house where one drinks tea

Zarraba Canal

ALASTAIR SAWDAY'S
SPECIAL ESCAPES

Home • Search • Hotlist • Owners • Links

Shutters on the Harbour, St Ives

Cornwall, England

You'd never guess that this 1875 former fishermans' cottage in the belly of the old-town is the lap of modern luxury inside. Georgie and Janin have cleverly renovated this tiny dwelling into a funky palace with lots of surprising touches. Originally pilchards were pressed in the old lounge and shipped to Tuscany – now the only remaining sign is the wooden grooves in the stone walls. From the neutral stone-floored lounge with sheep-skin rugs on the rattan chairs, scamper into the shower/washing room to wash off the sand – perfect for surfers. Up to a suspended floor with the kitchen with round table, built-in benches and all mod-cons and a second chill-out space – from both look down to the lounge. A spiral stair leads up to the bedrooms. Here Janin's furniture-design skills were brought in to create wacky bedside tables using driftwood and stylistic shapes. There are painted wooden floors, funky light sculptures, neutral colours and portholes leading to the bathroom - separated by a vibrant sari curtain. It has a beach-house style with a modern home-spun element; they have carefully made the most of the limited space – it can be tight in some corners but somehow that adds to the fun. An ideal spot to make the most of St Ives.

'Shutters on the harbour' Bethesda Hill

Bedroom 1

Owner's Notice Board

BEAUTIFUL ST IVES

2 weeks still available in September - 17th and 24th - arguably the best time of year.. when the kids go back to school! STUNNING CONVERSION OF FISHERMAN'S COTTAGE IN HEART OF ST IVES

Note: This information has been provided by the owner or management of Shutters on the Harbour and is not verified or endorsed by ASP.

Details for Shutters on the Harbour

Contact Georgina Lenain

tel: +44(0)7770 431558

fax: +44(0)20 8877 0700

@ Send E-mail Enquiry

sleeps:

rooms: 2 doubles with shower; shower room.

price: £550.00 – £960.00. In winter short breaks negotiated

closed: Never.

changeover: Saturday - negotiable.

? Details Explanation

Currency Converter

? Symbol Explanations

Sitting room with winter rugs

Views on Porthminster Beach

A whole week self-catering in Britain with your friends or family is precious, and you dare not get it wrong. To whom do you turn for advice and who on earth do you trust when the web is awash with advice from strangers? We launched Special Escapes to satisfy an obvious need for impartial and trustworthy help – and that is what it provides. The criteria for inclusion are the same as for our books: we have to like the place and the owners. It has, quite simply, to be 'special'. The site, our first online-only publication, is featured on www.thegoodwebguide.com and is growing fast.

www.specialescapes.co.uk

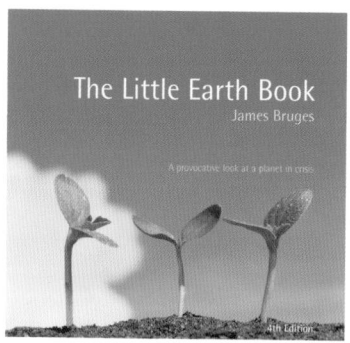

The Little Earth Book
Edition 4, £6.99
By James Bruges

A little book that has proved both hugely popular – and provocative. This new edition has chapters on Islam, Climate Change and The Tyranny of Corporations.

The Little Food Book
Edition 1, £6.99
By Craig Sams, Chairman of the Soil Association

An explosive account of the food we eat today. Never have we been at such risk - from our food. This book will help clarify what's at stake.

The Little Money Book
Edition 1, £6.99
By David Boyle, an associate of the New Economics Foundation

This pithy, wry little guide will tell you where money comes from, what it means, what it's doing to the planet and what we might be able to do about it.

www.fragile-earth.com

Order Form

All these books are available in major bookshops or you may order them direct.
Post and packaging are FREE within the UK.

British Hotels, Inns & Other Places	£13.99
Bed & Breakfast for Garden Lovers	£14.99
British Bed & Breakfast	£14.99
Pubs & Inns of England & Wales	£13.99
London	£9.99
French Bed & Breakfast	£15.99
French Hotels, Châteaux & Other Places	£14.99
French Holiday Homes	£12.99
Paris Hotels	£9.99
Ireland	£12.99
Spain	£14.99
Portugal	£10.99
Italy	£14.99
Mountains of Europe	£9.99
India	£10.99
Morocco	£10.99
Turkey	£11.99
The Little Earth Book	£6.99
The Little Food Book	£6.99
The Little Money Book	£6.99
Six Days	£12.99

Please make cheques payable to Alastair Sawday Publishing. Total £

Please send cheques to: Alastair Sawday Publishing, Yanley Lane, Long Ashton,
Bristol BS41 9LR. For credit card orders call 01275 464891
or order directly from our web site www.specialplacestostay.com

Title   First name   Surname

Address

Postcode   Tel

R2

If you do not wish to receive mail from other like-minded companies, please tick here ☐
If you would prefer not to receive information about special offers on our books, please tick here ☐

Report Form

If you have any comments on entries in this guide, please let us have them. If you have a favourite house, hotel, inn or other new discovery, please let us know about it. You can e-mail info@sawdays.co.uk, too.

Existing entry:

Book title: _____

Entry no: _____ Edition no: _____

New recommendation:

Country: _____

Property name: _____

Address: _____

_____

_____

_____

Tel: _____

Comments: Report:

_____

_____

_____

_____

_____

_____

_____

_____

Your name: _____

Address: _____

_____

_____

Tel: _____

Please send completed form to ASP, Yanley Lane, Long Ashton, Bristol BS41 9LR or go to www.specialplacestostay.com and click on 'contact'. Thank you.

Booking form

À l'attention de:
To: _____

Date: _____

Madame, Monsieur
Veuillez faire la réservation suivante au nom de:
Please make the following booking for (name):

Pour nuit(s)	*Arrivée le jour:*	*mois*	*année*
For night(s)	Arriving: day	month	year
	Départ le jour:	*mois*	*année*
	Leaving: day	month	year

Si possible, nous aimerions	*chambres, disposées comme suit:*
We would like	rooms, arranged as follows

À grand lit	*À lits jumeaux*
Double bed	Twin beds
Pour trois	*À un lit simple*
Triple	Single
Suite	*Appartement*
Suite	Apartment

Nous sommes accompagnés de   enfant(s) âgé(s) de   ans.
Avez-vous un/des lit(s) supplémentaire(s), un lit bébé; si oui, à quel prix?
We are travelling with   children, aged   years.
Please let us know if you have an extra bed/extra beds/a cot and if so, at what price.

Nous aimerions également réserver le dîner pour   personnes.
We would also like to book dinner for   people.

Veuillez nous envoyer la confirmation à l'adresse ci-dessous:
Please send confirmation to the following address:

Nom: Name: _____

Adresse: Address: _____

_____

Tel No: _____ Email: _____

Fax No: _____

la réservation – Special Places to Stay

Quick reference indices

Index by property name

Index by town

Desert oases

Dar Azawad
Douar Ouled Driss, BP 16, M'Hamid

The desert sand flows seamlessly up the solid walls of this very civilised base for exploring the barren lands and fabulous dunes that lie beyond M'Hamid, the southernmost village of Morocco. Vincent, a charming, energetic Arab-speaking art collector, has fulfilled his dream of creating a high-class trekking centre in a tiny palm grove. He has done it with true French refinement: sober, local style outside, some zinging colours on tiles, sabra-silk bedcovers, bright Berber rugs and remarkably original bathrooms inside. You sleep either in an individual miniature kasbah or in a bright-doored cabin with a camel-hair roof (they can get very hot). Each room is different, full of personality, yet calm and comfortable with a fascinating tadelakt bathroom. The tent corral washroom is unbelievably smart – tadelakt basins topped with copper taps and brass-framed mirrors; the dining room is a mass of fabulous pieces from Vincent's collection; the lovely pool is in the centre of the 'hamlet'. Come to discover the desert – on foot, dromedary or 4x4. It may seem expensive but there's none other like it.

rooms	6 + 7: 5 doubles, 1 suite. 7 tents for up to 4.
price	Half-board 1,000Dh–1,200Dh for two. 700Dh per tent for two half-board.
meals	Half-board only. Lunch 110Dh.
closed	Never.
directions	From Zagora south to M'Hamid 86km. House on right 900m after Ouled Driss sign.

	Vincent Jacquet
tel	+212 (0)44 84 87 30
mobile	+212 (0)61 24 70 18
fax	+212 (0)44 84 87 30
email	vincent@darazawad.com
web	www.darazawad.com

Small hotel

Map 5 Entry 142

Explanation

1 region, district

2 write up
Written by us.

3 rooms
Assume rooms are en suite; unless we state otherwise. If a room is not 'en suite' we say with separate, or with shared bathroom: the former you will have to yourself, the latter may be shared with other guests or family members. When an entry reads 4+2 this means 4 rooms and 2 self-catering apartments or similar.

4 price
The price shown is for two people sharing a room. Half-board prices are per person. A price range incorporates room/seasonal differences.

5 meals
Prices are per person. If breakfast isn't included we give the price.

6 closed
When given in months, this means for the whole of the named months and the time in between.

7 directions
Use as a guide and travel with a good map.

8 symbols
see the last page of the book for a fuller explanation:

&#x267F;	wheelchair facilities		good vegetarian dinner options
	easily accessible bedrooms		owners' pets live here
	children of all ages are welcome		At least one bedroom has air-conditioning.
	no smoking anywhere		pool on the premises
	payment by cash or cheque only		bikes on the premises to borrow or hire
Hello	your hosts speak some English		tennis on the premises
			information on local walks

9 map & entry numbers

The World Wide Web is big - very big. So big, in fact, that it can be a fruitless place to search if you don't know where to find reliable, trustworthy, up-to-date information about fantastic places to stay in Europe, India, Morocco and beyond...

Fortunately, there's **www.specialplacestostay.com**, where you can dip into all of our guides, find special offers from owners, catch up on news about the series and tell us about the special places you've been to.

WWW.SPECIALPLACESTOSTAY.COM